THE GANG 0s

vere

If you're un ry.

If you're ove unforgettable.

Shrewd old Ma Barker with her dumb sons and their smart buddy Alvin Karpis . . . the amiable oaf called Machine-Gun Kelly and the beautiful girl who made his reputation . . . bank robber Harvey Bailey, a real pro . . . the Barrow-Parker gang, kill-happy small-timers who never scored for more than $1,500 . . . Homer Van Meter, Harry Pierpont, John Hamilton, and their peerless leader, John Dillinger, who despite FBI claims to the contrary probably never killed a soul . . . murderous Lester Gillis, who was known as Baby Face Nelson . . . and Charles Floyd, the Oklahoma Robin Hood, whom they called Pretty Boy.

PRETTY BOY, BABY FACE– I LOVE YOU

The gangsters of the
'30s and their molls

by LEW LOUDERBACK

CORONET BOOKS
HODDER FAWCETT LTD.

First published by Fawcett Publications Inc., New York
Coronet Books Edition 1969

SBN 340 10873 8

Printed in Great Britain for Hodder Fawcett Ltd.,
St. Paul's House, Warwick Lane, London, E.C.4,
by Hazell Watson & Viney Ltd., Aylesbury, Bucks

All photographs by courtesy of Fawcett Publications, Inc., New York

INTRODUCTION

The New-Style Badmen

In the early 1930s a new kind of criminal appeared in this country.

The trend during the previous decade had been toward combination and monopoly, away from "free-lancing." The big syndicates had been established in the twenties, and law-breaking had been managed systematically—with book-keepers, crooked attorneys and graft. It had been a business.

As Repeal drew nearer and the Depression deepened, this picture changed.

The criminals who now began to crop up were loners: desperadoes who rode by night, traveling with a few accomplices, "kicking in" banks, hightailing it from city to city, state to state.

They used cars instead of horses, Thompson submachine guns rather than Colt .44s—but these were simply new wrappings on what was essentially an old American package—the frontier badman.

They were an anachronism, this new breed, a throwback to an earlier period when "honest thieves" had preyed on a simple, rural society with weapons. Their reappearance in the 1930s was completely unexpected and probably wouldn't have happened except for the Depression.

They flourished only briefly—1931 to 1936—and in a limited area, the Midwest "Crime Corridor," where outlawry had been something of a tradition since the Border Wars of the 1860s.

They left no heirs. Their influence on the overall history of American crime was negligible.

But who will ever forget them?

Ma Barker. Machine Gun Kelly. Bonnie and Clyde. Pretty Boy Floyd. Dillinger. Baby Face Nelson. Alvin Karpis.

The very mention of their names once provoked something close to mass hysteria. But time lends perspective. Looking back at them across the events of the past thirty-five years, we see them not as the beginning of a "new, terrible phase in crime," but as the tail end of an earlier tradition. It's clear now that the Old West didn't end at Coffeyville in 1892, but in a blaze of machine gun fire at Oklawaha, Florida, in 1935.

Looking back, we also see that the total damage caused by these "Public Enemies" was peanuts compared to the illicit billions that are raked in annually by organized crime. Clyde Barrow's biggest job netted him $1,500. Capone gave away more than that in tips when he threw a party. The Dillinger gang's lifetime take was around $250,000—less than an afternoon's action in the numbers racket.

They were surprisingly nonlethal, too. Some were worse than others that way, but even the worst weren't as bad as their Old West forebears. Cole Younger personally killed sixteen men; Wes Hardin more than forty. But the deadliest of the Depression gangs—Clyde Barrow's—accounted for only thirteen deaths all told.

The gangsters of the thirties were essentially armed bandits. They were bone-hard, all of them, and fast on the trigger, but they didn't go swaggering up and down the streets, rolling into saloons, shooting out the lights. Their business was robbery, and they stuck pretty much to their last.

They survived as long as they did because the law was ill-prepared for them. In the early 1930s there was no widespread police radio system. "In those days," W. D. Jones of the Barrow gang reminisced recently, "all we had to do to make a getaway was cut the phone lines. Today," he added, "Bonnie and Clyde wouldn't last a week."

Today the whole picture of crime has changed anyway. As the Depression gradually eased, the "lone raiders" vanished. They were replaced by the new style of outlaw—the self-made executive playing the percentages from the inside. Mafiosi in business tweeds.

There are still some old-style heist men around, but they too have turned to simpler, more lucrative crimes, notably hijacking. Renting a truck tractor and hooking it onto an unguarded trailer at a terminal is a lot easier—and safer—than walking into a bank with a submachine gun.

The bank jobs have been left to amateurs—the so-called "Nervous Nellys," lonely, frightened individuals who are "feather-fingered" enough to shoot in panic or throw a vial of acid if their demand for money is refused. Ironically these amateurs are stealing more each year than their hard-eyed ancestors stole in the entire Public Enemy Era.

The only real monument that the gangs of the thirties left behind is the FBI.

Before their appearance few persons outside official circles even knew that the Bureau existed. But by 1935 the FBI had become a household word, and the valorous doings of its "G-men" had been invested with fantastic glamour by an almost incessant drumbeat of high-powered publicity.

Time has cooled some of the hot rhetoric that accompanied the Bureau's rise to prominence and has deflated a few of the monstrous caricatures that ambitious lawmen and irresponsible city editors created back in the thirties. What we see now, under the pearl-gray fedoras and the blue pinstripe suits, are not J. Edgar Hoover's "craven beasts," "public rats," and "vermin," but simply old-style American badmen, sprung from the same soil as Jesse James, the Daltons, and Belle Starr. Theirs were the bucolic virtues, no matter how "big-cityish" they later became. The important things were hardihood, close-knit family ties, fierce independence of outside authority. And physical courage—they were like Red Indians that way.

These "new" old-style badmen appeared on the scene at a time when millions were unemployed and desperate, when ruinous dust storms were beginning to move across the plains. It was a time of "wintry despair," in the words of one historian, "of lives stunted and people demoralized." The daring deeds of the Public Enemies were the cheapest form of entertainment available. If a man had the price of a paper or a radio, he could follow the daily adventures of his favorite outlaw, as he might a Wild West serial. Only it was even better than fiction. It was really happening. It was as real as the latest headline.

Great segments of the population not only followed the outlaws' adventures, but found themselves secretly sympathizing with them. And why not? They only robbed banks, after all—hardly the most popular institutions in the country in 1933.

Harry Pierpont, a Dillinger gangster, sensed the spirit abroad in the land. "I'm not the kind of man you are," he sneered at the prosecuting attorney during his trial, "robbing widows and orphans. You'd probably be like me if you had the nerve."

The little man, crushed beneath the weight of the Depression, dreamed his forbidden dreams: of "packing a gat," of "taking it on the lam," of traveling with a good-looking moll, his pockets full of crisp greenbacks, of floorboarding his V-8 sedan along highways that ran like unswerving scars across the flat wheat plains of the American heartland. And in the end, when the real outlaw was riddled by lawmen's bullets, the little man could wake up and be glad it was only a dream and tell himself that crime, after all, didn't pay.

The Public Enemy Era was very therapeutic that way.

CHAPTER ONE

Ma Barker—and Her Boys

"Mother of Bandits"—that was what they called Missouri. And by the turn of the century there was no denying it. She had produced more outlaws than any other state in the Union.

Ma Barker was born there in 1872, the year the James-Younger gang held up the First National Bank of Kansas City.

She was born Arizona Donnie Clark in a pocket of the Ozarks some eighteen miles northwest of Springfield. Her folks were Scotch-Irish, the descendants of mountaineers who had moved from Kentucky in an oxdrawn wagon back in the 1830s.

Her childhood was normal for that section, that period.

The Ozark "hollers"—narrow, creek-carved slashes between rugged hills when darkness dropped quickly on cabin door-yards—had been home base for Quantrill's raiders during the Civil War. Now they were paying for it. Villages had been destroyed, farmhouses burned, fields that had once raised corn were weed patches. At night bands of ex-soldiers fired into the homes of Southern sympathizers. No man, when he laid himself down at night, knew if he would wake in the morning.

Men who had once been easygoing farm boys were now brigands. There was no other way to live. They "took to the brush," gathered into bands of five to fifty, stole horses, and rode down into the rich delta of the "boot heel" to rob and plunder.

The hill people, with their strong sense of family, clan, and honor, stuck by them, sheltered them, hero-worshipped them. Arch Clements, Tucker Bassham, Dick Liddil, George Shepherd—these were the childhood heroes of anyone growing up in "Hell's Corner" during the '70s and '80s.

When Arizona (called "Arrie" by her friends) was ten, the greatest hero of them all was killed. Jesse. His memory was everywhere about her as she grew up. During recess at the country school the kids used to run around shrieking, "The dirty little coward that shot Mr. Howard has laid Jesse James in his grave." And they meant it.

There were cabins all through the Ozarks where Jesse and his men had stayed a night, eaten a chicken dinner on their way back from a robbery, watered their horses. In nearby Carthage was a man who had even ridden with Jesse.

In nearby Carthage, too, was the old Shirley farm, where Myra Belle Shirley had been born. By the time Arrie Clark was a young girl, Myra Belle had flashed across the skies as Belle Starr, "the notorious bandit and outlaw woman of Arkansas and the Indian Territory." Back in the Ozarks she was remembered mainly as a spy for the Confederacy, the heroine of Newtonia. As far as the hill people were concerned, she could do no wrong.

Arrie Clark became "Kate" in her teens. She was a short, dark-haired girl, with direct, penetrating eyes. There was nothing unusual about her, no "streak of criminality" beginning to show, no suspicious restlessness. She was simply typical of the mountain breed: tough, fierce in her affections and loyalties, suspicious of outsiders. The instruments of her culture were the fiddle and the Bible. She never missed a church "sing." No one in the hills did. They were a singing people, and God-fearing.

In 1892, the year the Dalton boys caught theirs at Coffeyville, Kate Clark married. The groom was George Barker, a farm laborer from Lebanon, Missouri. The couple settled down in nearby Aurora, where Kate became known as "a good wife, devoted to the Presbyterian church, a fair housekeeper, and averse to back-fence gossip."

There in Aurora Kate's sons were born: Herman first, then Lloyd and Arthur—called "Dock" by his mother (the press would later spell it "Doc")—and her special favorite, the baby of the family, Freddie.

Herman and Lloyd grew to school age in Aurora; the others were still infants when the family moved out of the Ozarks to Webb City, Missouri, a lead- and zinc-mining town near the Kansas border.

Webb City was an overnight boomtown. Fifteen years before it had been an empty cornfield. Now a large semicircle of mines half surrounded a gritty, mud-and-tarpaper city of some eight thousand people. George Barker found work in one of the mines. Kate and the boys moved into a dilapidated house on the north side.

Soon there were complaints. The Barker boys were rowdy youngsters—window-breakers, petty pilferers. The father turned the complaints aside with a shrug. "You'll have to talk to Mother," he would say. "She handles the boys." But when the neighbors took their complaints to Kate Barker, she would fly into a rage, call them liars, and insist that her boys were good. The people who remembered her from this period said that the transformation was startling. Even grown men were afraid of her when she got into a temper. Her eyes, always queerly direct and penetrating, took on a kind of smoldering intensity that scared even her husband.

"She'd pack up those boys and take them to Sunday school every week," he remembered years later. "I don't know just why. Because when I'd try to straighten them up, she'd fly into me. She never would let me do with them what I wanted to."

Slowly Kate Barker began to change. Criticism of her offspring had triggered some indefinable shift in her chemistry. Her mountaineer's touchy pride, her fierce resentment of outside authority became more pronounced. Always close-mouthed and somewhat secretive, she seemed to draw into herself even further. She cut people in the street and stopped going to church. "If the good people of this town don't like my boys," she announced, "then the good people know what they can do."

It was the same route Belle Starr had taken. Loyalty to outlaw Cole Younger, the father of her illegitimate daughter, had turned Belle against her family, then against the society they represented.

When police picked up Kate's oldest son, Herman, for petty thievery, Kate Barker stormed down to the station house and raised such hell that they released him. Witnesses to this and later scenes with the police were convinced that Kate wasn't kidding. She really believed that her sons were being persecuted, that the townspeople had it in for them.

By 1910 each of the four boys had been arrested at least once. They were the "town toughs," certain to be part of any trouble that was around. In 1915 the police of nearby Joplin arrested Herman for highway robbery. Once again Ma got him off. She told neighbors that she'd had it, though. She was getting out. The boys would always be "persecuted" if they stayed in this neck of the woods.

She moved the family to Tulsa, a booming, two-fisted oil town across the line in Oklahoma. Husband George dutifully found work there while Ma and the boys got settled in a two-room shack near the Santa Fe railroad tracks.

"Tulsey Town" was a free-wheeling, wide-open place in those days, hip-deep in mud, oil, and trouble. The Barker boys took one good look at it and waded in, grinning. Within a couple of weeks they had organized the Central Park gang, a rough-and-tumble group devoted to all forms of adolescent thievery.

When merchants along Sixth Street complained, the police rounded them up—and once again Ma swung into action.

Her style was an unsettling mixture of tears, scathing tirades, and motherly pleading. It was effective. The police let them go. All of them. Ma had fought as hard for the other boys as for her own sons—a significant point. When she got them home, she lashed into them, not for breaking the law, but for getting caught at it. Why had they answered questions when they were picked up? she demanded harshly. The person who talked was the person who lost. Say nothing, lose nothing. She repeated it over and over and over, striking the table for emphasis. No kid who had grown up in "Hell's Corner" in the '70s would ever forget that lesson. Their kinfolk's lives had often depended on it.

It was around this time that Fred went to visit Herb Farmer, a neighbor from Webb City days. Herb had just gotten out of the state pen. A number of ex-cons were stopping at his place. Fred invited them to drop by Ma's whenever they were in Tulsa. They did—and hit it off famously with her.

Slowly word began to spread through the tristate area: there was a "cooling-off joint" in Tulsa where a fellow in trouble could get not only protection, but even, on occasion, some shrewd advice.

Kate Barker had taken another step along Belle Starr's route.

Belle had started by sheltering a few of her husband's friends, then more and more, until every bandit in the Indian Territory knew he would find a welcome at "Robber's Roost." Belle had gradually become their guiding spirit, their "brains." And it wasn't such a big step from that to saddling up with them, riding out to rob and plunder.

All that had happened only thirty years before, and a little less than seventy miles away, in the Cookson Hills.

Many of the men who now came trooping through Ma's shack were the descendants of outlaws that Belle had sheltered. Some of the older ones had even ridden with Bill Doolin, Cherokee Bill, and the Al Jennings train-robbing gang. Ma liked them all. They were the kind of "hellers" she had known and admired back in the Ozarks.

Later, when she really got rolling, the press would turn Kate Barker into a monster. There would be a great deal of panting prose about "an unnatural mother's viper brood." Accounts of her life would make it seem that she had sprung in full, evil bloom from an otherwise immaculate community.

Actually, sixteen years passed between the time she first defended her boys in a police station and the time when she herself finally became a fugitive.

No one will ever know the nature of her madness during these years or the substance of her delusions. But one thing is certain. Ma Barker, circa 1915, was not unlike a lot of other people along the Middle Border.

They all felt a kind of sneaking admiration for outlaws. When Robert Pinkerton, of the Detective Agency, arrived in the tristate area to check on the James-Younger gang he found the populace "willing to lie about the deplorable robbers." He gave it up and went back to Chicago, where people had a "higher standard."

And later, when Bill Doolin was captured and brought handcuffed to the federal prison at Guthrie, Oklahoma, he was welcomed by a cheering crowd eager to shake his hand in admiration.

The truth is, people found it hard to dislike men who plundered banks and railroads. Everybody hated the railroads. They grabbed lands made valuable by the struggles of early settlers, fenced off grazing areas, and bypassed communities that refused to co-operate with them. Banks were unregulated; they charged usury; they cheated farmers in freight rates and on land deals.

Oklahoma had been a state just eight years when the Barkers arrived in Tulsa. Before that it had been the Indian Territory, and as such it had attracted a swift influx of hardened outlaws among its horde of settlers. The outlaws were still there in 1915, hiding out in the Cookson Hills, occasionally dashing forth to shoot up towns and rob banks.

Statehood had brought a measure of law enforcement. It had also put a gravel-top surface on what had been cattle trails. And it had brought the telephone.

For a while it looked as if that combination, plus the fences that were going up everywhere, might cramp the outlaws' style. Then a desperado named Henry Starr made an interesting discovery.

Henry was a half-breed Cherokee who had started out as a horse thief back in the '90s. He had switched to banks somewhere along the line and had knocked over some forty-eight of them. Until 1914, or thereabouts, he and his gang had always made their getaway on horseback. Then one day they decided to use an automobile. It was a grand success. So they used it again. And again. Henry kept right on using it, as a matter of fact, until he was killed busting open a Harrison, Arkansas, bank in 1921.

No bugle fanfare accompanied that moment of historical transition, but it marked, indelibly, the end of the Old West and the beginning of the Public Enemy Era.

One of the outlaws who occasionally holed up at Ma's Tulsa shack during the early '20s was a disciple of Henry Starr, a man named Al Spencer. A native of the Cookson Hills, Spencer had started life as a cattle rustler. Then he too had gone motorized and had switched to banks.

Spencer was a quiet, competent professional. He didn't drink, didn't smoke, didn't fool around with women while working. His raids were carefully planned and smoothly executed. His gang made little effort to conceal their identity, depending on swiftness and the security of their hideouts to carry them through. They often robbed three and four banks a week in the tristate area. Officers set traps, posses pursued them and staged gun battles with them, but the gang's high-powered roadsters gave them an unbeatable edge.

Spencer's men had all been recruited from the Cookson Hills. There was swarthy, balding Frank Nash, who would later play an important role in one of the Public Enemy Era's bloodiest encounters; smiling, freckle-faced Earl Thayer, one of the best shots and the most fearless of the group; and Ray Terrill, "a criminal genius" who would later lead his own gang.

These men and their new high-speed techniques had a profound influence on Kate Barker.

She started out just listening. There were always two or three men holed up in the shack, and there wasn't much for them to do but talk or play cards. Ma would listen as they went over past and future jobs, arguing over approaches, getaways, hideouts, and diversionary tactics.

Gradually she joined in, offering an occasional suggestion. The men listened. They liked what they heard. They started asking her advice on different jobs. She always had some idea, some improvement that would make the operation safer, more effective.

On August 21, 1923, the Spencer gang pulled their most spectacular heist. They held up the *Katy Limited*, the Missouri, Kansas & Texas Railroad's crack passenger train, near Okesa, a lonely flag station on the edge of the Cookson Hills. The robbery netted them $20,000 in Liberty bonds and considerable cash.

The heat that followed was intense. Five of the seven who had taken part in the job were flushed out of the hills and captured. Frank Nash was caught on the Texas border after fleeing into Mexico. Spencer himself was trailed to Coffeyville, Kansas, where he was betrayed and riddled with police bullets before he could reach for his guns.

Nash and the others received twenty-five years apiece in Leavenworth.

Ray Terrill, who hadn't taken part in the *Katy* job, was still on the outside, however. He joined with Matthew and George Kimes, two Cookson Hill boys, to form the Kimes-Terrill gang.

Terrill was suave, intelligent, and crafty, more a burglar than a bandit. He introduced a new wrinkle to bank robbing: he would simply back a truck up to the bank door and winch its portable safe out, load it aboard the truck, and drive off to crack it at his leisure.

The technique was effective. During the mid-twenties Oklahoma and Texas suffered an epidemic of bank robberies, most of them attributed to the Kimes-Terrill gang. Their biggest recorded haul was $35,000—winched out of a bank in Pampa, Texas, in 1927.

Ma Barker, meanwhile, had moved into a more active role. She was now planning entire jobs from start to finish in return for a cut of the proceeds.

The money went to bailing her sons out of trouble. First one, then another forfeited bonds in serious cases. But Ma never stinted them. She was always there with another $10,000 when they needed it.

By 1927 three of them were beyond her help. Lloyd had been the first to take a fall. He'd been caught holding up a post office in 1922 and was now sitting still for twenty-five in Leavenworth.

Dock and Freddie hadn't been too clever, either. Dock had been tagged for the theft of a government-owned automobile in 1918. He had escaped, been caught, had broken jail again, and was now about to stand trial for the murder of a night watchman at St. John's Hospital in Tulsa.

Freddie, her baby, had been picked up first for vagrancy, then for robbery, then for bank robbery, once again for burglary, and finally for assault with intent to kill. He had been wounded by the Kansas City police, had escaped, been recaptured, and was now sitting out a 5-to-10 set in the Lansing, Kansas, state pen.

Only Herman, her eldest, was still free. He was riding with the Kimes-Terrill gang and, like a good son, was sending home part of his earnings. It wasn't enough, though. Ma needed thousands of dollars for attorneys' fees in her tireless campaign to free the other boys. There was only one way to make that kind of money —plan bigger and better jobs for other gangs.

Ma loved her sons dearly, but she was a realist. She knew that except for Herman they were small potatoes. They lacked the flair and imagination of a Ray Terrill, the polished professionalism of an Al Spencer or a Frank Nash. They were well-meaning boys, but they needed strong direction. She meant to provide that direction—as soon as she could get them out of stir.

Early in 1927 Dock was convicted of killing the night watchman and was sent to the Oklahoma State Penitentiary for life.

Ma felt very bitter about it. Dock had sworn to her that he hadn't done it, and she believed him. (Surprisingly enough, it was true; years later a man in California confessed to the crime.)

Ma severed her last connection with the noncriminal world after that, leaving George Barker and moving to a dilapidated bungalow on Tulsa's North Cincinnati Avenue.

There another—even worse—blow fell. One that, in J. Edgar Hoover's words, turned Kate Barker "from an animal mother of the she-wolf type to a veritable beast of prey."

Herman and Ray Terrill were caught breaking into a bank in

Missouri. Both escaped, Terrill within sight of McAlester Penitentiary, Herman from jail in Washington County, Arkansas, where he had been taken for questioning. They rendezvoused at Ma's, then made a dash for the Kansas line.

There had been a holdup that night at Newton, Kansas. Cops flagged down their car. Guns blazed. J. E. Marshall, a traffic officer, was killed as the car roared away through a hail of bullets. Witnesses said that Herman, who was driving, had also done the fatal shooting. The next morning his body was found in a weed patch on the outskirts of Wichita, Kansas. He had been wounded in several places, but the cause of death was a bullet through the brain. Officially his death was listed as suicide. Ma claimed it was murder. A police execution.

Death brought Ma and George Barker together briefly as they stood beside an open grave in a windblown little cemetery near Welch, Oklahoma. Then, with the earth mounded, they parted. This time for good.

Ma was all alone now. She was fifty-five years old, a short, stony-faced woman beginning to go to fat. She had gray hair, thin lips, and a scrawny neck. Her usual getup was a sack dress and a shapeless hat. Only her eyes set her apart. They were dark, intense, queerly penetrating. And if you were a cop, there was something else, too, that hadn't been there before—hatred.

In the next few years she hounded parole boards with appeals for Lloyd, Freddie, and Dock. She also continued to harbor wanted men in her bungalow. And she set up jobs for various gangs, working them out to the last detail in return for extremely fat cuts.

On March 20, 1931, her youngest and dearest, Freddie, was finally released from the Kansas State Pen.

That May his best friend at Lansing, a tall, sour-faced boy named Alvin Karpis, was also paroled. He joined Freddie and Ma and her current lover, Arthur V. ("Old Man") Dunlop, in their Tulsa bungalow.

Alvin, born Francis Albin Karpaviecz in Canada in 1907, was the son of Lithuanian immigrants who had moved to Topeka, Kansas, when the boy was four. He grew up there, becoming the city marbles champion in his early teens. In 1926 he was implicated in a robbery and was sent to the Kansas Reformatory. He did "hard time" there, violating so many rules that he spent most of his stay in solitary. In 1929 he escaped, found work in a bakery in Chicago, then suddenly threw it over.

"What I wanted," he said later, "was big automobiles like rich people had and everything like that. I didn't see how I was going to get them by making a fool of myself and working all my life. So I decided to take what I wanted."

He returned to Kansas, where he was picked up almost immediately for auto larceny and safe blowing. He was sent back to the reformatory. They found him too tough to handle, though, and passed him on to the state pen. He was assigned to work in the coal mines there and immediately turned it to his advantage. It was the custom to reward extra production by lopping days off a man's sentence. Karpis quickly saw the flaw in the plan. Lifers had little incentive to extra production because no days could be deducted from their sentences. But lifers *could* be stimulated to extra work by money. "I agreed to pay them retail price on all extra coal they'd mine for me," he said later. "I turned all this in on my account and got good time for it—that put me on the street way ahead of time."

Ma took an instant liking to this twenty-four-year-old kid with the hard, narrow mouth and the old man's eyes. She saw in "Creepy" (the name celebrated his rare, rather ghastly smile) many of the qualities that her own sons lacked—intelligence, coolness, and skill.

Under Karpis' personal direction, and using her plans, the Barker boys could probably stay out of the law's hands for months, maybe years.

No sooner had Ma reached this conclusion than Alvin and Fred were both arrested on suspicion of robbing a jewelry store.

Reluctantly Kate Barker decided that it was time to shake Tulsa. "Old Man" Dunlop, a billposter by trade, was sent on ahead to rent a tourist cabin in Thayer, a small railroad town on the Missouri-Arkansas line. Ma and the boys followed and immediately got down to work, mapping large-scale operations in both states. They needed living money, meanwhile, so Fred and Alvin stuck up a store in nearby West Plains, Missouri.

Fine. Only Alvin was apparently as chuckle-headed as Fred when it came to details.

Under Ma's system of evading pursuit, the '29 DeSoto they had used in the stickup would have remained hidden for months. But the boys didn't ask Ma's advice. Only a few days after the robbery, they drove the DeSoto into a West Plains garage for repairs. The sheriff saw it there, saw the two men sitting in it, and approached to ask questions. A gun roared. C. R. Kelly was the name they put on his grave.

Now the running began.

Ma herself wasn't a fugitive yet. She didn't have to go with them. But she knew that if she didn't, Fred and Alvin would get themselves into a mess as sure as God-a-mighty made little green apples.

So the three of them, plus an extremely reluctant Arthur V.

Dunlop, roared north through the dark Ozark night, heading toward St. Paul, Minnesota.

The three most important "cooling-off joints" in the Midwest, circa 1931–32, were Joplin, Missouri; St. Paul, Minnesota; and Hot Springs, Arkansas. Ma chose St. Paul because Frank Nash, Al Spencer's old lieutenant, had been holed up there since busting out of Leavenworth earlier that year, and Frank was a solid, dependable kind of man she knew she could lean on in her troubles.

As for St. Paul itself, it was as safe as houses. The city that U.S. Attorney General Homer S. Cummings would later call "a poison spot of crime" had been a layover town for top heist men since back in the '80s when John J. ("The Big Fella") O'Connor had run it.

Under O'Connor's rule and that of his successors, Paddy Griffin and "Dapper Danny" Hogan, out-of-town criminals were welcome as long as they reported in regularly to the police and didn't try to pull any local jobs.

"Dapper Danny" had gone up with a bomb in '28, though, and his successor, Harry Sandlovich, better known as Harry Sawyer, was having a hard time controlling the hoodlum empire that he had inherited. Visiting gangsters still had to check in or risk arrest, but what they did after that was anybody's guess, including Harry Sawyer's.

The town was ripe for plunder, and a lot of the thieves holed up there knew it.

After checking in at Sawyer's saloon, the Green Lantern, the Barkers were assigned a rented house on South Robert Street in West St. Paul. There, in the weeks that followed, they met with Frank Nash and two other Leavenworth escapees, Francis Keating and Thomas Holden.

Keating and Holden were Chicago boys, bank and payroll robbers. Nash told them about Ma's skill at fingering jobs. They asked her to set a couple up for them. Ma did, taking a cut in the proceeds. Everybody was happy, including Alvin and Fred, who now had an opportunity to see how the "big boys" did it. As he got into the swing of things, Karpis was beginning to show the form that she had known he had in him all along.

As for Freddie—well, Freddie was always going to be Freddie, but he was her own flesh and blood, her best-loved "young-un." As always, she clasped him to her with emotional bands of steel.

Nash had brought Al Spencer's bank-robbing methods north: impeccably planned, lightning-fast kick-ins with plenty of heavy fire power backing up each stage of the operation. Thompson submachine guns, the bootlegger's weapon of the '20s, were standard armament. Gas-operated automatic rifles, air-cooled by radiator fins, sawed-off shotguns, and semi-automatic .45s were also favored.

Three or four "clean" cars would be stashed within a fifty-mile radius of the target. "Run and gets"—getaway charts with signals on them—would be prepared. The route would be run five or six times over, with maybe as much as half a day spent on eight or ten miles of ticklish road.

Kate Barker, meanwhile, brought her own peculiar talents to the fingering part of the operation. "When Ma 'cased a joint,'" J. Edgar Hoover later wrote, "nothing was left unnoted. Her eyes were keen, her ears sharp, her appearance and mannerisms of a type which dulled suspicion. Few persons indeed ever suspected, after a bank had been 'torn open,' that the 'nice little old woman' had furnished much of the brainwork of the job."

The team, known still as the "Holden-Keating gang," worked their way through a string of bank, payroll, and post office robberies in the Northwest that winter. Then, on April 25, 1932, the roof fell in.

The landlady at South Robert Street had noticed that every time the Barkers left the house, one of them carried a violin case, yet no sound of music ever came from their apartment. She mentioned this to her son, and he went leafing through some back issues of detective magazines—and sure enough, there were pictures of Fred and Alvin, wanted for the murder of that Missouri sheriff.

At 1 A.M. the landlady phoned the St. Paul police and with touching innocence told the desk sergeant that the desperadoes were asleep and that they could come and get them. Six hours later Harry Sawyer's police ambled over. It was okay, though. No embarrassment. The gang had had plenty of time to clear out.

That same morning the nude, bullet-riddled body of Arthur V. Dunlop was found on the shores of Lake Freasted near Webster Wisconsin. A woman's bloodstained glove lay nearby. The "Old Man" had been a reluctant partner from the start. He was forever whining about the running and the hiding. When the St. Paul police had called, the gang had apparently added two and two—and gotten five.

They moved on to Chicago, then to Kansas City, with Ma acting as an advance agent. The Depression was now two years old, and expensive apartments were going begging. Some buildings in the better parts of town had only three and four tenants in them. So what landlord was going to demand references of a little old lady who smiled pleasantly and took a great interest in quiet, respectable surroundings?

In Kansas City Ma rented a luxury apartment in the Country Club Plaza district. Holden and Keating arrived in town a few weeks later. Frank Nash had remained in St. Paul, but his place was taken by that dean of American bank robbers, Harvey Bailey.

"Old Harve" was a legendary figure by 1932, recognized throughout the underworld as a boss artisan when it came to "cracking a jug." Back in '22 he, Chi Slim, Big Fitz, and Jim Ripley had robbed the U.S. Mint in Denver. In '31, he, Eddie Bentz, and others had hit the Lincoln National Bank and Trust Company in Lincoln, Nebraska, for *one million dollars* in cash and negotiable securities. It was the largest bank robbery ever brought off in the U.S. It started a run on the bank, which closed its doors and was later forced to liquidate.

That a man of Bailey's caliber was willing to work jobs that Ma fingered shows how quickly she had arrived. Less than a year before, Kate Barker had been unknown outside the Tulsa area. Now she was working with the top heist men in the country.

Most of her earnings continued to go to lawyers who swore they could get Lloyd and Dock out of jail.

Lloyd's case seemed hopeless. (It was. He never joined the gang.) But by May 1932 things began to look brighter for Dock. Oklahoma Governor William H. ("Alfalfa Bill") Murray said he would study the case and issue a recommendation some time in the next six months.

This was music to Ma's ears. She went back to work with renewed vigor, humming hymns as she planned the details of the gang's latest job—a raid on a Fort Scott, Kansas, bank.

It was more a tactical exercise than anything else, a "shakedown run" to see how the new members of the outfit worked together.

The raid went off like clockwork in late June, with everybody functioning smoothly. The two newcomers, a Missouri gunman named Larry DeVol, and Bernard Phillips, a renegade policeman turned bank bandit, disported themselves well. The take was $31,000, and after splitting it, the gang filtered back to Kansas City in twos and threes to spend it.

Everybody was relaxed and happy. Ma organized an elaborate "coming out" party for one of Fred's Lansing classmates, William Weaver, an Arkansas gunman who was also known as "Phoenix Donald" and "Lapland Willie." He too joined the gang.

Ma and the boys went on picnics in Swope Park. Freddie occasionally got away from her and visited the bawdy houses out beyond the rusty viaduct on Wyandotte, but mostly he was good and kept his nose clean. Alvin Karpis, whose first love was fishing, spent his days at Lake Jacomo. The older men, Holden, Keating, and Harvey Bailey, were all avid golfers and whiled away the long summer afternoons on the Old Mission Golf Course—a serious mistake, as it turned out.

Charlie Harmon, a former member of the gang, had also loved golf. But the gang hadn't loved Charlie. They had grown tired of his mannerisms and his bungling methods, and had finally killed him during a bank getaway in Wisconsin the previous fall.

Ma had warned them to go back and strip the corpse. But the boys had felt that it wasn't worth the risk. So Charlie had rotted there in his clothes, and when Federal agents had come across him, they had checked his pockets and had found a Kansas City phone number. It belonged to a manufacturer of golf clubs. The Feds went to talk to him, learned about the trio's love for the game, and began checking public and private links around the city.

On July 7, as Holden, Keating, and Bailey were about to tee off at the Old Mission course, a dozen Federal agents leaped out of the bushes and surrounded them. There they were, America's three leading bank robbers, attired in sporty white knickers and argyle socks, and not even one lousy gun among them. It was humiliating.

Bernard Phillips, who was practising his putting a couple of hundred yards away, saw what was happening and raced to Ma's apartment with the news. She and the boys were just sitting down to a hot lunch when he came bursting in.

It was a close one. When the Feds arrived at the apartment a few minutes later, the food on the table was still warm.

The gang returned to St. Paul, where the heat generated by the Dunlop killing was beginning to dissipate. There was heat of another kind in town, though, so much of it through that sweltering summer of 1932 that Ma and the boys decided to move to a nearby resort called White Bear Lake. There, in a spacious two-story frame house in the wealthy Dellwood section, they began to pick up the pieces.

First there was an attempt to get Harvey Bailey off the hook. Underworld etiquette demanded it. They had worked a job together, and old Harve had been caught with a hot bond from that job in his pocket.

J. Earl Smith, a criminal lawyer from Tulsa, Oklahoma, was hired by the gang to defend Bailey. The evidence was too strong, though. Old Harve was convicted and sentenced. The gang felt that Smith had let them down. He received a phone call shortly after that, suggesting that he meet "the boys" in the vicinity of the lonely Indian Hills Country Club, fourteen miles north of Tulsa. They told him they might be able to throw some new business his way. Smith kept the appointment. The business was .38-caliber bullets. About ten of them.

Back at White Bear Lake Ma began to put together a new gang. Frank Nash had moved into a cottage a mile down the road. He visited her often. Larry DeVol had come north. A gunsel named Earl Christman had joined them.

Ma ruled over them all like a dowager empress. Even Frank Nash took orders. And why not? Holden and Keating were good examples of what happened to boys who didn't listen to Mother.

On the afternoon of July 25 members of the new gang left their hideouts and drifted south in small groups. The following morning they converged on the Cloud County Bank at Concordia, Kansas. They knocked it over with bewildering speed and precision, then scattered in all directions. When they reassembled at White Bear Lake a few days later, they were $240,000 richer.

They could take the rest of that summer off.

Christman had his girl, Helen, with him. Frank Nash had just gotten married a few weeks earlier. Larry DeVol was running around with two and three girls at once. Even Alvin Karpis stopped fishing long enough to drive in to St. Paul and pick up a pretty seventeen-year-old named Dolores Delaney.

Only Fred was without a girl.

It bothered him. But when he tried to bring one home, Ma came down hard on him. He had violated one of her three cardinal rules: don't talk, don't drink, don't run around with molls.

Fred pointed to the others. Ma told him to forget about the others. He was her boy and he wasn't going to run around with cheap sluts. There were endless arguments. Fred lost them all. Finally, unable to take any more of her possessiveness, he lit out on his own.

Ma was horrified—and had good reason to be.

On August 8 of that year he was identified as one of three gunmen who held up the Citizens' Security Bank at Bixby, Oklahoma. The take was chicken feed: $1,000 in cash. So there was Fred, a man who had just participated in a quarter-of-a-million-dollar robbery, risking his life for one third of a grand. It was enough to give Ma goose bumps.

Fortunately Dock Barker was paroled on September 27. Fred met him in McAlester, Oklahoma, and the two men headed back north together.

There was a happy—and relieved—family reunion when they reached White Bear Lake.

Volney Davis arrived a few days later. Ma had helped him get a parole, too. Davis had been sent up as Dock's accomplice in the killing of the night watchman. His alibi had been two girls with whom he had spent the night in Tulsa. Ma had asked him not to use them, since she had already gotten the girls to testify that they had been with Dock. Davis had gone along with it on the understanding that Ma would get him out later.

Davis had been born in the Cherokee Nation. He was a small, bushy-haired man, with sharp features and deep sunken eyes. He was only twenty-six but looked fifty. His first offense had been stealing a pair of shoes. They had given him three years for it, and he had come out dangerous.

For a while it was old home week. But Dock soon began to get restless. He wanted action. Ma told him no. Another one of her rules was: Don't work if you don't have to. And they didn't have to. They still had plenty of "paper" from the Concordia job. If they ran low on cash, all they had to do was sell a few more sheets of it to a hot bond pusher at fifty cents on the dollar.

In late November Ma took Volney Davis to visit her sister in California. Dock's restlessness increased. He drove in to the Twin City area and looked things over. He saw a bank he liked the looks of in Minneapolis. He cased it and headed back out to White Bear Lake.

Frank Nash didn't want any part of it. Alvin Karpis and the others were reluctant, too, but gradually allowed themselves to be talked into it. Dock was a small man, about five-four, weighing less than 120. He had his mother's face—the high cheekbones, the extremely intense eyes. And he had her persuasiveness, too. But not her sense.

On December 16 Dock, Fred, Alvin, Earl Christman, and Larry DeVol drove in to Minneapolis and hit the Third Northwestern Bank. The take was good ($20,000), but Dock's casing was downright miserable. Hidden alarms began clanging on all sides. The cops came running. Two of them were chopped down by the gang's machine gun fire. As the boys piled into the getaway car Fred spotted a civilian who looked like he was trying to memorize their license number. *Blam.* Down went the civilian.

Intense heat followed. The two policemen were dead, the civilian on the verge of death. The newspapers were screaming for blood. Harry Sawyer was aghast—it had happened in his own backyard. In the gang's, too—that was the unbelievable part. Frank Nash cut and ran. He knew what was coming. The gang was slower off the marks. Larry DeVol was the slowest of all; the cops nabbed him while he was still packing. The others raced to Reno, Nevada, where Ma joined them. There's no record of the tongue-lashing she gave them, but it must have been a sizzler.

The gang was down to four now: the two Barkers, Karpis, and Earl Christman. Bernard Phillips had pulled out, and Volney Davis, too. His sweetheart, Edna "The Kissing Bandit" Murray, had just escaped from the Missouri penitentiary, and the two of them were now on their second honeymoon.

The Barkers wintered in Reno, then packed up and headed to Chicago in late March. On their way Ma paused to finger a couple of banks in southern Nebraska. She was pleased to find them as stuffed as bed ticks despite the Depression.

She settled finally on the First National Bank in Fairbury. After chatting amiably with the vice-president for half an hour, she figured it good for at least a hundred and fifty thou.

In early April a souped-up black Plymouth jerked to a halt in front of the Fairbury bank. It was quarter to three in the afternoon—the best time, the vice-president had told Ma, to make a deposit. There was hardly anyone in the bank at that hour. The three hard-faced types who came piling out of the Plymouth didn't want to make a deposit, though. They had a large withdrawal in mind.

Fred Barker stayed at the wheel while Dock, Alvin, and Earl Christman hurried into the bank, looking like a string trio late for rehearsal. Inside the door they opened their violin cases and got everyone's attention by squeezing off a couple of noisy cadenzas.

Dock held down the lobby while Karpis and Earl Christman took the cages and vaults. Everything went smashingly until their exit. Then the vice-president went for a gun that he kept in his desk drawer. Dock caught the movement from the corner of his eye and swung toward him, shooting. The slugs lifted the VP out of his chair and flung him back against the wall, seriously wounded.

The bank guard saw that he wasn't covered and went for his gun. He managed to get off one shot before Dock nailed him to the floor with the Thompson.

Earl Christman dropped the sackful of cash that he was carrying and spun around, clutching at his chest. Karpis scooped the bag up and, with Dock's help, managed to drag the wounded gunman to the car.

The getaway went smoothly. The take was even a little better than Ma had figured—$151,350 in cash and securities. The VP's gun had been the only hitch, and Ma couldn't be faulted for that. She didn't have X-ray vision.

Earl Christman was badly wounded. He needed medical attention and immediately. The gang raced south and east toward Kansas City. They had an important underworld contact there, Verne Miller.

Verne had handled a submachine gun on a number of Holden-Keating raids. His usual slot was in the bank lobby. Sometimes he had been the tiger—the gunman outside the door. He was a tall, handsome man with silvery blond hair. He had been a parachute jumper at county fairs, a wrestler, a boxer, an expert machine gunner in the Army. He had come home from World War I a hero, and the folks had made him sheriff of his hometown in South Dakota.

Verne was a heavy drinker, though, a big spender. He had gone the embezzlement route. After two years in the pen, he had switched to bootlegging. Then the Depression had come, and he had switched again—to bank robbery. Recently he had switched professions a third time. He now managed a drop, or underworld post office, in Kansas City and also worked occasionally for the Syndicate as a torpedo, a hired killer.

The Holden-Keating crowd had never entirely trusted Miller. He was a hoodlum rather than a bandit. His real connections were with the mob. And there was the matter of his background, too. "Once a sheriff, always a sheriff"—that was Ma's opinion.

But now they needed him. Miller's home on posh Edgevale Road was an underworld clearing house. Contact could be made there with fences, crooked lawyers, and doctors who didn't report gunshot wounds.

The gang reached his place around midnight. Earl Christman was carried inside. Despite intensive medical care, he died toward morning.

The doctor's fees cost them plenty—and so did Verne Miller's funeral arrangements. As much as any gangster's funeral. Verne's services, as mob contact, didn't come cheaply. The ceremony was on the simple side, though. A car swung off a dirt road north of the city that night. In the glare of headlights, four men scooped out a shallow ditch and dropped Earl Christman into it. They kicked dirt over his stiffened body, climbed back into the car, and drove away.

Christman's girl, Helen, wanted to dig him up later and give him a decent funeral, but Ma Barker nixed the idea. "Dead men talk as much as live ones do," she ruled. "If they find him, they'll find us. He stays right where he's planted."

So far the Barker-Karpis outfit had covered their tracks well. Newspapers were blaming the Fairbury raid on "remnants of the old Keating gang led by Frank Nash." It would be the spring of 1934 before the name of Barker or Karpis would appear in print, and early 1935 before the Fairbury bank's vice-president would connect the "motherly-looking little woman" who had come in to see him with the, by then, notorious Ma Barker.

If the gang had continued to operate according to Ma's rules and under her personal supervision, chances are they could have gone another two or three years without fear of discovery. But it was around this time that the character of the gang began to change, and Ma Barker began to lose control of it.

It was mostly Harry Sawyer's doing.

Harry had gotten over his anger at the Minneapolis bank job.

In fact, it had given him an idea. There was hardly any profit left in supplying sanctuary to criminals. But with the police in his hip pocket, wouldn't St. Paul and Minneapolis make lovely places to plunder? Sawyer met with the boys in early May and discussed some targets. Ma refused to attend the meetings. She remained in Chicago, sulking. She disliked Sawyer, considered him a weakling. And she thought his wife, Gladys, a loud-mouthed troublemaker. She had advised the boys to have nothing to do with either of them, but they had ignored her.

Ma's preaching had been falling on many a deaf ear of late. Volney Davis had resumed his old romance with Edna Murray despite Ma's oft-stated dictum that the successful thief stayed away from liquor and women. And Alvin Karpis continued to share his quarters with Dolores Delaney. But the revolt that probably hurt Ma the most was Fred's. Her best-loved "young-un" had openly defied her by moving in with Tommy Harmon's libidinous widow, Paula.

These women had considerable influence on the boys and all of them had one thing in common: their dislike for Ma. And so the breach gradually widened.

On May 29 Harry Sawyer invited the boys to a meeting out at Jack Peifer's roadhouse, the Hollyhocks. He had, he said, a "fat cinch" of a job lined up. Were they interested? Dock said they were, and the gang's fate was twisted then and there.

The "fat cinch" was a kidnapping—the brainchild of Jack Peifer, a former bootlegger with Mafia connections, and two Chicago men, an ex-con named Charles J. Fitzgerald and another refugee from organized crime, Fred Goetz.

Goetz, also known as "Shotgun Ziegler," was a handsome rugged-looking man, the type one might run into in the locker room of a posh country club. He had been a student at the University of Illinois' School of Engineering and a campus football hero there, too. During the First World War he had been an enlisted flier. Then suddenly everything had fallen apart. While working as a lifeguard one summer, he had been arrested for the attempted rape of a seven-year-old girl, had jumped bond, and had vanished into the Chicago underworld. When he surfaced a few years later, it was as "Shotgun Ziegler," a torpedo for the Capone mob. His biggest contract was the St. Valentine's Day Massacre in 1929. Dressed as a policeman, he helped mow down six members of the Bugs Moran gang in a North Side garage. Now, with Repeal at hand and Capone in stir, he was casting around for a new way to make a buck.

The seven men discussed the kidnapping scheme. The intended victim was William A. Hamm, Jr., a wealthy St. Paul brewer. The job, Sawyer said, would be quick, safe, and clean, with his own police contacts keeping them informed of any progress that the Department might make.

After a few minutes' whispered conference, Karpis and the two Barker boys declared themselves in.

When they told Ma about it, she was aghast. Kidnapping was an amateur's game, she declared. "Good" criminals, the foundation blocks of the underworld, avoided it because it was a one-shot racket. Kidnapping was easier to solve than any other major crime. The life span of a kidnapping gang was exactly one kidnapping.

The boys pretended to listen, to think it over. They needed her. Goetz and Peifer had picked the victim; Fitzgerald would come up with the extra personnel and hideouts that a kidnapping required. But the plan itself would have to be theirs. They needed Ma's shrewd thinking to help them work out the details of the snatch and ransom pickup.

Gradually they managed to bring her around, to sweet-talk her into helping them, but only from a distance. She refused to become personally involved with Sawyer, Goetz, or that bunch. She didn't trust any of them.

By June 14, Ma and the boys had worked out a plan. Dock submitted it to Sawyer. He okayed it, and the following day the gang swung into action.

Hamm was seized as he stepped out of his office next door to the brewery. Two men pushed him into the back seat of a large black limousine. He was shoved face down on the floor, and a white hood was forced over his head as the car swung away from the curb and headed east.

That afternoon the brewery's sale manager, William V. Dunn, received a telephone call. A gruff voice at the other end demanded $100,000 in unmarked five-, ten-, and twenty-dollar bills for Hamm's safe return. Dunn consulted with the kidnapped man's family. His mother decided that the ransom should be paid. But she also wanted the police informed.

Dunn went to the police and told them what had happened. They presumably told Harry Sawyer, and Sawyer passed the information on, enabling the gang to follow the progress of negotiations from both ends.

Hamm was taken to Bensenville, Illinois, a small town twenty miles northwest of Chicago. There he was held in the home of Edmund Bartholmey, the future postmaster. He was treated well and fed simple but adequate meals. Fred Goetz was the only man to come in direct contact with him and he was careful to keep his face covered.

On June 17 Dunn received final instructions on how to deliver the ransom money. He was to travel north that night on U.S. 61

at twenty miles per hour, driving either a Ford or Chevrolet coupe with the doors off and the rumble seat removed and with a red lantern hanging on the back. Cars would pass him several times. When one of them blinked its lights five times, Dunn was to throw the money bag on the highway and proceed to the New Duluth Hotel to pick Hamm up.

Dunn did as he was told. North of White Bear Lake a big sedan roared past at seventy miles an hour, followed by a smaller car. They swung off the highway, let him pass, then sped by once more. This process was repeated several times. Finally Dunn saw the signal. A car's lights flashed five times. He flung the briefcase containing $100,000 onto the highway and continued north to the rendezvous point.

Hamm wasn't there, of course. He was released the following dawn at Wyoming, Minnesota, a small farming community forty miles north of St. Paul.

In their separate hideouts the gang celebrated. It had been a lead-pipe cinch. One hundred thousand dollars for three days' work. Everybody but Ma was impressed.

Two months later they were still in the clear. The snatch and ransom pickup had gone so smoothly and they had covered themselves so well that somebody else was now taking the fall for them. That somebody was Chicago gangster Roger Touhy.

The FBI was sure that Touhy had pulled the Hamm kidnapping. It didn't matter that Hamm was unable to identify Touhy and his confederates, or even that Touhy could prove that he had been elsewhere at the time. As far as the Feds were concerned, Touhy had done it.

On August 12 the Touhy gang was indicted for the Hamm kidnapping by a federal grand jury in St. Paul. Melvin Purvis, the FBI agent who had ridden herd on them, told newsmen: "We have an ironclad case."

Even as he spoke, the real kidnappers, still unknown to the world at large, were busy in another part of the city.

They were casing a payroll job. Apparently they didn't case it enough, though, for when they hit the Swift Company's messengers on the steps of the South St. Paul Post Office, three days later, things went badly. It was a messy job, ruled by violence. One policeman was killed outright, a second one badly wounded. The take: only $30,000.

The gang shouldn't have been working at all, of course—not with $100,000 in crisp new bills in their jeans.

But the money was worthless—a little something that Harry Sawyer had forgotten to mention to them. It was one of kidnapping's weak points, and there was nothing that could be done about it. The ransom money's serial numbers had been recorded and distributed to banks all over the country.

They could either sit and wait until things cooled off or sell the money now to underworld fences at ten cents on the dollar. The gang understandably preferrred to wait.

Meanwhile they had to live—and pay protection. Lots of it since the Hamm snatch. So the intervals between jobs got shorter, and the planning, no longer being done by Ma, got sloppier, more haphazard. There was almost always shooting now, and killing.

After the South St. Paul job the gang raced to Chicago and immediately pulled another one. Using armor-plated cars equipped with smoke screen devices, they ambushed a Federal Reserve mail truck. As they were escaping with several bags of worthless registered mail one of the cars became involved in a minor traffic accident at the corner of Jackson Boulevard and Halsted Street.

Patrolman Miles A. Cunningham saw the accident and approached. He knew nothing about the robbery, but that didn't matter—they couldn't let him take a close look at the car. Two machine gun blasts killed him.

Hotter than a two-dollar pistol, the gang fled back to St. Paul. Harry Sawyer was waiting for them. He had a bank job lined up, "a real soft touch," in his words.

Ma stayed in Chicago. She had had enough.

The gang had changed in the past year from a simple, old-fashioned heist outfit to a sprawling big city "mob" with connections reaching into the Syndicate, municipal politics, even into a couple of state capitals.

What had started out a tightly knit family group was now a cumbersome organization with a hard core of at least thirteen gangsters and their molls. Surrounding this core was a constantly changing cast of hangers-on. In fact, the gang was like a train: a minor gunsel got on and rode a way and then got off; then someone else came and took his place.

The quality of the personnel was changing, too. The Holdens, the Keatings, the Frank Nashes were gone, replaced by gangland topedoes and skittery drug addicts like Russell Gibson, alias "Slim Gray."

Alvin Karpis was still nominally the boss, sharing the decision-making with Dock and, to some extent, Fred Barker. But in reality, this trio had little control over such "marginal" members as Harry Campbell, Jesse Doyle, William E. Meade (known as "Christ Kid"), or Big Homer Wilson, alias "Charley Potatoes." And they had no control at all over Boss John J. McLaughlin, the Chicago ward heeler who now served as the gang's "hot money" agent.

Ma blamed it all on kidnapping. It had larded the gang's clean, muscular lines with go-betweens, hideout owners, money changers, molls, and camp followers. Parasites all of them, and as thick as lightning bugs on a June night. A beautiful beacon for the Feds, who were now moving in on the kidnapping racket in droves.

Ma sat in her Chicago apartment and waited, hoping that the boys would call her for advice. But the phone never rang.

In St. Paul, meanwhile, all was not right. In fact, things were in the deuce of a shape. Harry Sawyer had changed his mind about "the real soft touch" he had lined up. He no longer wanted the Commercial State Bank of Minneapolis robbed. He had a better idea. They could make more money by kidnapping its president, Edward G. Bremer.

Alvin Karpis was furious at this switch in plans. They needed cash—immediately. What good was more ransom money that couldn't be converted for months?

Harry Sawyer shrugged. If they weren't interested, he would find another gang.

He had them over a barrel, and they knew it. The gang hadn't gotten a plugged nickel out of that Federal Reserve mail robbery. They were in desperate financial straits.

Sawyer proceeded to sweeten the deal a bit. He would bankroll them for now, he said, and would also pass the ransom money for them. He guaranteed them an immediate forty cents on the dollar. Bremner, he pointed out, was loaded. They would demand twice what they had asked for Hamm—$200,000.

The boys talked it over among themselves. Finally Fred spoke and for the first time in his life he had a good idea. "Give us a couple of days," he told Sawyer. "We want to go to Chicago, talk to Ma about it."

Sawyer, a shrewd psychologist if he was nothing else, said that it was mighty strange that grown men couldn't make a simple decision without running to their mother. Stung by his criticism, the three of them reluctantly agreed to engineer the Bremer kidnapping.

Later Dock Barker would admit it had been the wrong decision. Ma had been right. Kidnapping was a mug's game. They should never have gotten involved in it. But now that they were, there was no getting free of it. They were like cats on flypaper. When they raised one foot, the other sank into the mess.

CHAPTER TWO

Machine Gun Kelly—and the Girl in Front of Him

From outside, the Hamm job looked beautiful. No sweat, no danger, and a payoff of one hundred thousand dollars. To those unable to see kidnapping's basic, built-in flaws, it looked like the key to instant wealth. A whole slew of abductions followed. And because nervous amateurs and psychopaths were often involved, a few ended in disaster.

The nation's traumatic reaction to the Lindbergh kidnapping had already brought prompt action from Washington. Abduction across a state line was now a Federal offense, with the kidnappers liable to life sentences.

That didn't seem to worry Kathryn Kelly.

Kathryn wanted to be a big-timer, to lead a gang of dashing desperadoes on a cross-country orgy of kidnapping and plunder. She wanted to be another Ma Barker, or her idea of what Ma Barker was, at any rate—a sequined, bejeweled Garbo with a machine gun, probably.

The trouble was, she had powerful poor material with which to work. Namely, herself and her husband, amiable, scatter-brained George (Machine Gun) Kelly.

Kathryn was born in Saltillo, Mississippi, in 1904. She was christened Cleo, but she felt there was something "frowzy" about the name and changed it later. She was an alert, imaginative child, dark-eyed, dark-haired, almost beautiful. Her father's side of the family was eminently respectable, but her mother was a Coleman, and in the Southwest a lot of the Colemans were operators of whiskey stills, counterfeiters, and prostitutes. They were thickest around the town of Coleman, in the county of the same name, Texas. When Kathryn was seventeen, her mother left her father and moved to Coleman. Kathryn, already married and divorced and with a two-year-old daughter of her own, went with her. Her mother opened a small hotel, which quickly gained an unsavory reputation. Kathryn became its bootlegger, driving a big roadster full of half-gallon fruit jars down from Fort Worth every other night. Eventually she moved to Fort Worth for good, leaving the baby with her mother. She worked as a manicurist and went to the movies a lot. She also dated—usually for money. Twice she was arrested for soliciting. Friends from this period remember her as a bewildering mixture of naiveté and toughness. She dressed well, even stylishly, used "far better than average" English, had a queer kind of "Southern Belle" charm. Yet at the same time, a man who dated her said, "She knows more bums than the Police Department, can drink liquor like water, and has some of the toughest women friends I ever laid eyes on."

When she was twenty, Kathryn married a bootlegger named Charlie Thorne. He built her a home on Mulkey Street in Fort Worth and another one in Coleman. They spent most of their marriage shuttling between the places, loaded to the gills and brawling. Charlie was an eye-blacker; Kathryn preferred firearms. Twice during these marital bruhahas she almost drilled him.

One night early in 1927 Kathryn drove into a Fort Worth gas station. "Where you all headed, Kathryn?" the attendant asked her as he serviced the car.

"I'm bound for Coleman to kill that goddamned Charlie Thorne," she said fiercely. Gears meshed, and the car roared away.

The next morning the bootlegger was found dead with a revolver at his side. A typewritten note said: *I can't live with her or without her, hence I am departing this life.*

Friends agreed they had never heard Charlie use that kind of language while he was alive. Most doubted his ability to even spell *hence.* A coroner's jury gallantly tipped their hats to Kathryn, though, and called it suicide.

Shortly after this the widow Thorne began to take long trips. She would be gone from Fort Worth for weeks at a time. She told friends that she was visiting her mother, now remarried and living on a ranch near Paradise, Texas. It was rumored, however, that she was fingering banks for bandit gangs and sharing in the proceeds.

On one of these trips Kathryn met George Kelly. He was a big, round-faced man with piercing blue eyes and slicked-back hair. He had once been a "society bootlegger" in Memphis but had been run out of town and had shifted operations to New Mexico. After serving a few months in the state pen there, he had moved on once again, this time to Oklahoma City, where he was now drinking almost as much bathtub gin as he sold.

Kelly was all mouth. The way he told it, he was the most dangerous man alive: wanted in twelve states for murder, bank robbery, and kidnapping. He would never be taken alive, he vowed. "Come and get me, coppers!" he would snarl at imaginary posses, his trigger finger tightening around the stem of his glass.

Kathryn was amused by him. But she also caught something in him. Some quality that could be developed, possibly exploited. She noticed that other people were impressed by him. Some who should have known better even feared him. He was a big man and he talked hard; and in a world of surface impressions that went a long way.

Kathryn decided to organize a Kelly promotion campaign. She was rather disgruntled with the cuts she had been receiving on certain jobs. If word got around that her man was tough, maybe she could get him into a gang. This would automatically double her take, and also place her own personal agent in a strategic spot.

The campaign she mounted would have impressed George Washington Hill. Kelly was marketed like a new brand of soap suds. Everywhere Kathryn went, she talked him up, telling endless stories about his violence, his daring depredations, his running battles with hordes of police.

She had taken the precaution, meanwhile, of removing the object of the campaign from circulation. According to Kathryn, he was on the lam somewhere, fighting off posses. Actually, Kelly was on her mother's ranch, fighting off the DT's.

As soon as he was sufficiently dried out, Kathryn bought him a submachine gun and forced him to start practising with it. In time he became rather adept in its use. According to Kathryn, he could knock a row of walnuts off the top of a fence. The spent cartridges from these sessions were gathered up, and Kathryn passed them out to underworld acquaintances with the message: "Here's a souvenir I brought you. It's a cartridge fired by George's machine gun—Machine Gun Kelly, you know."

She couldn't watch him all the time, though, and one day George escaped. When next heard from, he was in Oklahoma—and in jail. The charge: smuggling liquor into an Indian reservation. It was a Federal offense, and so the amiable Kelly was shipped off to Leavenworth, where he was liked by everyone, including the guards.

Kathryn didn't give up. She bided her time, guarding the legend, nurturing it. The Leavenworth part sounded good; she glossed over the humiliating circumstances that had landed him there.

He was released in 1931, and this time Kathryn married him. It was the only way she could really keep tabs on him. She also got him a job with a couple of small-time bank-robbing gangs. It's known that he helped knock over a jug at Tupelo, Mississippi, and another at Wilmer, Texas. And there may have been others.

As the Depression deepened, Kathryn's mind turned to kidnapping. The successful Hamm job provided the immediate inspiration, but the whole idea of kidnapping was in the air that spring of 1933.

Old-time heist men spurned the racket. It seemed wrong to them in a way that taking bank money didn't. It was beneath their dignity, somehow, like picking pockets or shop-lifting. But the small-fry on the edges of crime, the ones who were beginning to find bank robbery increasingly dangerous and difficult, they went for it and in a big way.

That spring saw the Mary McElroy kidnapping, the Charles Boettcher abduction in Denver, and, of course, the Hamm job.

Now Kathryn Kelly decided to have a try at it.

Her first attempt was pitiful. She, Kelly, and a bank-robbing companion went to South Bend, Indiana, looked in the directory, and found the name of an influential businessman. They put the snatch on him and asked for $50,000. The man had been hard hit by the Depression, though. He didn't even have $50. They held on to him for a while, wondering what to do, then finally released him when he promised to raise the money if they would let him go. Naturally that was the last they heard of him.

Kathryn began to get the picture. They needed somebody with brains in the gang. The two-bit bank bandit was bounced, and Kathryn sent for Albert Bates, an old friend.

Bates was a middle-aged swindler and con man who had done time in three different state pens. He and Kathryn selected Guy Waggoner, son of a millionaire Fort Worth banker, as their next victim.

Bates' brains were no match for Kathryn's tongue, though. At a party she threw that spring in her Mulkey Street home she got drunk and outlined the whole snatch plan to a couple of detectives she had befriended. Kathryn thought she was using them to gain information about law enforcement activities; actually they were using her to get information about the underworld.

The two dicks, Ed Weatherford and J. W. Swinney, hurried away from the party and warned the prospective victim of his danger. He was immediately put under heavy guard. And that was the end of that.

Undaunted, the gang switched their attention to Charles F. Urschel, a wealthy Oklahoma City oilman. They decided to ask $200,000 for Urschel's safe return, and to use the Paradise, Texas, ranch as the abduction hideout.

The man Kathryn's mother had married, balding, hawk-nosed Robert G. Shannon, was already running a busy cooling-off spot there. Outlaws were constantly coming and going, paying up to $50 a night for the privilege of hiding out.

It was hardly the coolest spot in the Southwest, but Kathryn decided it was just the place to conceal Urschel. Kelly didn't argue with her, and Bates, while he didn't like it, couldn't figure out a better setup.

On the night of July 22 Urschel and his wife were sitting on the screened sun porch of their Oklahoma City mansion, playing bridge with their neighbors, Mr. and Mrs. Walter Jarrett. Suddenly the screen door was thrown open, and Machine Gun Kelly and Bates entered. Both carried Tommy guns.

"Stick 'em up," said Kelly. "Which one's Urschel?" Neither man said anything. Kelly glared at one, then the other. "All right," he said finally, "we'll take both of you."

Kelly warned the women not to move until they heard a car start in the driveway. Then he and Bates moved off into the darkness, herding their captives before them. As soon as they were gone, Mrs. Urschel rushed to the telephone and called Oklahoma City's chief of police. He advised her to call the FBI in Washington on the special kidnap line that had just been installed. She did, and found herself talking directly to J. Edgar Hoover. She explained the situation, and Hoover reassured her, saying that his department would do nothing to endanger her husband's life. Even the ransom payment question would be left up to her.

As soon as he hung up, Hoover threw all the Bureau's investigative machinery into action. He volleyed orders to the FBI's Oklahoma City office. He rounded up agents from surrounding districts and sent them hurrying toward the Urschel home.

The kidnap car, meanwhile, had reached the city limits and had turned off onto a dirt road. After bumping along it for some twelve miles, it stopped. Urschel and Jarrett were forced to empty their pockets. Urschel's identity was established from papers he had in his wallet, and Jarrett was put out of the car, which then disappeared to the south.

So far, so good. The case was a blank as far as the investigators were concerned.

But Kathryn couldn't leave well enough alone. As soon as Urschel arrived at the Shannon ranch in Paradise, blindfolded and with cotton taped over his ears, she decided to drive in to Fort Worth and find out if the law had any leads. They didn't, of course, but she would now provide their first.

She phoned one of her two detective friends and invited him to drop by her place on Mulkey Street. She said she had something she wanted to tell him. (Unbelievably, she had never figured out the connection between the two dicks and the sudden security net that had been thrown around their prospective victim, Waggoner. As far as Kathryn was concerned, she was still using them rather than vice versa.)

The detective stopped by and found that Kathryn had nothing specific to tell him. She just wanted to chat. That made him suspicious and therefore observant. She told him she had just driven in from St. Louis, but he noticed that she didn't seem tired from the trip. Furthermore, there was an Oklahama City paper on the front seat of her sixteen-cylinder roadster, and the red clay of Oklahoma on the tire rims.

As he was leaving, Kathryn suddenly—rather impusively—asked him a favor. In case her husband or his partner, Albert Bates, ever got in trouble out of the state, would he wire that they were wanted for bank robbery in Texas? "Why, sure," said the detective, grinning, and went straight to the FBI with the information.

That night Urschel was transferred from the main ranch house to a smaller cabin. He was made to lie down on a quilt and was handcuffed to a baby's high chair. He heard voices through the cotton in his ears. They belonged to Robert Shannon's son, Armon, and his young wife. Kelly had talked them into taking Urschel in. The main house was going to be filled with outlaws for the next few days. An escape party from the Kansas State Pen led by old-time bank robber, Harvey Bailey, had just arrived.

The next morning the kidnappers told Urschel that Oklahoma City was crawling with Feds, and it would be safer to make contact in Tulsa. Did he have a trusted friend there? Urschel did—an oilman named John G. Catlett.

The following day a package was delivered to Catlett by a Western Union messenger. It contained three letters. One was addressed to Catlett, another to Urschel's wife, and a third—typewritten—to E. E. Kirkpatrick of Oklahoma City, an old friend of the family. This letter, appointing Kirkpatrick go-between, demanded $200,000 for Urschel's safe return. If his family agreed to pay the demanded ransom, they were to insert a carefully worded advertisement in the *Daily Oklahoman*'s classified ad columns.

After a family conference, the ad was inserted. It read:

FOR SALE
160 Acres Land, good five-room house, deep well.
Also Cows, Tools, Tractors, Corn, and Hay.
$3750 for quick sale . . . TERMS . . . Box H-807.

Fort Worth detectives, meanwhile, had placed Kathryn's Mulkey Street home under surveillance, and J. Edgar Hoover had ordered an investigation into the Kellys' recent activities.

Two days after the ad appeared in the *Daily Oklahoman*, the Urschel family received another letter of instructions, this one mailed from Joplin, Missouri. Acting on it, Kirkpatrick left Oklahoma City carrying $200,000 in new twenty-dollar bills stuffed inside a briefcase. Their serial numbers had of course been recorded by the FBI.

He boarded *The Sooner*, as instructed, and proceeded to the last coach. He was to watch for two successive fires on the right side of the railroad tracks, then toss the briefcase from the observation platform.

Kirpatrick watched all the way to Kansas City but saw nothing. He was practically beside himself with worry. Had he somehow missed them? Or worse, had he endangered Urschel's life by bringing along John Catlett?

In Kansas City the two men proceeded to the Muehlebach Hotel, and Kirkpatrick registered there as E. E. Kincaid of Little Rock, Arkansas, as instructed. There was nothing to do now but wait. And hope.

At ten o'clock the following morning a postal telegram arrived. It read: UNAVOIDABLE INCIDENT KEPT ME FROM SEEING YOU LAST NIGHT WILL COMMUNICATE ABOUT 6:00 O'CLOCK. E. W. MOORE.

The "incident" had been Machine Gun Kelly's usual bumbling. In his nervousness he had flooded the engine of the gang's new Buick, and they had arrived at the rendezvous point too late to light any fires. They had been unable to follow their own elaborate, uncompromising instructions and had been forced to stand there in the darkness while the train—and $200,000—had roared past them.

The next contact attempt was more successful. The phone rang at 5:45 that same afternoon, and a husky voice told Kirkpatrick to take a Yellow cab to the La Salle Hotel and walk west with the briefcase in his right hand. "Can I bring a friend along?" Kirkpatrick asked.

"Hell, no!" the voice exploded. "We know all about your friend. You come alone and unarmed."

Twenty minutes later Kirkpatrick set out from the La Salle, walking west on Linwood. He noticed two cars parked across the boulevard and thought he saw a figure step out from behind one of them. Moments later a tall, heavyset man caught up with him. The man didn't stop, though. He kept walking, glancing furtively at Kirkpatrick from the corner of his eye. A few yards farther up the street he suddenly stopped and turned. "Mr. Kincaid, I'll take that bag," he whispered.

Kirkpatrick stalled. "How do I know you're the right party?"

"Hell, you know damned well I am."

"Two hundred thousand dollars is a lot of money," Kirkpatrick said, as his eyes took in every detail about the man—the black hair, dark skin, the stylish summer suit, the two-toned shoes, and the turned-down Panama hat. "I want some kind of assurance."

Kelly tugged nervously at his hat brim. "Don't argue with me!" he rasped. "The boys are waiting."

Kirkpatrick sensed that he had the upper hand. He put the briefcase on the sidewalk between his legs. "Tell me definitely what I can tell Mrs. Urschel. When will her husband be home?"

Kelly was shifting nervously from foot to foot now, his face red with mingled rage, anxiety, and embarrassment. "Inside of twelve hours," he promised hoarsely.

Kirkpatrick decided that he had pushed him far enough. He didn't want to jeopardize the transaction. He left the bag where it was and walked away without looking back.

Kelly and Bates headed to the Paradise ranch with the ransom money. They arrived there at two o'clock the following afternoon. Kathryn was waiting for them. The three of them divided up the loot. The Kellys got half, Bates half. The expenses had come to $11,500. That left each of them with $94,250 profit.

Bates packed up his share of the money and went out to the back porch to clean up. There sat Harvey Bailey. Bates was aghast. Had he heard them arguing? "Listen," he told the bank bandit nervously. "This place is hot. I told the others to get out. Why didn't you go with them?"

Bailey pointed to his leg. He had caught a bullet while exchanging shots with a posse. The leg looked bad. Bates peeled off $500 of the kidnay money and handed it to Bailey. "Here. You better get going," he said. "Go see a doctor."

Bates drove out to Armon Shannon's cabin and told Urschel he was going to be released. The oilman's nine-day beard was shaved off, and he was loaded into Bates's car, still blindfolded.

Nineteen miles from Oklahoma City the car stopped. Urschel was given a hat and a ten-dollar bill and was told to start walking. There was a gas station up ahead where he could call a cab.

An hour later Urschel arrived home. After he had rested, he gave FBI men a detailed account of everything that had happened to him. While he couldn't provide any direct clues to the identity of his kidnappers, the FBI claimed he had observed a lot of significant details.

These included an accurate guess as to the make of the car in which he had been carried, the amount of time he had traveled, and an important snatch of conversation that had occurred just before they had reached their destination. The car had stopped at a gas station where a woman had filled the tank. "How are crop conditions?" one of the kidnappers had asked her.

"The crops around here are burned up," she had replied, "although we may make some broom corn."

He had noticed other things, too. Water being drawn by bucket from a well outside the house in which he had been held prisoner.

Water with a strong mineral taste. And the sound of an airplane passing overhead twice a day, at 9:45 in the morning and 5:45 at night. One day it had rained, though, and that day—Sunday, July 30—Urschel had not heard the morning plane. (Though the kidnappers had taken his watch, Urschel told FBI men that he had figured the time out by mentally counting off five minutes, then casually asking one of his guards what time it was.)

FBI agents now went to work with this information. They checked airline schedules for a radius of six hundred miles around Oklahoma City, then began to compare schedules with meteorological data. They learned that an American Airways plane on the Fort Worth-Amarillo run had been forced to make a wide detour to the north on July 30 to avoid a heavy rainstorm. U.S. Weather Bureau records in Dallas confirmed another important fact. That entire section of Texas had been suffering from heavy drought. The corn had begun to burn in the fields before the July 30 rains had brought relief.

The FBI men concentrated on the American Airways schedule now, calculating that planes on the Amarillo-Fort Worth run would pass over a point near Paradise, Texas, at the hours recalled by Urschel. A search of the surrounding countryside located a farmhouse that matched Urschel's description. There was a well to the northwest of it, and the water from it had a strong mineral taste.

Bureau agents swooped down on the farm. Mr. and Mrs. R. G. Shannon were questioned. They confessed that they had helped guard Urschel. The actual kidnappers, they said, were Mrs. Shannon's daughter, Kathryn, her notorious husband, George (Machine Gun) Kelly, and his confederate, Albert L. Bates.

This tale of Holmesian detection thrilled the nation. It had been a brilliant performance, everyone agreed, achieved in the face of almost insurmountable odds. The Bureau, only a few months earlier the target of such criticism that there was talk around Washington that it would soon be disbanded and its functions turned over to the Department of the Interior, was now eulogized in newspapers, magazines, radio, and newsreels.

Overlooked in the general chorus of praise, however, was a rather significant point. The Bureau, thanks to that tip from the Fort Worth detective, had started investigating the Kellys *before* Urschel's release. They knew about Kathryn's mother, and they knew about the ranch she lived on near Paradise. Checking the ranch out was routine police procedure. The brackish well water, the airline schedule, and the comment about the burned-up crops made good, colorful copy, but it had little bearing on the decision to investigate the place.

Nor was the raiding party made up exclusively of FBI men. There were four federal agents in the group, a deputy sheriff from Oklahoma City, Urschel himself, and eight police officers from Fort Worth and Dallas, including the two who had originally provided the government with the tip, Detectives Swinney and Weatherford.

The fourteen men piled out of their cars just after dawn on August 12, 1933, and spread out, moving across the sandy, rutted fields toward the ranch house. Special Agent Gus T. Jones spotted a man sleeping on an improvised bed in the backyard. Cautiously he edged his way around the house, machine gun ready. He recognized the man. It was Harvey Bailey. Beside him on the bed were a fully loaded automatic rifle and a .45 automatic pistol.

"Get up, Harvey," Jones said softly. Bailey's eyes snapped open. "If a shot is fired, I'll riddle you."

"I'm here alone," Bailey said. "You've got me." Cautiously, without moving his hands, he crossed his legs. "Well, after all," he chuckled, "a fellow has to sleep sometime."

For a while Bailey's capture overshadowed the rest of the case. His name, from the early '20s on, had been a kind of catch-all for every major criminal catastrophe in the U.S. Old Harve had been blamed for the St. Valentine's Day rubout, the Columbus Prison Riot, the Lindbergh kidnapping, even the Kansas City Massacre.

After working the Fort Scott, Kansas, job with the Barker-Karpis gang the previous spring, Bailey had been caught, convicted, and sent to the Kansas State Pen. There he had immediately gotten down to work organizing his escape. On Memorial Day he and ten other cons had come barreling out, kidnapping the warden and two guards and heading south toward the Cookson Hills.

Wilbur Underhill, a cop killer known as the "Tri-State Terror," was a member of Bailey's crashout party, and so were Bob Brady, Ed Davis, Jim Clark, and Frank Sawyer, all of them extremely desperate Oklahoma outlaws.

They robbed banks, stole automobiles, kidnapped motorists, and battled posses as they fled southward. Four were killed and two captured before they reached the sanctuary of the hills. There, Bailey split away from the others, making his way slowly south to Paradise, Texas. His eventual destination, some say, was Mexico.

Now, once again, Bailey was in the hands of the law. The raiding party searched him and found $500 of the Urschel ransom money in his pockets. Old Harve explained how it had gotten there, but the lawmen just laughed.

That was probably what hurt the most. Harvey Bailey, dean of

American bank robbers, the last of the Old West badmen, accused of participating in a chintzy, amateurish kidnapping.

They made the charge stick, though. He was sent to Leavenworth on a life sentence and wasn't paroled until 1962. (And even then the AP dispatch that announced the event described him as "the kidnapper of Urschel.")

There was still one last, typical Bailey touch to the whole affair, though. While awaiting trial in the Dallas jail in September 1933, old Harve sawed his way to freedom. It wasn't a difficult job because when Bailey's arm got tired, the jailer, Thomas L. Manion, would take his place at the bars. The saw had a tendency to stick, so Manion went to a local hardware store and bought a can of oil that made the sawing easier. All this on the strength of Bailey's promise to cut Manion in on his next three bank jobs.

When Bailey hit the street, he stole the first car he saw. Roadblocks were immediately set up, posses formed in four states. Finally after a wild, gun-blazing finale Bailey was trapped in Ardmore, Oklahoma, and returned to Dallas. His only comment as he puffed reflectively on a cigarette was: "Well, I got out, didn't I?"

The very same day that the Shannon ranch was raided, Albert Bates, by the sheerest coincidence, was arrested out in Denver on suspicion of passing stolen Express Company checks.

Albert was extremely nervous. He still had Urschel money in his pockets. He had to get out before they began checking the serial numbers. Remembering the deal that Kathryn had set up with the two Fort Worth detectives, he sent word to his wife to summon them. Within hours a telegram was on its way to Weatherford and Swinney. It read: HELD IN DENVER WANTED IN BLUE RIDGE, TEXAS, BANK ROBBERY. WILL WAIVE EXTRADITION. COME AT ONCE.

They came at once, all right, but from Washington. Feds by the dozen.

"Oh, my God," croaked Machine Gun Kelly as he read the news in a hotel room in Des Moines. "It's all over."

He and Kathryn had been on the run from the moment they had released Urschel. They had traveled north to Omaha, then to Chicago, finally to Minneapolis, where underworld bankers had bought part of the ransom cash at cut-rate prices.

They had moved on to Cleveland next, looking gaudier than a Memphis whorehouse. Anyone else on the run would have done his best to look average, which in 1933 meant poor. But not Machine Gun and wife. Kathryn was still driving her big sixteen-cylinder roadster, silver fox furs flying from her throat. She had also added a gold watch set with two hundred and thirty-four diamonds to her finery, plus a thousand-dollar dinner ring and a large collection of Chanel originals. George, for his part, had become a platinum blond (through misreading the directions on a bottle of hair dye) and, to top things off, had taken to wearing blue-tinted octagon glasses. Wherever they went, heads understandably turned.

They fled Cleveland when the Minneapolis money changers were nabbed by the Feds, stopped briefly in Chicago, then moved on to Des Moines.

And that's where they were on August 12, the day the sweet-smelling hit the fan.

The Shannons and Albert Bates nabbed the same day! How could it have happened?

Kelly lost what was left of his cool. J. Edgar Hoover later recorded the scene for posterity: Machine Gun pacing back and forth, bellowing at his wife, "I was the biggest damn fool in the world to ever let you suck me into this thing. Here I was, making fifty grand a year knocking over these tin-can state banks. But that wasn't good enough for you. Now we've got G-heat smeared all over us. It's a fine mess you've got us into."

But Kelly's Oliver Hardy-like tirade was nothing to what Kathryn gave him back. It was all his fault that her mother now faced life imprisonment for harboring Urschel, she stormed. He was yellow, a phony, a cheap, sniveling punk that she had built up into a national menace.

Kelly tried to weather the storm with gin, but there was no letup. Finally, just to stop her voice, he agreed to surrender himself if the government would free Kathryn's mother and stepfather.

Negotiations were immediately begun through underworld contacts. But word came filtering back from the government—no trade. Everyone involved in the Urschel kidnapping would be prosecuted to the full extent of the law.

By now the Kellys were low on money. With their usual shrewdness, they had buried most of the ransom loot on the Texas ranch of one of Kathryn's relatives. Now, with every relative being watched around the clock, there was no way they could get to it.

Kathryn headed south anyway, driving a dusty Ford pickup truck and wearing a red wig. George remained hidden in a cooling-off joint in the Oklahoma City area.

The great dust storms had already begun that summer, raking the topsoil from the dried-out fields of Texas and Oklahoma, filling the air with towering clouds of chocolate and tan dirt that blotted out the sun. By autumn the first refugees had appeared on the roads: gaunt men in faded overalls and squashed-down hats, and barefoot women, leading strings of corn-headed, wide-eyed children.

Outside Hillsboro, Texas, Kathryn came across three of them, hitchhiking along the edge of the highway. "Can I give you a lift?" she asked. She could, indeed. They were an itinerant farm laborer, his wife, and twelve-year-old daughter, Geraldine.

Where were they headed? Kathryn wanted to know. The man shrugged. "Anywhere but here," he said. "There ain't nothin' here. Fifty cents a clean acre for choppin' cotton, an' folks beggin' for the chance to chop."

An idea began to form in Kathryn's mind. She treated them to meals and put them up at a cabin that night. She also bought clothes for Geraldine, who, as she put it, "reminds me so much of my own dear little girl."

The next morning she suddenly said, "I can fix it so you can make some money. Can I trust you?" They said she could, and Kathryn announced dramatically. "I'm Kathryn Kelly. You've seen my name in the newspapers. I'm on the run and I need your help."

What she needed, specifically, was the man's services as a messenger. He was glad to oblige her, and in the days that followed he was sent to a lawyer's office in Fort Worth to inquire once again into the possibilities of a Kelly-for-Shannon trade and, when that fell through, to a lawyer in Memphis to try and arrange a dig-up of the ransom loot.

When the lawyer visited the ranch where it was buried, however, Kathryn's relative, Cassey Coleman, was so scared he pretended he didn't know what the man was talking about. It was hopeless, the lawyer reported back to Kathryn. "Tried to get later appointment but prospect was afraid. Impossible to change his mind."

A new idea began to take shape in Kathryn's hot little brain. Since the government already had her real daughter in custody, the Feds wouldn't be looking for a man and a woman traveling with a child. "I'd just love to take Geraldine on a little trip with me," she told the mother. "It'll only be two hundred and fifty miles."

It was many times that, for the child was perfect camouflage, and enabled the Kellys to flee back north to Chicago.

George was drinking heavily now and writing threatening letters to everyone involved in the Bates-Shannon trial in Oklahoma City. One of these letters, addressed to "Ignorant Charles" (Urschel), stated:

". . . if the Shannons are convicted look out, and God help you for he is the only one that will be able to do you any good. In the event of my arrest I've already formed an outfit to take care of and destroy you and yours the same as if I was there. I am spending your money to have you and your family killed—nice—eh? You are bucking people who have cash—planes, bombs and unlimited connections both here and abroad."

The tougher he got on paper, the more Kelly fell apart personally. By the third week of September he was practically a basket case. Kathryn had to take him by the hand at one point and lead him to a neighborhood grind house. Leaving him huddled in the darkest part of the theater, she calmly went about renting a new hideout.

Chicago started to heat up, though—the result of the postmarks on the numerous threats that Kelly had been mailing to everyone.

Once again they had to flee, this time to Memphis, where Kelly still had some contacts from his bootlegging days. Geraldine was beginning to get underfoot, though, so Kathryn sent her home to her parents. A fatal mistake, for the Feds had already picked them up.

The girl was questioned closely. She told FBI men that the Kellys were living in Memphis with a man whose name she didn't know but whom they called "Tich."

Word went out to the Memphis police: Did they know any underworld figure with that nickname? They did. J. C. Tichenor. He had a bungalow on the edge of town. Federal agents were immediately rushed into Memphis by airplane.

The rest of the story is one of those classic FBI cameos: a dawn raid and Kelly, caught without a machine gun in his hands, cringing before the officers, pleading, "Don't shoot, G-men! Don't shoot, G-men!"

It was the first time the public had heard the term. The first time according to the Feds, that they themselves had heard it. They reportedly asked Kelly what it meant, and he (reportedly) told them that it was underworld parlance for "Government men," a dread term, he added, that meant only one thing to every crook—the jig was up.

It was a short, colorful name, ideal for headline purposes. The press seized on it. Magazines and movies took it up. It became as much a part of the language of the thirties as Mickey Mouse, Joe Louis, Popeye, or "They Satisfy." It put the FBI inside every home, on bubble gum cards and breakfast cereals, and it had a lot to do with making that organization as sacrosanct in time as apple pie, Mom, and the American flag.

There's still debate, though, over the word's actual origin and doubt as to whether Machine Gun Kelly ever really used it. After some of the excitement had died down, Memphis police gave

Howard McLellan of *Harper's* their own version of the historic capture.

For one thing, there were more city detectives in the raiding party than Federal men, they said, and it was one of their own boys, Detective Sergeant W. J. Raney, who made the actual pinch. He slipped into the bungalow around 6 A.M. while the others covered him. As he tiptoed through the front room the bedroom door suddenly swung open. Kelly stood there, an automatic in his hand. He hesitated just a fraction of a second—and Raney made his move. He shoved his shotgun barrel into Kelly's stomach and said, "Drop that gun." Kelly dropped it.

"I've been waiting all night for you," said Kelly, grinning.

"Well," said Raney, "here we are."

If Kelly used the word "G-men," Memphis police didn't hear it. It would have been a word of his own invention, too, for one thing is certain: *G-man* was *not* an underworld term prior to Kelly's capture on September 26, 1933. Nor did criminals use it after that except in a derisive sense. The common, everyday term for FBI agents, both before and after the Memphis raid, was *Feds.*

Kelly, in captivity, was his old self once again—calm, amiable, even charming at times. He seemed relieved that it was over.

FBI men, meanwhile, had recovered what was left of the Kellys' share of the ransom loot: $73,250, found buried in a two gallon Thermos jug on the Coleman ranch in Texas.

The trial that followed was unprecedented in many ways. The prosecutor was Joseph Keenan, the Assistant Attorney General of the United States. He got life sentences not only for the Kellys and Albert Bates, but also for Harvey Bailey and the Shannons. He also fought for, and got, unusually heavy sentences for the Minneapolis money changers, Bates's lawyer, and a number of other people accused of harboring the kidnappers.

It was obvious that this was a "show trial," a declaration of war by the Justice Department on kidnappers in general. There could be no loose ends in a harsh example of this kind. Its deterrent value depended upon a clean, across-the-board sweep. So a lot of people who had merely touched the ransom money at some point also ended up serving long jail sentences.

The Kellys were small potatoes right to the end. They blamed each other for everything. Kathryn wept and decried the hoodlum who "had brought this disgrace upon her family." George said that if it hadn't been for him, Urschel would have been rubbed out.

The Justice Department sided with Kelly's version of events. Kathryn became the mastermind, the instigator. Kelly's mild, easygoing manner made him a lousy "heavy." Only the dupe's role really fitted him. As he was led from the courtroom in the custody of U.S. Marshals, Oklahoma City newsboys were already on the streets, shouting, "Paper here! Read all about it. Popgun Kelly gets the limit. It's life for Kelly!"

He served most of it on The Rock. Shortly before his death at Leavenworth in 1954, he wrote to Urschel, the man he had helped kidnap: ". . . these five words seem written in fire on the walls of my cell: 'Nothing can be worth this.' "

Kathryn Kelly remained in prison until 1958. At that time the government let its case against her drop.

The circumstances are interesting.

Kathryn's new attorney claimed that her original trial had been unfair. His argument was that the Department of Justice, in their eagerness to secure life sentences for all the principals in the Urschel kidnapping, had cut a few corners in establishing her personal involvement. What he specifically had in mind was their contention that she had signed one of the threatening letters to Urschel. Kathryn maintained that she had not. A local handwriting expert had testified that the signature was hers. The new attorney argued that Kathryn should have been permitted to call in another handwriting expert.

The Federal judge who heard this argument ordered the prosecution to produce the twenty-five-year-old records of the case. The Department of Justice refused. So the judge set aside Kathryn's conviction and freed her on bond pending a new trial.

According to Edward Bennet Williams, the famous Washington defense attorney, the reason the government had refused to produce their files was that the FBI had in its possession, at the time of Kathryn's trial, evidence that she had *not* signed the letter in question. That evidence was the testimony of their own handwriting expert, Charles A. Appel. Rather than reveal this deliberate suppression of vital evidence, the government chose to keep the files closed and forget the case.

The Urschel kidnapping is the cornerstone of the FBI's Public Enemy Era reputation, a vital part of the Bureau's overall legend. The keepers of that legend do not want anyone dislodging the cornerstone at this late date. It might weaken the whole edifice.

CHAPTER THREE

Clyde, Bonnie, Buck—and the Boys

"Machine Gun Kelly!" Clyde Barrow sneered the day he read of his capture in Memphis. "I've forgotten more about a Tommy gun than that phony creep ever knew."

It was probably true. The pint-sized Texan with the weak chin and the soft hazel eyes had no equal for sheer gunmanship. Guns were more than just the tools of his trade. They were objects of beauty to him, almost of veneration.

Ray Hamilton, who ran his mouth a lot after he was captured, told how Clyde was always fussing with his extensive collection of weapons, modifying them, oiling them, polishing them, holding them up to the light admiringly.

Clyde was the most heavily armed outlaw of the thirties. His arsenal included several submachine guns, a half dozen automatic rifles, and a bewildering variety of shotguns, automatics, and revolvers. When he ran low on ammunition or needed more guns, he backed his car up to a National Guard Armory and filled it—at gunpoint.

His aim was deadly. Target practice was a daily ritual with him. Anybody who rode with him had to be good, too. He drilled them until they were. His diminutive blonde traveling companion, Bonnie Parker, was said to be able to shoot the pips out of a playing card at twenty paces. Clyde himself could slice the card sideways, shoot the head off a dove in flight.

The speed of his draw was equally phenomenal. He carried a sawed-off shotgun in a zippered compartment in his right trouser leg, and was proud of the fact that he could draw it almost as fast as he could his pistol. His gunfighting attitude was Billy the Kid's: "It's a game for two—and I get there first."

The Barrow gang robbed and killed in five states before the law finally caught up with them. They never made a big score, never, to anyone's knowledge, tried for one. Their favorite targets were gas stations, luncheonettes, variety stores, plus an occasional small-town bank. Their biggest haul was $1,500.

They moved across the countryside aimlessly, heading anywhere—sometimes even in circles—to avoid their final destination. They had no political or legal connections, never had enough money to buy their way into established underworld retreats like Hot Springs and St. Paul, and were unwanted in such places anyway.

They were outlaws even to the rest of the criminal world. Most big-time heist men would have turned them in on sight. To them Barrow and his crowd were "kill-crazy punks" who were ruining the business for everyone else.

Yet today Clyde and his sweetheart, Bonnie, have the bigtime reputations, while the big-leaguers of their day—the Harvey Baileys, the Eddie Bentzes and Frank Nashes—are largely forgotten.

It's partly the work of the film: its appeal, particularly to the young, came from its portrayal of Clyde Barrow and his moll as a pair of displaced kids on the run, barreling along from crime to crime in a restless search for their place in the sun. As the screen Bonnie puts it: "When we started, I thought we were going somewhere, but we're just going."

Barrow and his girl are presented in the film as sad, murderous, dumb kids—confused neurotics rather than the old Hollywood "mad dog" stereotype. What they do is crazy and terrible, but it's never that far removed from the secret desires of a debilitated, apathetic population trapped in the economic decay of the Depression.

The film's period flavour—the cheesebox sedans, the moneyless banks, the hopelessness on every face—underscores this message. So do scenes of the gang in repose—listening to Eddie Cantor on the radio, playing checkers, taking endless pictures of themselves with a Kodak. They're just folks and, like the rest of us, disorganized, confused, frustrated.

So far, so good. This is what the real Bonnie and Clyde were probably like. Even the neurotic sensualities that plagued the two star-crossed lovers are there. Granted, their sexual hang-ups have been changed a bit, but at least they're present. They would have been glossed over completely in a standard Hollywood "shoot-'em-up."

Biographically the film sticks close to the facts. The screenwriters have left out some things and have shifted others around to tighten the plot, but many of the scenes, particularly the action ones, re-create in faithful detail exactly what happened.

Where the film and reality go their separate ways, however, is in the suggestion that Bonnie and Clyde were Robin Hood figures to the poor people of the Southwest. That is simply not true. Other outlaws—Dillinger, Pretty Boy Floyd, even the

Barkers—robbed the wealthy and left the poor alone. But not Bonnie and Clyde. They preyed on their fellow poor and they killed them when they got in their way. The Barrow gang was universally feared, and most of all by those likeliest to encounter them—the poverty-stricken farm folk of the Dust Bowl.

It's been argued that Bonnie and Clyde don't really deserve a place in American folklore because of this. Maybe they don't, but the argument is academic. The two of them are already there, enshrined beside Billy the Kid and Jesse James, and no amount of debunking is going to dislodge them now.

It isn't just the film's doing. It began in their own lifetime with the discovery of a handful of snapshots and one of Bonnie's poems, "The Story of Suicide Sal." The photos and the verses gave people an intimate, keyhole view of what it must have been like during those two years of driving, killing and hiding.

It struck a nerve. The poetry was bad, little more than doggerel, really. The emotions expressed were often trite and sentimental. But there was the thrill of its having been composed in the heat of action. And there was something else, too—a strangely detached, abstracted view that Bonnie had of Clyde and herself and of their crazy, pathetic ride to nowhere.

The real Clyde was born on a farm near Telice, Texas, on March 24, 1909. He was one of eight children. His father, Henry, was a tenant farmer. Clyde was farmed out to relatives when he was five, living first in Dallas, then in Corsicana and Houston. He was in trouble right from the start. At age nine he was committed to the Harris County School for Boys as an "incorrigible truant, thief, and runaway." He served three years. He was released to his parents after Henry Barrow finally gave up the land for good and moved to Dallas, finding work in a gas station.

Clyde's first serious brushes with the law involved cars. He loved them, tinkered with them, stripped them down, drove them fast. Speed intoxicated him. He never voluntarily stopped for anything, including red lights. The police started chasing him, but Clyde just drove faster. "It's easier to run than explain," he told his older brother, Ivan Marvin ("Buck") Barrow.

What he needed, he stole. Clyde had a feeling for music, so he swiped a saxophone. It went everywhere with him. Clyde had a date with a girl in San Antonio. His roadster burned out that same day. So he rented a car and kept it. He was arrested and charged with auto theft. His parents dug up the money, and he was released.

Buck, meanwhile, had been getting into trouble on his own. He had started out peddling hot turkeys, had graduated to stealing cars, and was now doing it professionally, turning the vehicles he clipped over to a hot car ring for a cut of the resale price.

Clyde wanted to work with him, but Buck didn't want his kid brother in the racket. He advised him to go straight.

Clyde did—to Houston. His traveling companions were two West Dallas toughs, Frank Clause and Raymond Hamilton. Clause was a small-time sneak thief. Hamilton, the descendant of one of the Southwest's most noted outlaw families, had never seriously considered any life other than crime.

The three of them gravitated to Houston's Fifth Ward, a section so tough that oilman Glenn McCarthy would later recall that ". . . the cops were afraid of the people, and there was almost always a dead man somewhere in the street in the morning." There they enrolled in the Root Square Gang, a finishing school for burglars. Soon Clyde was hard at work with the others, learning how to break and enter, strip cars, and roll drunks.

Graduation day saw him holding up a Fort Bend gambling spa with a rusty "Saturday Night Special" that wouldn't even fire. It didn't matter, though. Before housemen could figure the odds, Clyde had lifted a couple of long-barreled .38s from two off-duty deputies. That gave him the winning hand—a pair of sixes.

The gang returned to Dallas, where an impressed brother Buck and a youth named "Dapper Dan" Black joined them. After pulling a string of robberies in the Dallas area, the group headed across the line into Oklahoma, where Hamilton had kinfolk.

They hit a whole flock of grocery stores and gas stations in the Choctaw country, high-tailing it from town to town along the back country roads. Clyde was the wheelman and a damned good one. He could maneuver their sedan along the rutted roads at eighty-five and better, bucking through the gulches between the clay cuts and the trees, sucking the dust out of the cornfields into their wake, boiling it up into a thick white cloud that choked the pursuing posses.

At Henreyetta, Oklahoma, the gang stole a new car and started back to Dallas, pulling holdups and burglaries along the way.

In Denton, Texas, they stuck up a gas station and when they couldn't open a small safe, they heaved it into the car. Outside of Lewisville a police car jumped them. Clyde was driving. He floorboarded her. The police started shooting. Bullets shattered the rear window, slammed into the metal door stanchions. Buck pitched forward. "I'm hit," he grunted as he clutched at his right shoulder.

Clyde had her up to ninety when he came to a right-angle turn with no road signs to warn him. He stood on the brakes, but it was too late. The car careened across a ditch and ploughed into the chaparral, both axles snapping. The men leaped out and started running. All except Buck escaped.

The next morning the police came for Clyde. Everybody in

Dallas knew that the two brothers were working together. Clyde made a deal—the only one, it's said, of his career. He sold Clause and Black out on a burglary charge. Buck drew a five-year jolt at the Eastham prison farm. Clause and Black got suspended sentences.

Clyde went back to work with Ray Hamilton, pulling a series of jobs in the Waco area. He was arrested three more times for investigation of burglary and car theft. None of it stuck. He was only five feet, six and three-quarters inches tall and had the face of a choirboy. People simply couldn't believe that a boy like that would do anything bad.

Clyde met Bonnie Parker in January 1930. He was twenty-one, she was nineteen. They met through Ray Hamilton, who had been her husband's friend and was now hers. The husband, Roy Thornton, was chopping cotton at Eastham and would be at it for the next ninety-nine years. Bonnie had his name tatooed on her right thigh, along with two hearts, but that was the limit of her devotion. At the time she met Clyde, she was working as a waitress in Dallas and was juggling dates with several men on the side.

She was a tiny girl, less than five feet tall and weighing only ninety pounds. She had boyishly flat flanks, an angular body, and an almost pretty face that was spoiled by an overly hard mouth. She had come to Dallas from Cement City, one of those arid, innocent North Texas towns where nothing happens in even the best of times. Before that there had been another town, Rowena, where she had been born, the daughter of a bricklayer, and where nothing had happened, either.

Bonnie wanted desperately to make something happen that winter of 1930. She wasn't sure just what or how. All she knew was that she was "bored crapless" and had been most of her life. Then Clyde came along—an unimpressive little squirt who parted his hair in the middle, had long eyelashes, small delicate hands, and a slightly effeminate manner.

In the film version Clyde was pretty explicit as to what he was offering: excitement and fame. It's doubtful that the real Clyde offered Bonnie anything of the sort. Or that he even thought of himself in those terms.

Clyde Barrow, in 1930, was essentially a burglar and a car thief. He had yet to fire his gun in anger or desperation. All that would come later. After Eastham.

Bonnie saw some quality in him. What it was, we will never know. They started keeping company. They were together the night the law came for Clyde—"mooning on the sofa," according to one of the arresting officers.

It seemed that Clyde had forgotten to wear gloves on a couple of jobs in Waco. And if that didn't stick, Chief of Police Hollis Barron had him nailed on five car thefts, too.

Clyde pleaded guilty, and a McClellan County judge sentenced him to two years on each count. The court allowed the sentences to run concurrently, but that didn't cheer Clyde up any. He dreaded prison. He had a claustrophobic horror of locks and bars, a hangover from those early years he'd spent in the Harris County School.

Then, on March 2, 1930, his brother Buck came busting out of Eastham like a bull through a corral fence.

Inspired, Clyde began to make plans of his own. His cellmate in the Waco jail, William Turner, told him he had a gun hidden away in his house, a .38 Colt with a slim Bisley handle that would fit through the bars. Clyde sent Bonnie to get it. She came back with it taped to the inside of her thigh and managed to slip it to him without the guard noticing.

That night, when the jailer brought them their supper, Clyde pressed the barrel into his neck. "Open up," he said. "Fast."

Clyde and Turner went barreling out. Bonnie had a car hidden behind the K. C. dance hall. She wanted to go with them. Turner nixed the idea, and since the gun was his, the play was, too, and Clyde backed him on it.

The two of them raced to Abilene, then to Wichita Falls, where they switched to a stolen Graham coupe. It was a good car, with new tires, and they burned up the roads with it. When it ran out of gas, they abandoned it and hopped a freight. Railroad dicks grabbed them a few days later at Middleton, Ohio, and sent them back to Texas in handcuffs.

This time the law didn't kid around. Clyde was sent to replace his brother in the cotton fields at Eastham.

Back in the '30s Eastham was known among cons as the "Burnin' Hell" of the Texas prison system. Sadism was the order of the day there. Men were beaten by wardens, by trustees, by one another. In the fields whippings were regular and almost maniacally brutal. The men were underfed and dressed in tatters. They slept on bunks, jammed one against the other, in barracks that stank of excrement.

The slightest infraction of the rules meant a hitch in the "barrel cavalry." This was a roughhewn pickle barrel mounted on a sawhorse in the blazing sun. Prisoners were made to straddle the barrel for hours at a time. Even the strongest eventually collapsed. Some of the weaker ones died or "lost it" (went insane).

Clyde's sentence had been beefed up since his escape try. It no longer ran concurrently. He was in now for the full fourteen years.

In desperation he chopped two toes off his right foot with an ax. He hoped it would get him transferred to the "Walls" at Huntsville. It didn't. It didn't even get him out of the cotton fields. The guard captain reassigned him to a hoe squad as soon as his foot stopped bleeding.

At Eastham Clyde was involved in murder—his first. He and some other cons had been sentenced to the "barrel cavalry" for gambling. They all knew who had fingered them—the barrack stoolie, Ed Crowder.

When the punishment period was over, they trapped Crowder in a secluded section of the prison yard. Clyde had a length of lead pipe. The others had homemade knives.

There were no repercussions. At Eastham one more death was hardly noticed.

Clyde had served twenty months of his sentence when Buck Barrow surrendered outside the walls at Huntsville. His mother, Mrs. Cumie Barrow, had talked him into it. "I'll go back, do my time," he told her, "so long as it's not at Eastham."

Mrs. Barrrow went to Austin now, where she managed to secure a personal meeting with Governor Ross Sterling. She made an impassioned plea for both her sons. The Governor promised to review their cases.

A month later Clyde was granted a parole.

It came too late, though. Eastham had done its work. He "hit the ground" on February 2, 1932, and he hit it running. It would take almost two hundred rounds of ammunition to finally stop him twenty-six months later.

Bonnie described the change in him in "The Story of Bonnie and Clyde":

> They class them as cold-blooded killers,
> They say they are heartless and mean,
> But I say this with pride,
> That I once knew Clyde
> When he was honest and upright and clean.
>
> But the law fooled around,
> Kept tracking him down,
> And locking him up in a cell,
> Till he said to me,
> "I will never be free,
> "So I will meet a few of them in hell."
> This road was so dimly lighted
> There were no highway signs to guide,
> But they made up their minds
> If the roads were all blind
> They wouldn't give up till they died...

Bonnie was exaggerating, of course. She had never known Clyde when he was "honest and upright and clean." No one had. But at the same time she was right. Clyde had gone into Eastham a burglar and a car thief who avoided gunplay. He came out the most dangerous Texan since Wes Hardin.

In March he and Bonnie went on the road together for the first time. It was a false start, though. The car was hot, and the law jumped them outside Mabank. There was a wild chase along U.S. 175. Clyde skidded the car off the highway and onto a backcountry road, where it immediately got bogged down in mud. Clyde, Bonnie, and the kid who'd been riding with them took to the fields. Bonnie lost her shoes and was caught.

She sat for three months in the jail at Kaufman, Texas. The jailer's wife had advised her mother not to make bail. The theory was that a session in the pokey would cool Bonnie's ardor for Clyde.

To an extent it did. She was deeply hurt that he never tried to spring her. The experience probably contributed to her later poem, "The Story of Suicide Sal."

While Bonnie sat brooding, Clyde was busy robbing. He had teamed up with his old buddy, Ray Hamilton, once again. On March 25 the two of them hit the Sims Oil Company in Dallas and escaped with several hundred dollars.

Hamilton was a small, wiry youth, smaller even than Clyde. He walked with the swaying strut of a rooster about to crow. He was talkative, quick to anger, and as jumpy, a friend once said, "as a stud horse in a box stall." He had a cruel streak in him that verged at times on the sadistic. All in all, bad news, particularly for someone standing across a gun from him.

On the night of April 30 that was John N. Bucher, a 65-year-old jeweler and service station operator in Hillsboro, Texas. Bucher's wife had just opened the safe so that he could give Hamilton and his companion change of a ten. Both youths suddenly whipped out guns. "We'll take it all, old man," snapped Hamilton. Bucher's hand darted toward the drawer where he kept his gun. They blasted him. Then, after scooping just forty dollars out of the safe, they ran for the car. A third youth was waiting behind the wheel, the motor running.

Later Mrs. Bucher identified her husband's killers from mug shots: Clyde Barrow and Ray Hamilton.

Clyde's relatives denied it. His mother claimed that Clyde had told her he was the wheelman on that job, that he'd been waiting out in the car when the shooting had taken place.

Maybe so. But it didn't matter now. The chase was on. Governor Sterling offered a $250 reward for Bucher's killers, a lot of money in the Depression. Dallas newspapers, meanwhile, went ahead and convicted Clyde. He was described as "the killer of John Bucher," even though he had only been charged with the crime.

The third member of the old "Root Square" trio now joined Hamilton and Barrow. Frank Clause had apparently forgiven Clyde for fingering him after the Denton job. The three of them hit several gas stations in the Lufkin area in early May, then sped back to Dallas to knock over a liquor store on May 12. The take: a spectacular $76.

In June the Kaufman Grand Jury met and no-billed Bonnie. She returned home and told her mother that she was finished with Clyde.

The gang was in Oklahoma now. Dallas had gotten too hot. They were staying with some of Hamilton's relatives near Tishomingo. Clause had been replaced by a local gunsel.

On the night of August 5, as the three men were cruising through the Choctaw country around Atoka, they passed a barn dance. Hamilton, who was driving, sniffed the air. "Poontang," he said, grinning, and whipped the car into the parking area.

Clyde didn't want to stop. Neither did the other man. Hamilton ignored them. He was a billygoat who had to have his daily exercise. Clyde got into an argument with him. Their voices became loud.

Atoka sheriff, C. G. Maxwell, and his deputy, Eugene Moore, heard the commotion and approached. They thought the three of them were farm boys who had come out of the hills to attend the Stringtown dance. "What's going on here?" drawled Maxwell. "You boys been drinking?"

Clyde and Hamilton whirled, saw the stars on their shirtfronts and opened fire. They emptied their .45s, then reached into the car for replacement weapons.

Deputy Moore was killed instantly. The sheriff staggered back against a car, fumbling for his pistol, but he was dropped by a second barrage of bullets before he could reach it.

Several men came running out of the dance. They leaped for cover as Clyde leaned out the car window and swept the front of the building with a raking fire from a Browning automatic rifle. Hamilton threw the car into reverse and floorboarded her. The machine hung there a second, wheels spinning in the gravel: then it shot out of the lot like a cork out of a bottle.

Hamilton spun the wheel hard left. With a clash of gears, the car roared off into the darkness.

The road was slick from a recent rain, though, and a few minutes later they went slithering off the shoulder into a ditch. Cursing, the three men climbed out and looked around. A farmhouse lay a hundred yards down the road. As they approached it Clyde spotted the silhouette of his favorite car, a Ford V-8, in the front yard. They knocked on the door and asked the farmer who answered if he would help get them out of the ditch.

The farmer nodded and climbed into his V-8. Clyde, Hamilton, and the third man piled into the seat behind him. "Never mind pulling us out," said Clyde, as he pressed the muzzle of the BAR into his neck. "Just start driving."

The farmer drove too hard. The engine soon began to sputter and clank. It had thrown a rod. Another car came along. Clyde flagged it down and asked the driver if he wanted to trade. He said he didn't. But he traded anyway and was glad to do so.

They drove the new car to Clayton, fifty miles east of Stringtown. There Clyde spotted a brand-new V-8 parked on a side street. He couldn't pass it up. He jumped the switch on it, and the gang piled in. With Clyde behind the wheel now, they roared out of town, heading through the Kiamichi mountains toward the Arkansas line.

Several days later Bonnie received a phone call. "Pack your clothes," said Clyde. "Then turn on the radio. When you hear the Neuhoff Company has been robbed, be ready to leave."

That same afternoon, August 12, the bulletin came over the radio: two men identified as Clyde Barrow and Raymond Hamilton had just held up the Neuhoff Packing Company offices in downtown Dallas. The two, sought for the recent murder of an Atoka County sheriff and his deputy, were heavily armed. They had escaped with approximately $1,100 and at last report were driving west toward Fort Worth at high speed.

Bonnie got ready. The Parker home was on the Fort Worth Turnpike, not far from Arcadia Park. She kissed her mother good-bye and told her that she had a ride to Wichita Falls. A new cafe had just opened there, and she thought she might be able to find work.

A car honked, and Bonnie ran out to meet it. Mrs. Emma Parker glanced out the window. The car was a dusty V-8 sedan with Oklahoma plates. As it pulled away Mrs. Parker caught a glimpse of the two men sitting in the front seat with Bonnie. One of them looked an awful lot like Clyde Barrow.

In the car there was backslapping and laughter. It was a happy reunion. For all three of them. They decided to honeymoon in New Mexico, where Bonnie had an aunt. Clyde drove the whole distance with lead in his foot.

Bonnie's aunt gave them a big welcome when they pulled into Carlsbad the next morning. It was certainly nice of the two young men to have brought her niece all the way from Dallas for a visit. "Glad to be of service, ma'am," said Clyde, grinning. "I'll just get our things from the car."

He turned—and stopped short. A tall man wearing a gun belt was looking over their car. "Howdy," said the man. He came sauntering up the walk, and Clyde saw the silver star on his shirt-front.

Clyde and Hamilton had left their guns under the car seat. Because of that, Sheriff Joe Johns lived to tell the story to his grandchildren. "I was just passing"—the sheriff smiled amiably—"an' I saw the out-of-state plates an' wondered who was visitin' Missus—"

He felt a sudden pressure between his shoulder blades and turned. A tiny, freckle-faced blonde in a dark blue beret was holding a shotgun on him. "Don't move, damn you!" she snapped.

Clyde leaped forward, snatched the sheriff's pistol out of his holster, and prodded him in the belly with it. "Get in the car," he snarled.

The aunt stood watching from the porch, eyes wide with disbelief. Bonnie had sighted the sheriff through the window, had raced to her uncle's room, grabbed his shotgun, and skinned out the back door to sneak up behind him—all in thirty seconds flat.

The four of them were in the car now. It roared away in a cloud of dust. The aunt went back into the house and had herself a good case of hysterics.

The trio drove the sheriff all the way to San Antonio. It was a nonstop trip with Clyde, as usual, keeping the needle hovering between ninety and a hundred.

Hamilton didn't want to release him. "We either got to kill him or keep him with us," he kept saying. But Clyde overruled him. They couldn't take him with them, and as for killing—that was out. Clyde never killed a hostage. It was a quixotic quirk of his. He would kill in the heat of action and never think twice about it. But a hostage was different. A hostage presented no immediate threat, and Clyde, to his credit, killed only when threatened.

After dropping the sheriff off along the highway between Beckman and San Antonio, the gang drove east toward the Gulf.

In Victoria Clyde spotted a new V-8. Naturally he had to have it. He and Bonnie clouted it, and Hamilton followed them in the other car. The theft had been seen, though, and reported to the local sheriff. He got on the phone to Wharton, describing the two cars that were headed their way.

There was only one bridge across the Colorado River, a narrow trestlelike affair on U.S. 59 just outside Wharton. A dozen armed officers hurriedly took up positions at either end of it.

The two cars came roaring along the highway. The Wharton sheriff tried to flag them down, then jumped for his life as Clyde opened up with a pistol, shooting around the edge of his windshield. The other officers returned the fire. A deadly fusillade tore into the two cars as they roared onto the bridge.

The men at the other end got ready, zeroing in on the first car. Suddenly Clyde spotted them. He threw the V-8 into second gear, cocked the wheel and hit the accelerator, bringing the rear end skidding around in a perfect 180-degree arc. It was the famous "bootlegger's turn," flawlessly executed.

He went roaring back across the bridge with a dozen pistols, rifles, and shotguns spitting hell at him. Bonnie stuck her twelve-gauge out the window and let the ambushers have it. Hamilton, still right behind them, was driving with one hand, shooting with the other.

It was Bonnie's first taste of combat, the first time she had heard the angry buzz of bullets around her head or felt the thud of buckshot ripping into glass and metal. It didn't bother her a bit. She handled herself with an easygoing skill that won the instant admiration of both men. "That Bonnie," Clyde said later, as they licked their wounds in an empty field near Yoakum, Texas, "she's sure full of piss and vinegar."

They hid out in an abandoned farmhouse at Grand Prairie for the next few weeks. From here Clyde and Hamilton raided the National Guard armory at Fort Worth, returning with boxes full of submachine guns, automatic rifles, shotguns, and extra ammunition. The Wharton ambush had taught them the importance of firepower.

From here, too, they pushed off against the Abilene State Bank on October 8, 1932. Bonnie was the wheelman on that job, Hamilton the center fielder. Clyde took the cages. It was their biggest haul so far—$1,400.

They headed north and east from Abilene, intending to swing up into the Choctaw country. At Sherman, in the Red River Valley, they stopped for food and supplies. Bonnie and Hamilton waited in the car while Clyde entered a small general store. Casually he looked around. He saw only two attendants working amid the jumble of dried sausages, meal, flour, and fly swatters—Homer Glaze, at the cash register, and Howard Hall, behind the meat counter.

After Clyde had ordered everything on his shopping list, he showed Glaze the .45 he was carrying. "Open the register," he said. Glaze's pupils shifted slightly. Clyde swung around just as the butcher leaped toward him, a meat cleaver in his hand. Three of the four shots he squeezed off found their mark. Clyde scooped $50 out of the till, grabbed his groceries, and ran. The butcher was dead on arrival at the Dennison Hospital.

The trio worked their way north, riding the back country roads by night, sleeping in the car or beside it. They lived on sandwiches and on coffee, which they brewed over an open fire. On the rare occasions when they slept in a bed, it was in remote tourist cabins or fishing resorts where there were no telephones, newspapers, or radios.

They were famous now. Newspapers in the Southwest called Clyde the "Texas Rattlesnake." Bonnie hadn't been identified by name as yet; she was simply his "quick-shooting woman accomplice." They had a good description of her, though, and they kept running it in the papers and on the radio.

So the gang stayed off the main roads as they moved north that fall, heading through the Ozarks to Illinois, and up through Indiana to the North Woods of Michigan. The car was the focal point of their lives. They relaxed only when they were in it or near it. The gas tank was kept full, the motor tuned to perfection. Their belongings were in the trunk, their arsenal on the back seat, together with a four-day supply of food, a first-aid kit, Clyde's saxophone, and a five-gallon jug of drinking water.

The outdoor life didn't appeal much to Ray Hamilton, though. He began to get restless. Finally, in late October, he announced his decision: he was going to strike out on his own. "All right," said Clyde. "But you'll get caught, and I'll have to get you out. You ain't smart like I am."

Hamilton returned to Texas, where he recruited his former girl friend's brother, Gene O'Dare. The two of them hit the Carmine State Bank at LaGrange on November 9, and then, with a gunsel named Les Stewart in center field, the Cedar Hill State Bank in Dallas on the 25th. The take from that job was $1,800, more than Hamilton had ever made with Bonnie and Clyde. Who was smart now?

Clyde pulled only one job during the same period—a minor one. With Bonnie behind the wheel, he took the Oronogo, Missouri, bank for a few hundred dollars on November 15. Then, because Bonnie was homesick, the two of them returned to Dallas and hid out with relatives.

While there, they shopped for Hamilton's replacement. They found him just down the street from Henry Barrow's filling station. He was a seventeen-year-old car thief named William Daniel Jones. Most people called him either "W. D." or "Deacon," a tribute to his guileless appearance.

In the film his name became "C. W. Moss," and he was supposedly picked for his mechanical skills. Actually, he didn't have any. Nor much criminal experience, either. But he had other attributes: vacant, blue-eyed good looks, an almost overbearing innocence.

"Want to take a ride with us?" Clyde was said to have asked

him. "I'm Clyde Barrow and this is Bonnie Parker. We rob banks."

Awed beyond belief, the seventeen-year-old climbed into their V-8 and was swept off into thirteen months of "living hell," during which he was shot at, unnaturally assaulted by both of them, kept in chains, and forced, while fleeing from police, to fire a submachine gun.

That's W. D.'s story at any rate—the one he told police when he was finally picked up. His remarkable 28-page confession is a goldmine of information about Bonnie and Clyde and the way they lived while on the run. Most of it has an authentic ring to it, particularly the parts about their sex lives. W. D. was an innocent at heart, a Panhandle fundamentalist who believed that fleshly sins deserved fleshly punishment. His profound shock at some of the stuff that went on is apparent in every line of the confession.

The three of them left Dallas on December 22 and headed south.

Ray Hamilton was back in town—in police custody, just as Clyde had prophesied. Hamilton had gone tomcatting all over the country with the Cedar Hill loot and had naturally been collared. Now he was busy running his mouth for the benefit of police and press.

Clyde, Bonnie, and young Jones drifted quietly south. As they drove through Temple, Texas, on the afternoon of December 23, Clyde spotted a new V-8 parked along a quiet, residential street. He turned to W. D. "Go get it, boy."

Jones trotted over to the Ford obediently, climbed in, and started fussing with the ignition wires. A minute passed. Two minutes. Nothing happened. Sighing, Clyde got out of the car and walked over. "Not that way," he said. "This way." But Jones was nervous now and lost the contact after the motor had turned over once with a loud growl.

That brought the Ford's owner, Doyle Johnson, charging out of his house. He'd been in the middle of dinner and was still wiping gravy off his chin. "Hey! That's my car!" he shouted. "What are you fellows doing?"

Clyde whirled, drew, and fired in one motion. Johnson dropped to his knees, a surprised look on his face. He clutched at his stomach and slowly toppled forward, dead.

Bonnie had the other car in motion, doors open. Clyde tumbled in, cursing, pushing W. D. ahead of him. Bonnie slammed the accelerator to the floor, and the car vanished around the corner, tires squealing like pigs being slaughtered.

In Dallas, meanwhile, a jury listened to the evidence against Ray Hamilton and decided that he needed to do some time in the cotton fields of Eastham. They thought two hundred and sixty-three years would be about right. Hamilton was returned to the Hill Country Jail to await transfer. While there, he hit the panic button.

Clyde had a pretty extensive communications network set up by now. He could be contacted, or make contacts, through strategically located "drops" in Texas, Oklahoma, and Louisiana.

Hamilton's message reached him in late December. It was short and to the point: "Get me out." Clyde decided that it might be a good idea. It would stop that nonstop mouth of his, at any rate. He made arrangements to visit Ray's sister in Dallas, Mrs. Lillie McBride. She would be the go-between.

The McBride house was already under surveillance, though. Odell Chandless and Les Stewart had robbed the Grapevine Bank on December 31. Texas Rangers had nabbed Stewart, and he'd told them that Chandless was supposed to visit Mrs. McBride on the night of January 6.

That was the night that Clyde decided to come calling.

The house was packed with Rangers and Tarrant County sheriffs and deputies, all heavily armed.

Clyde cruised past the darkened house twice. Instinct told him something was wrong. He had W. D. park directly in front. "Keep the motor running," he told him. He slipped a sawed-off twelve-gauge into the zippered compartment of his pants leg and told Bonnie to cover him. As he moved through the shadows and up onto the porch, Bonnie trained a .30-.30 Winchester on the front of the house.

Inside, Ranger J. F. Vannoy heard Clyde's footsteps. He tapped Ray Hamilton's 18-year-old sister on the shoulder and signaled her to go to the door and open it.

As she started forward Clyde suddenly cut loose. He hadn't heard anything, hadn't seen anyone. It was just a sudden "feeling" he had. His automatic shotgun blasted out a second-story window. Tarrant County Deputy F. T. Bradberry dropped to the floor, cut by flying glass.

Vannoy and his men opened up from inside now, firing blindly through doors and windows. As they did, Deputy Malcolm Davis raced around from the back of the house. He saw Clyde starting down the steps. He leaped onto the porch, gun in hand. "Hold on there!" he shouted. Clyde spun toward him. His twelve-gauge roared. The load of buckshot caught Davis in the chest, catapulting him backward to the ground, killing him instantly.

Bonnie opened up with the Winchester as Clyde ran for the car. The withering fire from her .30-.30 kept Vannoy and his men inside the house until the car was in motion. W. D. had them halfway down the block and pushing seventy by the time the first officers reached the street and opened fire.

Dallas County was immediately sealed off by roadblocks. Rangers and city police armed with riot guns began raiding every known gangster haunt. Clyde, Bonnie, and W. D. Jones were far away, though, roaring through the red clay cuts of Oklahoma.

Back in Texas things were looking up for Clyde's older brother, Buck. Mrs. Miriam A. ("Ma") Ferguson had replaced Ross Sterling as governor in January. "Ma" was famous for granting pardons. She had issued more than two thousand of them during her first term in office back in the '20s.

Buck's wife, Blanche, mother of three children and about to give birth to a fourth, saw her chance. She hitchhiked to the state capital with the kids and made a tearful, in-person plea. "Ma" was so moved that she granted Buck Barrow a full pardon. He walked out of Huntsville on March 20, 1933 a free man.

He hung around Dallas until Blanche gave birth. Then both of them suddenly vanished, leaving all four kids behind. Mrs. Cumie Barrow told police that Buck had gotten a letter from Clyde and was on his way to see him to try and talk him into going straight.

She must have got the message wrong, because Buck's next public appearance was in a jewelry store stickup in Neosho, Missouri. A few days later he and his brother popped up again, not to surrender, but to get themselves some new guns out of a federal armory in Springfield, Missouri. Three days after that they appeared once again, using their new arsenal to kick in a loan office in Kansas City.

Then they went to ground, renting a garage apartment in Freeman's Grove Addition, a suburb of Joplin, in early April.

Clyde didn't like the idea. He preferred to be in, or near, his car, with open country on all sides of him. But Blanche was still kind of "delicate." So he let himself be talked into it.

The five of them took life easy for a while, sleeping late, playing cards, admiring the Kodak snapshots they had taken of each other.

The Texas license plates were noticed, though, and a delivery boy got to wondering why the women never let him into the apartment with his packages. Both reports reached the ears of Sergeant G. B. Kahler of the Missouri Highway Patrol. He figured it for a bootleg liquor operation and decided to raid. He rounded up a highway patrolman, a Newton County constable, and two Joplin police detectives and, on the afternoon of April 13, the five men drove out to Freeman's Grove Addition in a couple of unmarked cars.

It was around 4 P.M. Clyde and W. D. Jones were standing in the garage, checking over their Marmon sedan. Blanche was upstairs cooking. Buck was sitting in his undershirt reading a newspaper. Bonnie was hard at work on her first poem, "The Story of Suicide Sal."

Clyde spotted the two cars coming up Oak Ridge Drive and got one of his sudden "feelings." He leaped into the garage, pulled W. D. in behind him, and slammed the doors.

Sergeant Kahler brought his car to a stop a few yards beyond the driveway. The second vehicle swung in, blocking the gang's escape route. The garage doors opened a crack, and a blast from a shotgun sprayed the car with lead. Newton County Constable Wes Harryman leaped out with his pistol drawn. He managed to squeeze off one shot before his head was practically torn from his body by a second blast.

Detective Harry L. McGinnis sprinted forward, firing his pistol. Suddenly his right arm was ripped off at the elbow. Buckshot showered his face and head. He dropped to the pavement, dying.

Upstairs Buck had grabbed his submachine gun. Bonnie ran into the bedroom and snatched up two pistols. Blanche just stood there, hands over her ears, screaming. It was her first taste of combat.

Detective Thomas DeGraff had taken cover behind the car. He fired into the garage as Sergeant Kahler and Patrolman W. E. Grammer moved to the left, trying to outflank the gang.

Suddenly W. D. Jones came running out of the garage, spraying the car with fire from a Browning automatic rifle. DeGraff was forced to retreat around the east side of the building.

Jones leaped over the two bodies and struggled with the hand brake on the police car. Kahler fired at him. Jones clutched at his head and staggered back into the garage.

Buck Barrow came charging out next, spraying machine gun fire in all directions. He ran to the police car, released the brake, and gave it a push. The car coasted down the driveway, slowly gathering speed, then shot across the street, bounced over the curb, and smashed into a red oak tree.

Blanche, still screaming at the top of her lungs, burst out of the building and went racing down the driveway into the street. At that moment the garage doors suddenly swung open, and the Marmon sedan roared out, gears clashing. Kahler saw three men and a woman in it. As the lawmen peppered the car with bullets, it swung left, chasing Blanche. It slowed down as it reached her, and Kahler saw a man lean out and pull her inside. Then it roared off in a whirl of red dust.

Kahler sent Patrolman Grammer for help. An ambulance came. It was too late, though. Harryman and McGinnis were both dead. Reinforcements arrived shortly after that. Half of them were sent after the Marmon. The rest made their way cautiously into the upstairs apartment.

There they found an arsenal of rifles, machine guns, and BAR's. And snapshots. One of Bonnie holding a shotgun on Clyde. Another showing Bonnie with one foot up on a car bumper, puffing on a cigar. And on the dining room table they found Bonnie's unfinished poem:

THE STORY OF SUICIDE SAL
By "Bonnie" Parker

We, each of us, have a good alibi
  For being down here in the joint;
But few of them are really justified,
  If you get right down to the point.

You have heard of a woman's glory
  Being spent on a downright cur.
Still you can't always judge the story
  As true being told by her.

As long as I stayed on the island
  And heard confidence tales from the gals,
There was only one interesting and truthful,
  It was the story of Suicide Sal.

Now Sal was a girl of rare beauty,
  Tho' her features were somewhat tough,
She never once faltered from duty,
  To play on the up and up.

Sal told me this tale on the evening
  Before she was turned out free,
And I'll do my best to relate it,
  Just as she told it to me.

I was born on a ranch in Wyoming,
  Not treated like Helen of Troy,
Was taught that rods were rulers,
  And ranked with greasy cowboys . . .

The press went to work on the legend. The "Battle of Joplin" shared the front page with the Japanese siege of Peking. The snapshot of Bonnie with the cigar appeared alongside Amelia Earhart's photograph in one of the more prestigious newsweeklies. Excerpts from "Suicide Sal" ran in practically every paper in the country.

The gang didn't learn about their new fame immediately. They were holed up in the swamps of Lincoln Parish, Louisiana, too hot to even venture out for food, let alone a newspaper.

W. D.'s head wound was more painful than serious. They were able to treat it with their own first-aid supplies. In his confession Jones said that he ran away from the gang at this point, stole a car, and fled home to Dallas, but that Clyde and Bonnie followed him and forced him to return.

The Barrow gang struck next in Indiana. The Lucerne State Bank. A small take but plenty of fireworks: two women bystanders wounded by machine gun fire. Eight days later, on May 16, they swooped into the First State Bank of Okabena, Minnesota. A redheaded woman stayed at the wheel of a dark green V-8 sedan. The townspeople opened fire from the sidewalks as the men came barreling out with their $1,500 take. Bullets thudded into the car as it pulled away. The gang shattered the car windows and fired back, with BAR's and shotguns. "The battle raged furiously," according to one account, "but it was impossible to face the outlaw barrage and live. Slowly the defenders fell back to the shelter of buildings, and the bandits escaped."

Bonnie was homesick. Clyde wanted to see his family, too. Buck said it was too risky. So he and Blanche were dropped off at a hideout in the Arkansas Ozarks, while Bonnie, Clyde, and W. D. ran the gauntlet into Dallas.

They met their families at an abandoned stone quarry off the Fort Worth Turnpike. There was time just for a few quick embraces, inquiries about each other's health, and a hurriedly gobbled picnic of cold chicken and homemade apple pie. Then the running started again.

Clyde raced north through the Texas Panhandle, the speedometer needle shivering, as usual, between 90 and 100 mph. They were to meet Buck outside Erick, Oklahoma, late that night.

Clyde didn't see that the bridge over the Salt Fork River north of Wellington was out. The car sailed off the edge, flipped over, and burst into flames on the dry river bed below. Bonnie was pinned beneath the wreckage. Clyde and W. D. were thrown clear.

Two farmers who had heard the crash came running. Bonnie was screaming, begging Clyde to shoot her so that she wouldn't burn to death. The farmers, Steve Pritchard and Lonzo Carter, helped Clyde and W. D. pull her free. She was badly burned. Her arms were seared to the shoulders. The lower part of her face was white with blisters. Her whole right leg was a mass of cooked flesh.

"This woman needs a doctor," said Pritchard.

"No doctor," said Clyde. "Where do you live?" Pritchard pointed, and Clyde said, "All right, carry her up there."

The two farmers looked at the automatic rifles the men were holding and did as they were told. At the farmhouse Mrs. Pritchard made up a paste of baking soda and spread it on the burns. Bonnie was writhing and moaning, obviously in terrible pain.

"I'm going back for the rest of the guns," Clyde said abruptly. He turned to W. D. "Keep them covered."

W. D. had been unnerved by the whole business, though. He was careless, and Lonzo Carter got away. The farmer ran through the darkness to a neighboring house and telephoned Sheriff George Corry at Wellington. Corry picked up City Marshal Paul Hardy and the two of them sped toward the Pritchard farmhouse.

Clyde returned with the guns and W. D. told him that Carter had probably called the law. Moments later, there was a knock at the door. Clyde whirled, snatched up his shotgun and fired.

A woman screamed. He swung the door open. There stood Pritchard's daughter-in-law, her right hand shot off. Clyde herded her inside with the others. "Get down on the floor, all of you," he commanded tersely. "Don't let me hear a sound out of you." He and W. D. carried Bonnie out of the house and into the underbrush. They made her comfortable on a bed of leaves, then waited there beside her, guns ready.

Sheriff Corry's car pulled up a few minutes later. He and Marshal Hardy got out and cautiously approached the farmhouse with drawn weapons. Clyde and W. D. stepped out of the darkness, shotguns aimed at their heads. "Back into the car," ordered Clyde. He forced the two of them to hold Bonnie on their laps in the back seat while W. D. covered them from the front.

Clyde drove west to Pampa at high speed, then north toward Erick, relaxing only when he had crossed the state line. "You're in a fine pickle," he shouted over his shoulder at the two men. "I'm Clyde Barrow. Guess what that means for you?"

The officers swallowed heavily, but Clyde was just kidding around. When they reached Buck Barrow's car and Buck asked if they were going to kill them, Clyde shook his head. "Naw," he chuckled, "I've had them with me so long I'm beginning to like them."

The officers were left bound to an oak tree with barbed wire. They managed to get loose a few hours later and limped into town to tell their story to a breathless world. "One thing's sure," said Sheriff Corry. "The woman's burned bad. She'll die if they don't get her to a doctor."

The gang knew that. They took Bonnie to an isolated tourist cabin near Fort Smith, Arkansas, and Clyde brought a doctor out to see her, explaining that his wife had been burned by an oil stove explosion at their campsite. The doctor treated her but said that she would either have to be taken to a hospital or have round-the-clock nursing. Clyde settled for the nursing. For a week he never left her bedside, day or night.

Bonnie kept begging for her mother in her delirium. So Clyde left Buck in charge and ran the gauntlet into Dallas once again. He refused to bring Mrs. Parker back, though. She would be recognized by the police. He settled instead on Bonnie's younger sister, Billie Jean.

Meanwhile, the medical bills continued to pile up, eating into the gang's slim reserves. By mid-June they were broke. Leaving W. D. in charge of the three women, Clyde and Buck drove forth to scare up some cash.

They knocked over the Alma State Bank on June 22, then raced north to hit a Piggly Wiggly store in Fayetteville. On their way back to Fort Smith on U.S. 71 they had to pass through Alma once again. A description of their car had been phoned ahead to Alma's marshal, H. D. Humphrey. He realized that it was the same car that had been used in the bank job—a '33 Ford V-8 with Indiana plates.

He and his deputy, A. M. Salyars, jumped into their patrol car and headed north to intercept them. Two miles outside Alma they saw a car approaching. They slowed down. So did the other car. The driver waved. It was Webber Wilson, night manager of a nearby garage, on his way to work. Wilson stopped his car and leaned out the window, about to say something.

At that instant Humphrey saw the second car. It was approaching at better than 90 mph. "Better not stop," he shouted to Wilson. "That fellow will run you over." Humphrey started forward, saw that it was the V-8 they were looking for, and jammed on the brakes.

The second car went ploughing into Wilson's. Metal shrieked. Flames burst with a roar from both cars. Humphrey was sure that no one could have survived the wreck. But to his surprise he saw Wilson crawl free and the Barrow brothers, too. He and Salyars leaped out, guns drawn. "Get them up!" they shouted, racing toward the wreckage.

Buck and Clyde took shelter behind the open doors. There was a quick burst of shots as one of them opened up with a Browning. Humphrey and Salyars fired back. Then a shotgun roared, and the marshal seemed to trip over his own feet and go sprawling face down on the highway.

Salyars kept firing until he was out of ammunition. Then he ran behind the corner of a farmhouse and reloaded. Buck and Clyde came charging out. Clyde stopped and leaned over Humphrey as his brother ran toward the police car. "I ought to finish you right now," he snarled.

"Go ahead," the marshal groaned. "I think you've already finished me." (He had. Humphrey died of his wounds four days later.)

Clyde ran on, leaping into the police sedan. It roared off, passing the terrified occupants of cars in the opposite lane. Deputy Salyars peppered it with shots but to no avail. It quickly vanished into the darkness.

Buck and Clyde drove to Van Buren. There they forced a Fort Smith couple to surrender their car. Clyde took a wrong turn a few minutes later, though, and got on a dead end road that petered out at the top of Mount Vista. Quickly a half dozen posses closed in on them.

The Barrows took to the brush, making their way on foot to a cabin in the Ozarks just north of Winslow. Clyde kicked in the door and ordered Mrs. John Rogers to hand over the keys to the ancient jalopy standing out in the yard. She refused. Clyde whipped out his shotgun. She still refused. The posses were so close now that the two men could actually hear them hallooing.

Buck picked up a trace chain and began to beat her with it. She still wouldn't give them the keys. Clyde tried to jump the switch meanwhile, but he wasn't familiar with a Pierce-Arrow's innards and had to give up. "Okay," he snarled, "we'll fix it so nobody can use it!" With Buck's help he gave the car a shove toward a nearby cliff. The woman leaped to her feet and ran after it. Clyde leveled his shotgun at her. "Don't touch it!" he yelled.

Mrs. Rogers ignored him. She leaped onto the running board and gave the steering wheel a twist that sent the car careening into a tree.

The Barrows had finally met their match: a hill woman who refused to be separated from her car.

Cussing wildly, the two of them fled into the woods in back of the cabin. Mrs. Rogers heard a great trampling behind her. She swung around. Possemen came streaming out from among the trees at the far end of the clearing. "They went thataway!" she shouted. "They're only seconds ahead of you!"

They were sure they had them now. Extra men were poured into the area with instructions to shoot first, then ask. Scouts went ahead of the main body to guard against ambush. Everyone regarded a major battle as imminent. Sheriff A. H. Maxey of Crawford County rushed men up State 59 to get ahead of the outlaws and throw out a net. The Barrows slipped through like minnows through a whale net.

They made it back to the Fort Smith tourist cabin and pulled out that same night. Bonnie's sister, Billie Jean, was sent home to Dallas; the others headed across the line into Oklahoma.

When the doctor stopped by the next morning and found them gone, he got suspicious and called the police. There could be no doubt from his description—he had been treating Bonnie Parker.

"They won't get far," he said. "She's an extremely sick woman. She shouldn't have been moved."

The gang surfaced next at Enid, Oklahoma, where they stole Dr. Julian Fields' car in order to get his medicine kit. Within the hour they knocked over the National Guard Armory, too, escaping with fifty Army automatics and armloads of ammunition.

Fort Dodge, Iowa, was next. On July 18 three men and two women in a Ford sedan robbed three filling stations in quick succession. One of the women, a redhead, had bandages on her face and arms. It was obviously the Barrow gang.

At ten o'clock that same night the five of them pulled up in front of the Red Crown Cabin Camp at the junction of U.S. 71 and State 59, six miles southeast of Platte City, Missouri. They rented a double brick cabin separated by two garages and paid the attendant, Delbert Crabtree, in small change. After backing the car into one of the garages and closing the doors, the group split up—three into the left-hand cabin, two into the right. A little later the bandaged redhead bought five sandwiches and five beers from Crabtree. Again she paid in small change. The next day the cabin rental was renewed, and the redhead bought five chicken dinners. The bill came to ten dollars and something. She paid it with nickels, dimes, and quarters.

Crabtree told his boss. His boss phoned the Missouri Highway Patrol. The lawmen listened to the description of the five, plus the fact that they paid for everything in silver, and realized that it was the group who had hit the Fort Dodge filling stations—and that spelled Barrows. They called Kansas City for reinforcements.

The extra men and equipment arrived shortly before midnight—sheriff's deputies, constables, and city police armed with shotguns, machine guns, automatic rifles, even an armored car mounted with searchlights. The small army moved quietly into position, confident that the gang was asleep.

Actually, every move they made was being watched.

W. D. Jones had gone into Platte City earlier that night to buy bandages and salve for Bonnie. While there, he had overheard a man in the drugstore mention "all the officers out at the highway junction."

Jones had alerted the gang, and they were now crouched in Buck's darkened cabin, watching as the armored car drove up and two helmeted figures set machine guns up behind steel shields. Suddenly the searchlights blazed on. There was a knock at the door. "Officers," a voice announced. "We want to talk to you."

"As soon as we get dressed," said Bonnie. Then, as W. D. slipped through the inside door connecting the cabin with the garage and got behind the wheel of the car, she added, "The men are on the other side."

"You had better come out," called the lawman.

The Barrow brothers were in position now: one at the window, one at the inside door. "Let the bastards have it!" yelled Clyde.

There was a sustained roar of gunfire. Bullets rattled off the steel shields as the machine gunners swung into action. Armor-piercing rounds sliced through the armored car as if it were paper. Deputy George Highfill crumpled, shot through both legs, but still shooting as he fell. Sheriff Holt Coffey went down, a bullet in his neck. His son, Clarence, pitched to the ground. Bullets had smashed his right arm, punctured his cheek.

A shotgun blast short-circuited the armored car's horn. It began a steady blast. The rest of the men thought it was a signal to charge and came rushing forward into the murderous cross fire.

A fragment of glass jammed the mechanism of one of the machine guns. "Let's get out of here," yelled Deputy James Thorpe, realizing that they were sitting ducks. He and Highfill managed to throw the armored car into reverse. They backed away from the garage doors as bullets continued to buzz around their heads like angry hornets.

Buck Barrow came charging out of the right-hand cabin now, a blazing automatic in each hand. Bonnie and Blanche were behind him, holding up mattresses as shields.

The posse directed its fire at the trio. As they did, a motor roared to life inside the garage. A man suddenly swung open the doors and hopped on the running board of the car that came shooting out. It was Clyde Barrow, hanging on with one hand and laying down a deadly barrage of sub-machine gun fire with the other. W. D. was behind the car's wheel, a cap pulled low over his face.

Bonnie and Blanche dropped their mattresses and began firing pistols as they ran toward the car. The officers returned their fire. Suddenly Buck staggered, shot through the temple. Blanche and Bonnie leaped to support him. They pulled him into the car. Blanche screaming that she'd been hit.

The car roared forward into a withering cross fire. Its windows dissoved into milky opalescence. The metal door frames seemed to actually shiver under the impact of dozens of rounds, a woman inside the car screamed in terrible, agonized pain. The vehicle swung onto the highway, careened wildly from side to side for a moment, then straightened out and disappeared in the direction of Platte City.

Though seriously wounded, Sheriff Coffey dragged himself to a telephone. Roadblocks were immediately set up on all major highways.

The gang had already swung east, though, and was traveling

along backcountry roads. About halfway between Platte City and Hoover they stopped and took stock. Buck was in the most critical shape; a bullet had entered his right temple and had exited from his left. Clyde had a scalp wound. Bonnie had a bullet burn along the ribs. Blanche's eyes had been cut by bullet-showered glass; she could only see vague, shadowy shapes and was in terrible pain. W. D. alone had come through unscathed.

At this point any other gang would have retreated to a city where the fix was on. Crooked lawyers would have arranged hide-outs; underworld surgeons would have treated their wounds. But the Barrows, with around $200 in nickels and dimes in their pockets, had only one alternative—keep running.

A vast manhunt was already in progress. The FBI, which had been keeping an eye on the gang since their raid on the Enid armory, sent agents to all hospitals in a five-state area, warning them to hold anyone with gunshot wounds. WDAF, the radio station of the *Kansas City Star*, broadcast detailed descriptions of the fugitives. A motorist near Mount Ayr, Iowa, just north of the Missouri line, heard one of these broadcasts. A few minutes later he spotted a car parked on a lonely side road. A man lay on the rear seat. Two men and two women were bent over a fire, burning bloody bandages. They leaped into the car and drove off the moment they saw him.

He reported what he had seen and the manhunt shifted to Iowa. Three days later a farmer came across a smoldering campfire and bloody bandages at a deserted amusement park halfway between the towns of Dexter and Redfield.

John Love, a member of the county vigilantes, hid in some nearby bushes and waited. He saw two cars drive up later that afternoon. Three men and two women got out. Love crept away and phoned Sheriff C. A. Knee of Adel. His description of the five matched the Barrows.

Knee called the sheriffs of surrounding counties and also the Iowa National Guard. By evening a good-sized army of officers had assembled at Dexter, its ranks swollen by dozens of local citizens armed with shotguns and squirrel rifles. With all possible escape roads sealed off, the posse moved in. They crept cautiously from tree to tree, slowly encircling the campsite. At dawn they began to tighten the noose.

Bonnie was brewing coffee over an open fire. Blanche was frying eggs. Clyde stood watching them, smoking a cigarette. W. D. Jones sat with Buck on the running board of one of the cars. Buck was clad only in a one-piece suit of underwear. Blanche, who wore riding breeches and boots, had a pair of dark goggles over her injured eyes.

Suddenly Clyde went diving towards his shotgun. He had

caught a glimpse of movement in the tree. "The law's coming!" he shouted. The coffee spilled into the fire as the others snatched up weapons. It was too late, though. They were surrounded. A murderous fusillade was already pouring into them from all sides.

"Get the car started!" Clyde shouted, as he fired back, trying to cover the others. W. D. ran toward it but was hit by a load of buckshot and fell, momentarily stunned. Still firing, Clyde shoved him into the back seat while Bonnie ran around to the other side and climbed in.

Clyde slid behind the wheel, and the car started forward. A couple of dozen guns roared. The machine was riddled. Clyde lost control of it as a bullet ripped into his arm. The car went ploughing into a tree stump.

The three of them leaped out and ran through withering fire to the second car. As it started up, a thunderous volley smashed into it, dissolving the windows, ripping the tires to shreds. They scrambled out and plunged off into the woods on foot with half the posse on their heels while the other half stayed to shoot it out with Buck.

Buck and Blanche were trapped behind a tree stump. Both had automatics. The posse surrounded them, called on them to surrender. Buck's answer was a curse as he opened fire. Bullets laced into them from all sides. Buck was hit twice but kept firing. Blanche huddled closer to him, handing him clips of shells. He jammed them into the gun, emptied it, then loaded up again. He was hit four more times. Blanche began to scream hysterically. Buck's head slumped forward, but he managed somehow to keep firing. Finally Doctor H. W. Keller of Des Moines, a national guardsman, rushed forward and kicked the gun out of his hand.

Blanche struggled with the possemen who seized her, hitting out at them blindly with her fists, spitting and cursing as they tried to drag her away. "Don't die, Daddy," she screamed. "Don't die!"

But there wasn't much else Buck could do. Blood was pouring from his old head wound and also from six new ones—all critical. He was taken to the Kings Daughters Hospital at Perry, where he died five days later.

W. D. and Bonnie, meanwhile, were fighting their way through the woods toward a creek that skirted the north side of the park. Clyde was right behind them, laying down a covering fire. All three were wounded—Clyde in the arm, Bonnie in the fleshy part of the back, Jones with a shoulder full of buckshot.

Possemen seemed to be lurking behind every bush. No matter which direction the trio headed, they found themselves trapped. "They fought desperately each step through the woods," an eyewitness report later stated, "darting from brush clump to brush clump. They made difficult targets and they were shooting with deadly accuracy."

They reached the stream and dived in, heading for the cornfield on the opposite side. The possemen halted at the edge of the clearing and took careful aim. Spouts of water rose around the fleeing outlaws. Bonnie screamed and sank out of sight. Clyde tugged at her but couldn't lift her because of his injured arm. W. D. gave him a push up the steep bank, then went back for Bonnie. The posse opened fire as he lifted her into his arms and carried her up the bank. W. D.'s head jerked to one side. The possemen cheered. They were sure they had gotten him. He didn't stop, though, and now the three of them were in the cornfield, and even the bravest members of the posse didn't want to go in after them.

A ring of men was thrown around the field, but it was too late. The three had already dashed out the other side, commandeered a farmer's Plymouth sedan, and fled north in it. An airplane was brought in to aid in the search. Two hundred possemen in cars followed it on the ground. Suddenly, near Guthrie Center, it dipped low, a signal that the outlaws had been sighted. An armored car was rushed to the head of the column to shield the possemen. This time they were sure they had them, but they didn't. The Plymouth ran the gamut of their fire and escaped.

They had Blanche, though. And after displaying her to the press, police tried to question her. She was incoherent. The months of running, the gun battles, her blindness, and now Buck's death had finally gotten to her. She subsequently served ten years in the Iowa State Prison for her part in the Dexter battle.

Clyde, Bonnie, and W. D. Jones stayed on the back roads that fall. They treated each other's wounds and lived on food that they stole from the fields.

The Fort Smith doctor had been right. Bonnie should never have been moved. Her burned leg had drawn up. She couldn't walk and was delirious much of the time. She had been a pretty twenty-year-old blonde only sixteen months earlier. Now, at twenty-two, she was scarred and crippled, and looked twice her age.

W. D. split with them some time in October. He made his way back to Texas and was arrested. He didn't seem unhappy about it. While awaiting trial, he dictated his twenty-eight-page confession, then pleaded for a life sentence. At least behind bars he would be safe from Bonnie and Clyde.

In early November the two of them dashed in to Dallas to see their parents. It was a foolhardy venture, but they brought it off, managing to spend almost an hour with them in a field near Grand Prairie. The parents noticed that they both seemed obsessed with thoughts of death. Bonnie even discussed funeral arrangements with her mother. When the two came home for another visit around Thanksgiving, those arrangements almost went into effect.

The Dallas County sheriff, Smoot Schmid, had heard about the last visit and had put tails on both families. When the two mothers drove to a lonely road off the Fort Worth Turnpike on the morning of November 22, Schmid concealed a group of heavily armed deputies in the ditches and woods on each side of the car in which they were sitting.

When Bonnie and Clyde showed up, the deputies let them have it. They blasted with machine guns, rifles, shot-guns, and pistols. They put seventeen holes in their car altogether. Clyde and Bonnie were hit in the legs but managed to drive away.

Clyde was furious that his mother's life had been endangered. He sent a message to Sheriff Schmid through a Dallas newspaper, warning him that if a hair of his mother's head was ever harmed, he would personally kill him.

The audacity of the threat appealed to the underworld. News of it traveled via the grapevine to Eastham, where Ray Hamilton decided that Clyde might be in the mood to spring him. Hamilton had been boasting that he was going to be sprung ever since they had put him away back in October. On checking into Eastham, he had told Warden B. B. Monzingo: "I won't be here long. Clyde Barrow won't let me lie around no prison farm." He had said it so many times that even his fellow cons had stopped believing him.

But now Clyde received Hamilton's message and was receptive.

On the morning of January 16, 1934, a party of ninety-five convicts marched through dense fog to the brush-covered river bottom where they had been clearing land. Three mounted guards were in charge of the detail. As the cons got down to work, Ray Hamilton slipped away from his squad and joined Joe Palmer and Henry Methvin. The three edged their way over to a large pile of brush next to a drainage ditch. Quickly they reached in—and came up with the .45 automatics that Clyde had hidden there.

The three guns roared in unison. Major E. M. Crowson was hit in the stomach by a shot from Hamilton's gun and toppled out of his saddle. Joe Palmer hit Guard Olen Bozeman as B. B. Bullard, a new screw, managed to bring up his shotgun. Nine pellets of buckshot slammed into Joe Palmer but didn't stop him. He swung toward Bullard, whose horse was rearing, and fired. The shot went wild as Bullard leaped from his saddle and dived behind a stack of cordwood.

Bozeman's horse bolted, with the wounded guard still clinging to the saddle. An auto horn had begun to blare, meanwhile, somewhere beyond the fence. Hamilton, Methvin, and Palmer asked who wanted to go with them. Convicts Hilton Bybee and J. B. French stepped forward. "Let's go, then," shouted Hamilton. The five of them slipped through the drainage ditch and ran toward the road.

Clyde and Bonnie were waiting beside two cars. As the men burst through the trees, they opened up with a submachine gun and a BAR, laying down a heavy barrage of covering fire. But no guards were following them. It had gone even smoother than expected.

Convict J. B. French split a few miles away from Eastham. He wanted to be on his own. He was recaptured the next day. Hilton Bybee was let out in Amarillo. He lasted a week.

The others hit a bank at Lancaster, Texas, then raced north to Oklahoma. It was like the old days, with Clyde, Bonnie, and Hamilton riding together once again. But with a difference. Now there was no refuge anywhere. They were too hot even for Hamilton's relatives. "Keep going," they were told. And so they drove north, out of Choctaw country, heading toward the Cookson Hills.

The heavily timbered hills had been a sanctuary for bad-men since the days of Jesse James and Belle Starr. The topography favored fugitives. It was wild, inaccessible, sinister country, honeycombed with caves and crisscrossed by chasms and gorges—2,400 square miles of roadless wilderness covered over with scrub oak and blackjack. A fugitive could step twenty feet off the main road—gravel-topped State 82—and be in Tibet, as far as anyone could tell.

Lawmen didn't enter the hills. It was a waste of time. Not only did the topography favor the outlaws, but so did the hill dwellers. They fed and sheltered fugitives, and even refused to take money from those they liked. But they wouldn't lift a hand to help the Barrow gang. Word had come down from the "Boss of the Hills," Pretty Boy Floyd: shun them, starve them out, if necessary lead the law to them. They were too hot for the Cookson Hills; they would ruin it for the other outlaws holed up there.

The Barrows got the message. They packed up. But it was already too late. Their two cars, as hot as their occupants, had been sighted turning off into the hills at Muskogee. It had been the final straw for the already hard-pressed Oklahoma authorities.

On the night of February 17, 1934, 1,000 lawmen, including four companies of Oklahoma National Guardsmen, began surrounding the Cookson country in drizzling rain. For the first time in history a large body of troops would be sent sweeping through the hills in search of outlaws. Their orders: shoot to kill.

At dawn they pushed off. Guardsmen set up Army machine

guns at all crossroads. Their instructions were to stop and search every car moving. If they refused to stop, shoot.

It was the biggest manhunt the press had ever had a whack at. Every newspaper in the Southwest sent reporters. Hubert Dail, of *True Detective* Magazine, was lucky enough to hitch a ride with an advance group. "Every officer was heavily armed," he reported. "Each police car carried bright red lights and signs reading: 'Stop! Sheriff!!' It was a weird scene, the darting cars with their red lights and the big shadowy trucks loaded with guardsmen lumbering along more slowly. A thin snow lay over the Hills and the dirt roads were deep in mud. Even the chill air seemed hostile. . . . The officers soon left all trails behind and trudged across the open country. Occasionally the rat-a-tat-tat of machine gun fire reached their ears. It meant that someone out along the road had refused to stop for questioning."

But all the rat-a-tat-tatting came to naught. Only nineteen people were caught in the dragnet, all of them small-fry. Pretty Boy Floyd got away. The Ford Bradshaw gang escaped. And so did the Barrow outfit.

They headed north once again, hitting banks in Michigan, Iowa, and Indiana before Joe Palmer, who had stomach trouble, left the gang. At Terre Haute, Clyde and Hamilton got into a squabble over Bonnie's share of the loot, and Hamilton bowed out, too.

That left Bonnie and Clyde alone with Henry Methvin, a shy Louisiana farm boy with blond hair and blue eyes. He was W. D. all over again.

Keeping Methvin with them was a mistake. But Bonnie and Clyde would never have time to regret it. They would discover their error and die in the same instant.

Death was all they could think about these days; and the news from home only confirmed the manner in which it would finally come to them.

The Texas Legislature was up in arms. Major E. M. Crowson had died of his wounds following the Eastham Prison Farm delivery, and lawmakers were talking about a "Wanted Dead" reward for Bonnie and Clyde.

T. H. McGregor, the representative from Austin, pleaded against the measure. "You are about to do in cold blood a thing which a mob does in the heat of passion," he cried.

That brought Congressman George Winningham to his feet. "I place Barrow and his gang beyond the category of human beings," he shouted angrily. "You are talking about according a trial to a beast. I say give him the same chance he gave those he murdered. Shoot him down like the mad dog he is."

A $2,500 reward was finally settled on, and the words "or alive" were added to the "Wanted Dead" posters that would be distributed. It was a victory for the moderates.

Lee Simmons, the general manager of the Texas prison system, didn't think that proclamations or rewards were going to do any good. He had his own ideas on how to get Bonnie and Clyde. He sent for Frank Hamer, a former captain of the Texas Rangers. The fifty-year-old Hamer was an almost legendary figure in Texas. An old-style lawman who always dressed in somber black, he was reputed to be the fastest draw south of the Red River. The sixty-five desperadoes he had killed in face-to-face encounters made Clyde's fatality list look pretty feeble.

Simmons gave Hamer a free hand, unlimited authority. "I don't care how long it takes," he told him. "I'll back you to the limit." And then he added, "I'd be foolish to tell you how to do your job, but the way I look at it, the best thing to do is put them on the spot, know you are right, and shoot everybody in sight."

On February 10 Hamer set out on his grim assignment. Like Clyde Barrow, he used a Ford V-8 and, like Clyde, he lived in it for days at a time. As he traveled through the Southwest Hamer stopped and interviewed anyone who had ever known Bonnie and Clyde. Slowly a picture of his quarry emerged—right down to the cigarettes they smoked, the food they ate, the kind of clothes they wore. A pattern of movement began to emerge, too. The fugitives traveled along a rough circle from Dallas to Joplin, Missouri, then over to Louisiana and back to Dallas.

In late February Hamer missed them by minutes at Texarkana. He was close again at Shreveport, then at a campsite outside Wichita Falls. Then suddenly the trail grew cold.

They had come to rest at the Methvin farm in Bienville Parish, Louisiana.

Bonnie had become obsessed with the idea of writing one last poem that would explain everything. She would send it to a newspaper and then the world would finally understand that they weren't as bad as they were painted. She sweated for some hours over the opening stanzas:

> You have read the story of Jesse James,
> Of how he lived and died.
> If you still are in need of something to read,
> Here is the story of Bonnie and Clyde.
>
> Now Bonnie and Clyde are the Barrow gang.
> I'm sure you all have read
> How they rob and steal,
> And how those who squeal,
> Are usually found dying or dead.

There are lots of untruths to their write-ups,
They are not so merciless as that;
They hate all the laws,
The stool-pigeons, spotters and rats.

After explaining how Clyde had been "honest and upright and clean" until the law had started hounding him, she elaborated on how every crime of the period was being attributed to them:

If a policeman is killed in Dallas
And they have no clues to guide—
If they can't find a fiend,
They just wipe the slate clean,
And hang it on Bonnie and Clyde.

She also recorded her version of the battles of Joplin and Platte City, concluding:

If they try to act like citizens,
And rent them a nice little flat,
About the third night they are invited to fight.
By a submachine-gun rat-tat-tat.

There was also a rather shrewd comment on their fame, and what it meant to some people during the Depression:

A newsboy once said to his buddy:
"I wish old Clyde would get jumped;
"In these awful hard times,
"We'd make a few dimes
"If five or six cops would get bumped."

Before she could finish the poem, the running began once again. State and Federal officers made a vice raid on nearby Ruston in mid-March, heating up all of Bienville and Lincoln Parishes.

Clyde, Bonnie, and young Henry Methvin drove west, crossing the Sabine River at Joaquin, Texas. They hid out in the "big piney" country for the next few weeks, then made a dash into Dallas on April 1.

It was Easter Sunday. Bonnie had bought a baby rabbit for her sister. At around 2 P.M. they arrived at the rendezvous point, a lonely country lane a hundred yards off the Preston Road near Grapevine, Texas. They tied a ribbon around the rabbit's neck and let it out to play in the grass.

As they stood watching it two motorcycle cops roared past on State 114. The cops glanced at the trio, then swung around and came back. It's thought that the two, State Highway Patrolmen E. B. Wheeler and H. D. Murphy, were just going to ask them to move on.

Clyde watched them rack their cycles at the edge of the dirt lane and start toward them. Casually he reached inside the car for his shotgun . . .

A lot of newsboys made a lot of extra dimes that night.

The reaction to the double killing was intense. Both officers had been young—in their early twenties. Neither had had a chance to unholster his gun. Clyde was made Texas' Public Enemy Number One.

Captain Hamer wasn't far behind as the trio sped north from Grapevine along backcountry roads. At Tioga he found a campsite. He knew it was theirs from the marks left by rabbit's teeth in some lettuce leaves. There were also stubs of Bonnie's Camels, one of them still warm. Hamer raced on.

The V-8 was found abandoned outside Cannon, Texas. There were no recent auto theft reports in the area, though, so gradually the trail began to cool.

Clyde, Bonnie, and Methvin surfaced five days later outside Commerce, Oklahoma. They were driving a new Plymouth now. As they jounced along a rutted dirt road known locally as The Lost Trail they got mired in the mud. Clyde tried to flag down a farmer, but the man caught a glimpse of the rifles stacked inside their car and sped away. He drove straight in to Commerce and told Police Chief Percy Boyd what he had seen.

Boyd picked up Constable Cal Campbell, and the two men drove out along the road until they spotted the Plymouth. They stopped and got out of their car. As they approached on foot, Clyde Barrow suddenly stepped out from behind the Plymouth. He had a Browning automatic rifle in his hands.

Campbell, a large man with a western-style mustache, was proud of his fast draw. He had his pistol out and was firing it before Clyde could get off a shot. His aim was wild, though. Clyde's wasn't. Campbell dropped, mortally wounded. Chief Boyd had also drawn and fired. He was sent spinning into the mud by a second blast from the BAR.

Barrow ran down the road while Methvin covered the two men. Clyde got a farmer in a truck to pull the Plymouth out of the ditch. Then the chief, who wasn't seriously wounded, was loaded into the back seat, and the four of them drove off.

That night they stopped at Fort Scott, Kansas, and Bonnie bought a newspaper and food, which they ate in the woods. They learned from the paper that Constable Campbell had died. "I'm sorry I killed the old man," Clyde told Boyd. "But I had to. He shouldn't have shot at me."

They released the police chief near Prescott, Kansas, an hour later. Bonnie's last words to him were that the much-publicized snapshot of her had been a joke. "Tell the public I don't smoke cigars," she called out as the car drove away. "It's the bunk."

Captain Hamer, as usual, was only a half hour behind them. He had been on their trail forty-five days now. It was a record. "Clyde Barrow," he would later tell newsmen, "was the smartest of them all. He was the most elusive and shrewdest man I ever tracked."

The FBI was too busy with the Dillinger case to waste much time on the Barrows, but one Special Agent, L. A. Kindell, had been acting as a liason between local police agencies and the Bureau.

In early April, Kindell discovered the identity of the third gang member, Henry Methvin. He took a trip to Louisiana and turned up another interesting fact—Clyde and Bonnie often visited Methvin's father, Ivan.

While poking around the Arcadia area, some eighty miles east of the Texas-Louisiana border, Kindell met Frank Hamer, who had also been drawn there by the Methvin angle. The two men went to see the Arcadia sheriff, Henderson Jordan.

He reported that Ivan Methvin had moved recently. At their request, Jordan tracked him down. Methvin was living on a rented farm about halfway between Arcadia and Gibsland. The three men went to see him. Methvin admitted that his son was involved with Bonnie and Clyde. But he refused to help them. "I've got my boy to think about," he said.

A few weeks passed, while the lawmen tried to figure out their next move. Then suddenly Ivan Methvin came to see them. Clyde and Bonnie had returned and had forced him to move once again. The four of them were holed up in an abandoned farmhouse deep in the woods. Methvin was now willing to cooperate with the law —for a price.

Hamer contacted Prison Manager Simmons and named the price. He could put Barrow and his girl on the spot, but it would take a full pardon for Henry Methvin.

Simmons went to Austin and conferred with "Ma" Ferguson. She agreed to issue the pardon if Methvin's father cooperated. Hamer passed the word on. Methvin was satisfied. He promised to help the lawmen and even suggested a plan.

The gang's routine, in the event they got separated, was to meet at the abandoned house. Methvin said he would tell his son to get lost, and when Clyde and Bonnie appeared at the rendezvous point, they could—well, be captured.

Ivan Methvin took his son aside that same night and told him the plan. Henry said they were going in to Shreveport the next day to do some shopping and that he would vanish at the first opportunity. He did. Clyde and Bonnie waited for him almost an hour. Then, figuring that something must have scared him away, they drove out to the abandoned house and waited.

Ivan Methvin sat watching them, sweat pouring down his face. But they apparently suspected nothing. Finally Bonnie said, "Maybe he got mixed up and went over to the rented place."

Clyde said to Methvin, "You better check on it. We'll meet you on the road between Sailes and Gibsland tomorrow morning at nine."

As soon as they were gone, Ivan rushed to Sheriff Jordan's house. Jordan phoned Federal Agent Kindell, but his office said he was out of town on an emergency assignment and couldn't be reached. Captain Hamer was in town, though, and came right over. With him was an old Ranger sidekick, M. B. "Manny" Gault, and two men from Sheriff Schmid's Dallas office, Chief Deputy Bob Alcorn and Deputy Ted Hinton.

After picking up Jordan's deputy, Paul M. Oakley, the six men drove back and forth between Sailes and Gibsland, looking for the best ambush spot. They finally settled on a patch of woods outside Mt. Lebanon. The road was narrow at this point and with steep banks on both sides. Clyde wouldn't be able to pull off his famous U-turn.

The men got into position behind the embankment. Captain Hamer and Sheriff Jordan had automatic shotguns. Hinton had a BAR. Gault, Oakley, and Alcorn had Winchester repeaters. All had a perfect field of fire.

Finally, around eight o'clock that morning, May 23, they heard Ivan Methvin's truck approaching. Sheriff Jordan flagged it down. Methvin was told to pull over to the side of the road and to take the truck's right front wheel off, as if he had a flat.

Then the waiting started once again. At nine o'clock several cars passed. The men tensed each time, but the cars sped by without stopping. Then, at nine-fifteen, a Ford V-8 suddenly appeared over the rise and came speeding toward the ambush site.

Clyde was at the wheel. He wore sunglasses and was driving in his socks. Bonnie sat beside him, munching on a sandwich. She had on her best dress, a flashy red one that she had bought in Terre Haute a few weeks earlier. Clyde's sawed-off twelve-gauge was propped between them. Their usual armory was on the back seat—eleven pistols, a revolver, three BAR's, and more than two thousand rounds of ammunition. Bonnie's overnight case was on top of it, together with Clyde's saxophone and some sheets of music.

Bonnie's poem wasn't in the car, though. She had completed it a few weeks earlier and had sent it to the Dallas *Evening Journal* with instructions to publish it after her death. The poem's final verses ran:

The road gets dimmer and dimmer.
Sometimes you can hardly see,
Still it's fight, man to man,
And do all you can,
For they know they can never be free.

They don't think they are too tough or desperate,
They know the law always wins,
They have been shot at before
But they do not ignore
That death is the wages of sin.

From heartbreaks some people have suffered,
From weariness some people have died,
But take it all in all,
Our troubles are small,
Till we get like Bonnie and Clyde.

Some day they will go down together,
And they will bury them side by side.
To a few it means grief,
To the law it's relief,
But it's death to Bonnie and Clyde.

Clyde saw Ivan Methvin's truck and slowed to a stop beside it. "Got a flat?" he called out. Methvin nodded nervously. "Did you find Henry?"

Methvin shook his head, then turned suddenly to Bonnie and asked her for a drink of water.

"Sure," she said, and reached for the thermos. Methvin dived behind his truck.

"Put 'em up, Clyde. You're covered!" Sheriff Jordan bellowed.

Clyde shifted into first, grabbed his shotgun, and swung the door open—all in one movement. Bonnie already had her pistol out.

The ambush party opened fire. Six powerful weapons poured nonstop streams of lead into the car. Bonnie and Clyde's bodies danced like puppets on a string. Clyde's jacket was literally torn from his body. He sagged against the wheel. His foot slipped off the clutch pedal. The car rolled forward against the embankment and there it bounced to a stop.

"Be careful, they may not be dead," Ranger Gault shouted as Captain Hamer cautiously approached the car.

One hundred and sixty-seven slugs had ripped into the vehicle, all of them breast-high on the two occupants. Yet there was still doubt in the lawmen's minds as to whether Bonnie and Clyde were actually dead. Such was the power of their legend.

The crowds got at the bodies immediately. They tore away scraps of their clothing and snipped off locks of their hair. They gathered up the empty cartridges and bits of broken glass.

The car was towed into Arcadia with the bodies still in it.

Photographs taken at the funeral parlor show the two bodies lying riddled and leaking on adjoining stone slabs, the tools of their trade piled on their chests, as crowds file past, gaping, hungry for one last thrill.

Captain Hamer's job was over. He had finally taken them—after 102 days of tracking. "There isn't much to it," he told the chief of the Texas Highway Patrol over the telephone. "They just drove into the wrong place. Both of them died with their guns in their hands, but they didn't have a chance to use them."

The news was flashed around the world. In New York City the *Herald Tribune* observed solemnly that "society is glad that Louisiana rubbed them both out."

They were not buried side by side as Bonnie had predicted in her poem. Clyde was buried beside his brother Buck in West Dallas Cemetery. Bonnie was lowered into the ground at Fish Trap Cemetery several miles away while a quartet sang "Beautiful Isle of Somewhere." Her body was later moved to Crown Hill Memorial Park.

The authorities were busy, meanwhile, rounding up the remnants of the gang. Ray Hamilton and Joe Palmer were caught and sentenced to death for killing Major Crowson during the Eastham bust-out. They made a spectacular escape from the Huntsville death house in July 1934 but were later recaptured and electrocuted.

Henry Methvin got his pardon from Texas, but Oklahoma officers were waiting for him. He was taken to that state and sentenced to death for the murder of Constable Cal Campbell. The sentence was later commuted, and he was paroled in 1942. A train ran over him in Sulphur, Louisiana, six years later.

Mrs Cumie Barrow and many other relatives of Bonnie and Clyde served prison terms ranging from a few days to years for having given "aid and comfort" to the pair while they were fugitives.

And that was supposed to be the end of it. Time would pass and people would forget. Instead the legend grew. Around Grand Prairie and the West Dallas viaduct it got more elaborate with every passing year.

There were the poems, and there was Clyde, who had carried Bonnie with him when she was crippled and no longer pretty, and there was Bonnie herself tough and hard-mouthed, a killer, yet capable of caring for him in some furious, half-crazy way.

After Bonnie was buried at Crown Hill Cemetery, her family had a plaque put over her grave. There were some verses on it. Not Bonnie's, just those standard lines that used to come with a certain price headstone back in the Depression. They read:

As the flowers are all made sweeter
By the sunshine and the dew,
So this old world is made brighter
By the lives of folks like you.

CHAPTER FOUR

Pretty Boy Floyd—the Robin Hood of the Cookson Hills

Pretty Boy Floyd had never liked the Barrow gang.

It didn't bother him that they were fast on the trigger or that they killed cops. He was fast himself, and as for the cops—they were paid to take risks.

What bothered him was the way they treated innocent civilians.

After the Cookson Hills manhunt, his dislike for them turned to active hatred. He had been flushed from cover by the manhunt, had been forced to flee, leaving behind people who had shielded him, who trusted him.

The law had not dealt kindly with them. The National Guardsmen had been okay. But the local sheriffs and their deputies had used the occasion to even some old scores. A lot of barns had been "accidentally" fired during the manhunt, and fences torn down, and livestock stampeded into the underbrush. And a lot of innocent hill people had been shot up in their cars when they hadn't stopped fast enough at roadblocks.

Floyd could have returned afterward. The people would have protected him still. But he never went back. He was afraid of bringing more hell down on their heads. He traveled north instead and tried to hide in the big cities. Hill folk had never done well in the cities. Floyd was no exception. On his own, without the help of his own kind, he lasted exactly eight months.

He was a unique figure in U.S. crime annals, this broad-shouldered, apple-cheeked bumpkin with the catlike reflexes and the stainless steel nerves. Floyd's use of his native terrain, his ability to live off a sympathetic population, suggests the present-day guerrilla more than the average apolitical gunman of the '30s.

"The guerrilla must swim amid the population as a fish must in water." Floyd had never heard of Mao Tse-tung's dictum, but he lived it. It was the secret of his success. The people of the Cookson Hills hid him, fed him, served as his communications network. Their loyalty to him took precedence over the law. As Pa Joad put it, in *The Grapes of Wrath:* "Sometimes the law can't be foller'd no way. Not in decency, anyways. . . . When Floyd was loose an' goin' wild, law said we got to give him up—an' nobody give him up. Sometimes a fella got to sift the law."

Floyd's people had a name by then. They had creaked westward from the Dust Bowl in their ancient jalopies, and by the time Steinbeck got around to writing about them in the late '30s, everybody knew them as "Okies."

But back in Floyd's day they'd had no name and no awareness of themselves as a unique, vestigial group, a casualty of agricultural progress. They had still been clinging stubbornly to their ruined land in the early '30s, holding off the bank's tractors with shotguns, daring any man to take what was rightly theirs.

Trouble was, they had pledged their property to the banks as security in the twenties, and by 1931 the banks wanted the land. The land companies—those were the banks when they had land—wanted tractors, not families, on the land. And so they proceeded to starve the people out.

The older folks didn't know what to do or where to go. And a lot of them actually did starve before the great westward migration began. The young ones refused to go hungry, though. They got themselves guns and became armed bandits.

They were a dangerous bunch, for they were crack shots from years of hunting and had courage born of desperation—courage enough to "charge hell with a bucket of water," as one awed sheriff put it. Those who had sampled jail swore never to go back. So there was only one way to really stop them—kill them.

They were bad medicine, all of them.

Ford Bradshaw, Wilbur Underhill, Jim Benge, Aussie Elliott, Tom Carlisle, Troy Love, Ed Newt Clanton—those were some of the wilder ones to come barreling out of the Cookson Hills in the early '30s. But even their names are forgotten today. Only one of their number has really survived in people's memories: Charles Arthur Floyd, of Akins, Oklahoma, the one who was called "Pretty Boy," though never by his own people.

Floyd robbed banks, and the hill folk loved him for it. "Give 'em hell, Chock!" a voice in the crowd shouted the day he held up the Sallisaw jug.

And he did. In 1931 and 1932 he knocked over so many one-horse banks in Oklahoma that the robbery insurance rates actually doubled. He even robbed two banks in one day—long the goal of every bandit in the tristate area. The Daltons had gotten themselves killed trying it at Coffeyville, and the Cook Brothers after them at Stroud. But Floyd brought it off—at Paden and Castle, Oklahoma, on December 12, 1931.

Floyd's basic equipment was a submachine gun and a bulletproof vest. He often worked alone and seldom with more than one

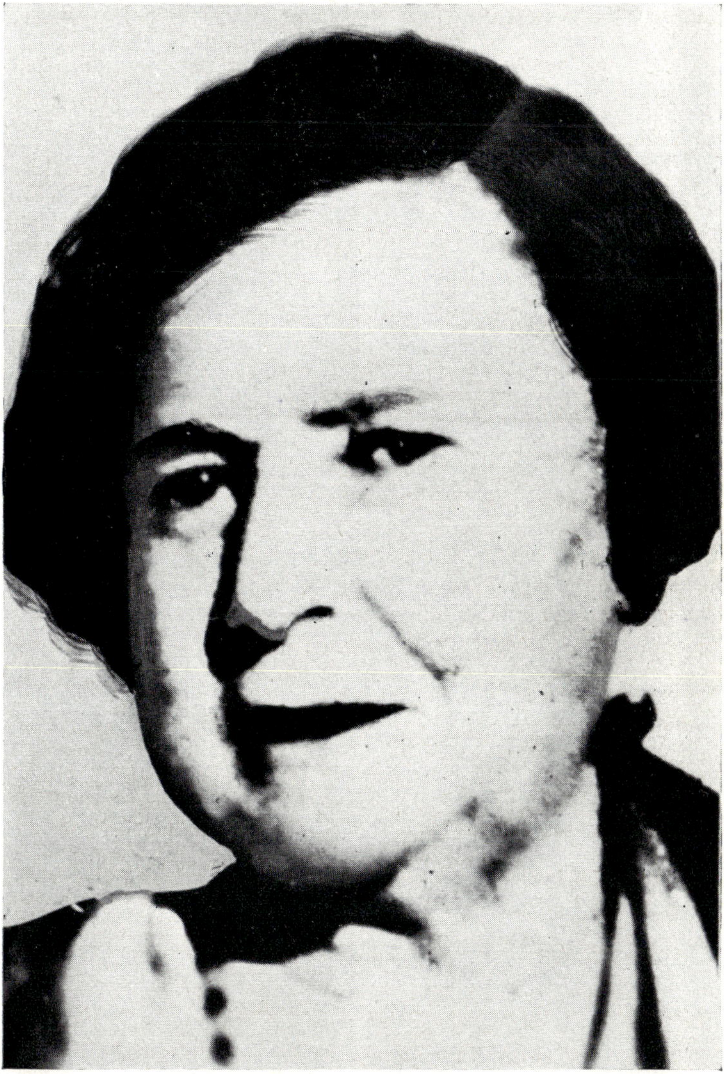

"Ma" Barker. Since she was never arrested, there are no mug-shots of her.

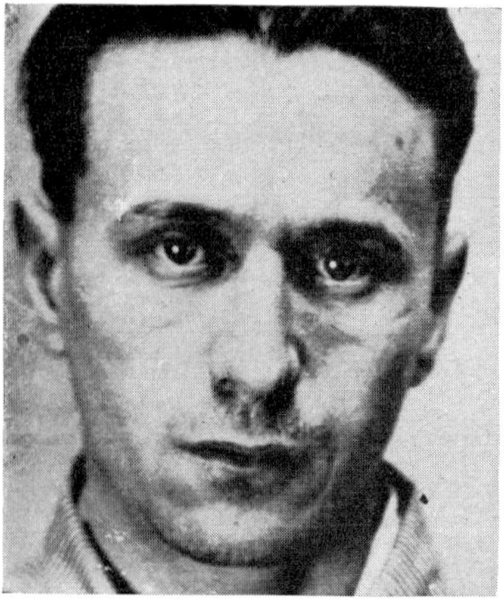

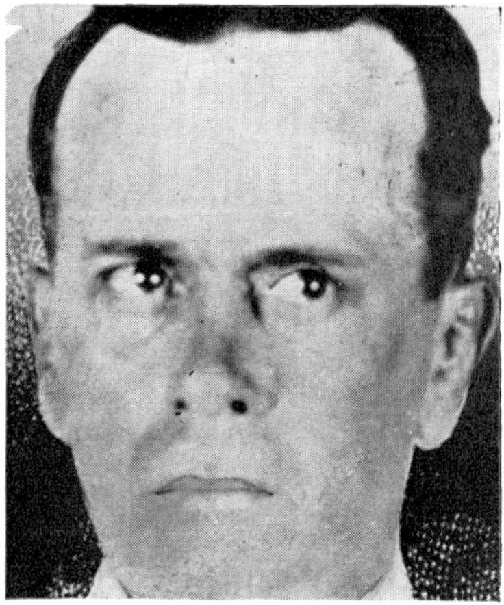

Top left: Fred Barker.
Top right: Dock Barker, Fred's older brother.
Bottom (left and right): Alvin Karpis—a cool cat, one of the ace performers of the era. Still alive.

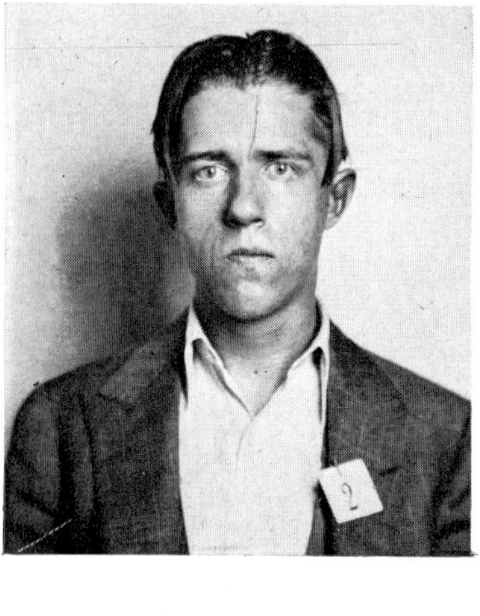

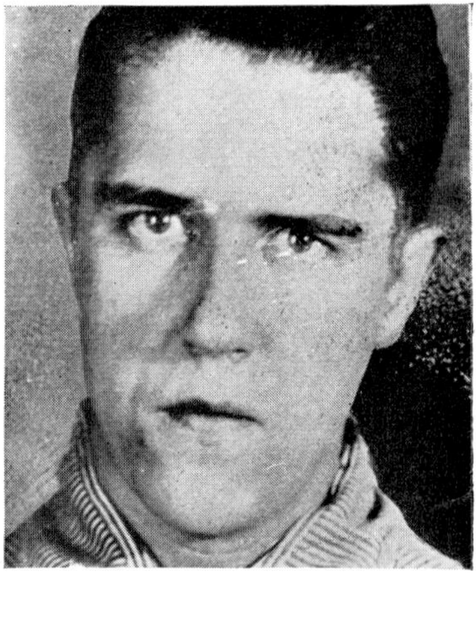

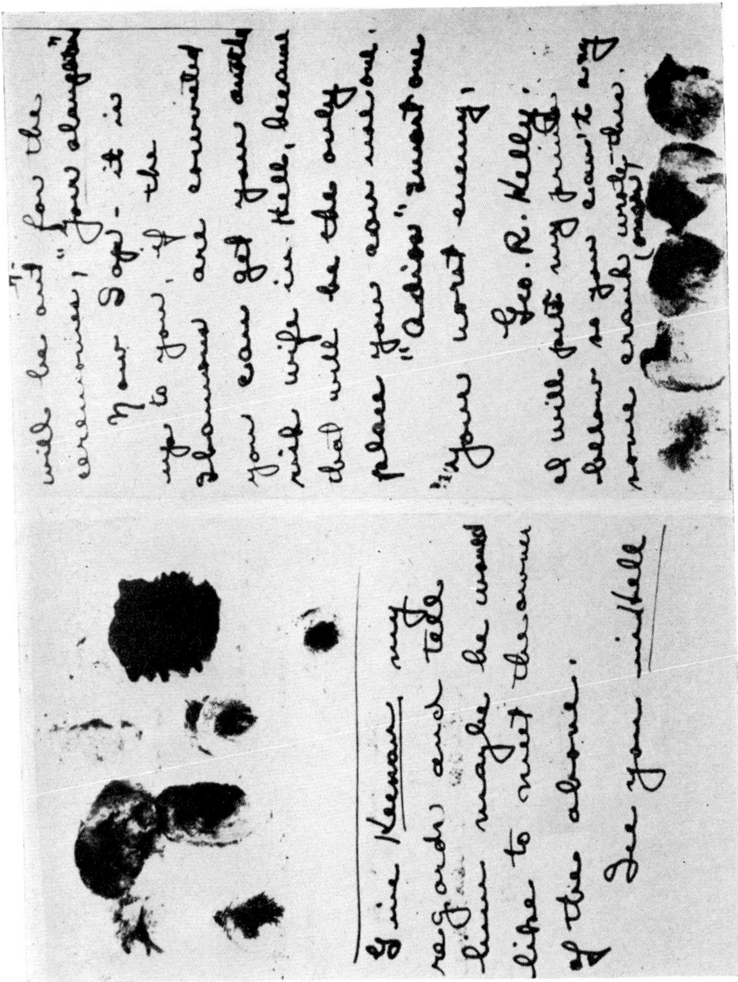

will be out for the
ceremonies; "Your Slaughter"
Now Sap - It is
up to you & the
Shannons and convicted
you can get your cut
with wife in Hell, because
that will be the only
place you can visit one.
"Adios" smart one
Your worst enemy,
Geo. R. Kelly.
I will put my prints
below so you can't make
some crack about under-three

Give Keenan my
regards and tell
him maybe he would
like to meet the owner
of the above.
See you in Hell

Part of the letter "Machine Gun" Kelly wrote to oilman Urschel showing bitterness at the arrest of his in-laws.

Bonnie Parker: the sweet, unassuming side that appeared for Clyde's camera.

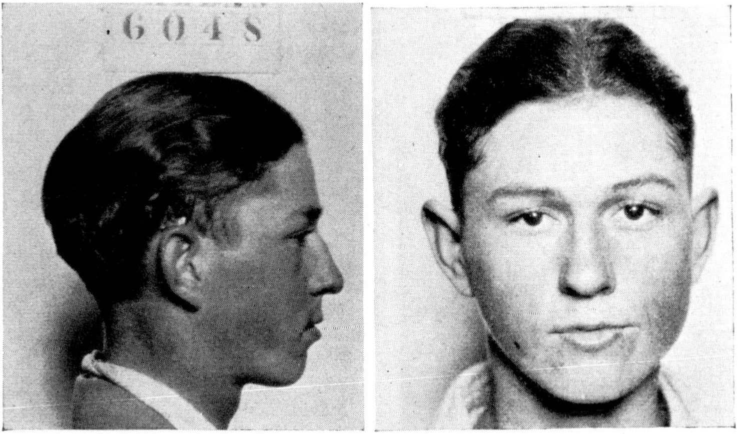

Top: Clyde Barrow: a sawn-off maniac with the face of a choir-boy. *Bottom:* Buck Barrow: small-time punk and turkey-thief, who advised his kid brother to go straight. Good advice, but over-sanguine.

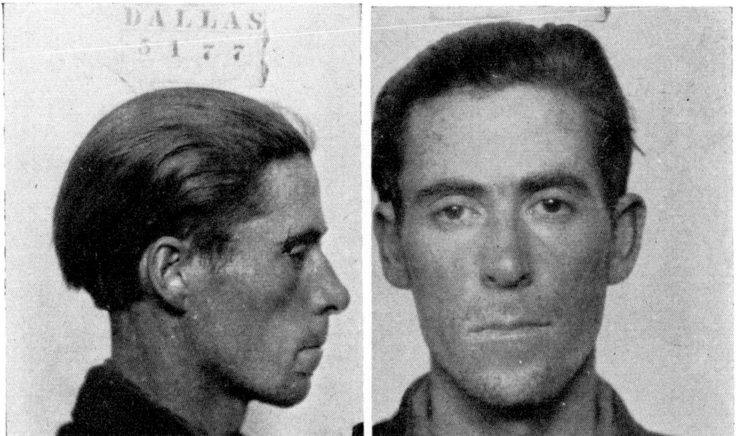

Clyde relaxing, with no cops in the vicinity to be bumped off.

W. D. Jones: raw, ravaged and totally guileless.

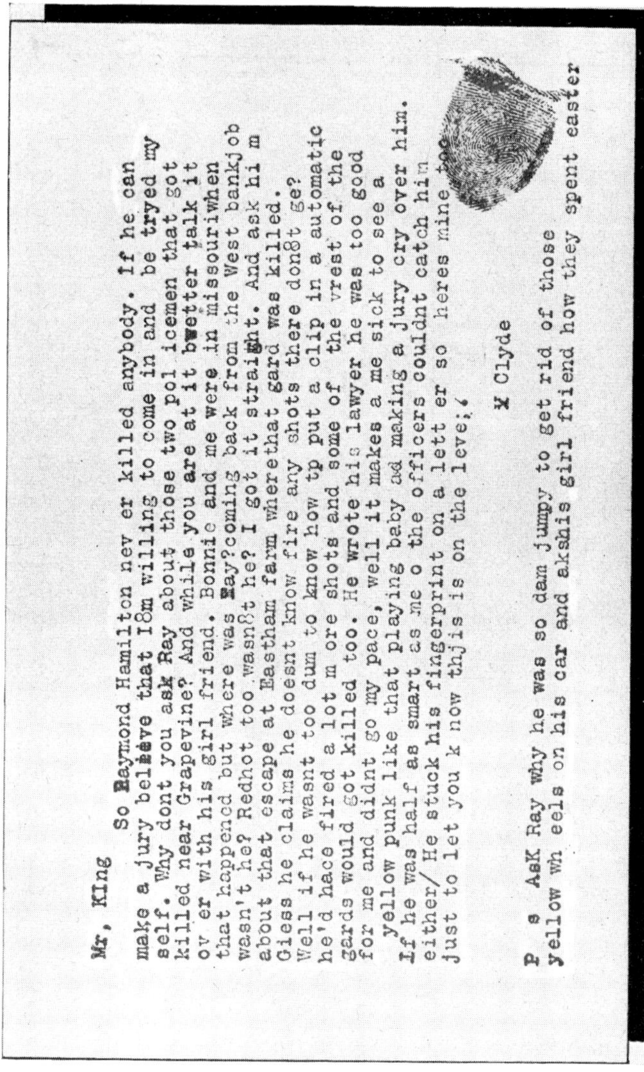
Mr, KIng

So Raymond Hamilton nev er killed anybody. If he can make a jury beleive that I8m willing to come in and be tryed my self. Why dont you ask Ray about those two pol icemen that got killed near Grapevine? And while you are at it bwetter talk it ov er with his girl friend. Bonnie and me were in missouriwhen that happened but where was Ray?coming back from the West bankjob wasn't he? Redhot too wasn8t he? I got it straight. And ask hi m about that escape at Eastham farm wherethat gard was killed. Giess he claims he doesnt know fire any shots there don8t ge? Well if he wasnt too dum to know how tp put a clip in a automatic he'd hace fired a lot m ore shots and some of the vrest of the gards would got killed too. He wrote his lawyer he was too good for me and didnt go my pace, well it makes a me sick to see a yellow punk like that playing baby ad making a jury cry over him. If he was half as smart as me o the officers couldnt catch him either/ He stuck his fingerprint on a lett er so heres mine too just to let you k now thjis is on the leve;

X Clyde

P s AsK Ray why he was so dam jumpy to get rid of those yellow wh eels on his car and akshis girl friend how they spent easter

Shortly after writing this letter to the trial judge, Clyde decided to spring Ray Hamilton in order to stop his non-stop mouth.

Charles Floyd: God-fearing heistman with fast trigger-finger and steel vest. Good nerves. Sobriquet—"Pretty Boy"—said to have been thought up by a Kansas City whore-house madam. Not proven.

TO r.J. scott

thanks for the

compliments and the pictures

of me in your paper

i'll be gone when you get this

jesse james wwas no punk himself

i'm not as bad as they say i am

they just wouldent let me alone

after i got out

yorus truly

Chas A Floyd

"Pretty Boy" had as bad a press as any in the Public Enemy Era. One of his many letters defending himself.

Left: John Dillinger whose success was matched by his popularity and sense of theatre.

Right: Harry Pierpont – the looks of a Scott Fitzgerald hero, and a heart as mean as any.

Top (left and right): Homer Van Meter – clown-faced joker, but all hell with the "fireworks".
Bottom left: John Hamilton – postgraduate criminal with heavy plotting brain.
Bottom right: Ed Shouse – former dirt track rider. Gangs could always use good wheelmen.

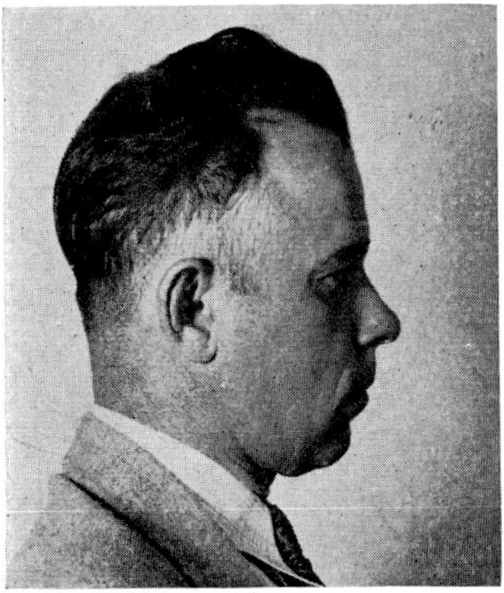

Top: Dillinger mug-shots – note the sardonic smile of a man who knew he would soon be sprung.
Bottom: In Crown Point jail, Dillinger rests on shoulder of prosecuting attorney, Robert Estill. This was the end of Estill's political career. Dillinger managed to stay in business.

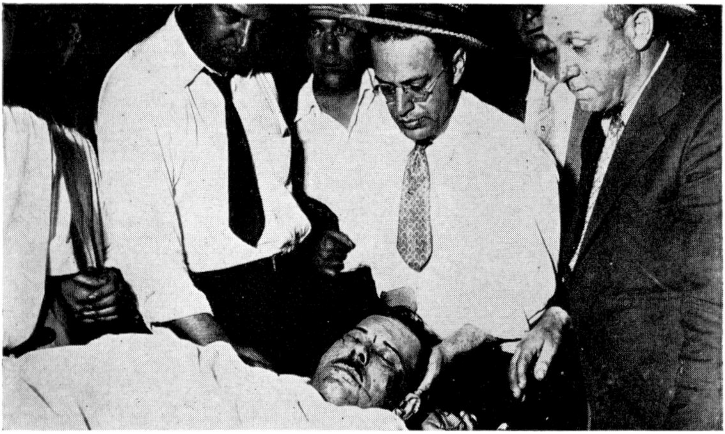

Dillinger in the morgue. Cuts on face the result of inept plastic surgery. Thousands of sensation-seekers filed past the icebox; thousands more were locked outside.

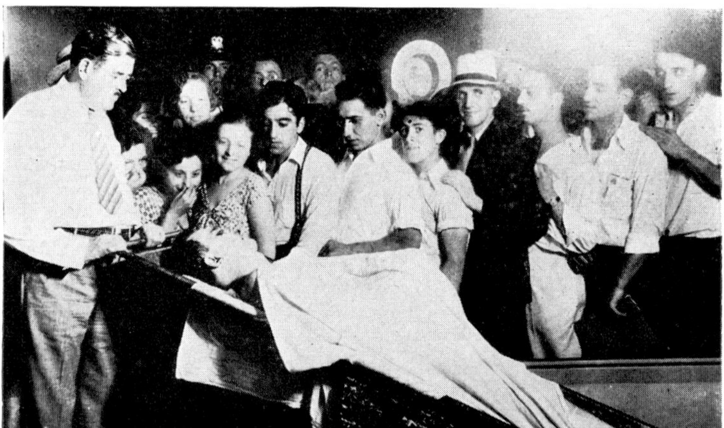

WANTED

LESTER M. GILLIS,

aliases GEORGE NELSON, "BABY FACE" NELSON, ALEX GILLIS, LESTER GILES, "BIG GEORGE" NELSON, "JIMMIE", "JIMMY" WILLIAMS .

On June 23, 1934, HOMER S. CUMMINGS, Attorney General of the United States, under the authority vested in him by an Act of Congress approved June 6, 1934, offered a reward of

$5,000.00

for the capture of Lester M. Gillis or a reward of

$2,500.00

for information leading to the arrest of Lester M. Gillis.

Nelson was furious that the reward money was less than half that offered for the capture of Dillinger. Typical.

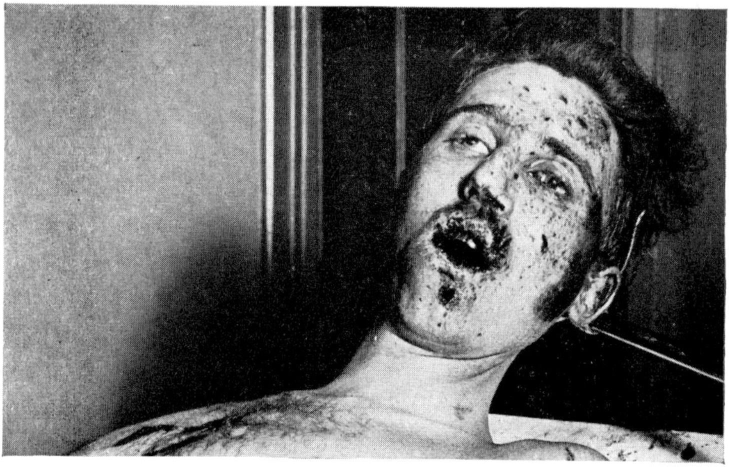

Top: Homer Van Meter before the cameras for the last time. Rigor mortis has set in.
Bottom: Nelson on slab. Autopsy accounts for stitches. Last recorded words after receiving 17 slugs in torso and limbs – "You better drive. I been hit".

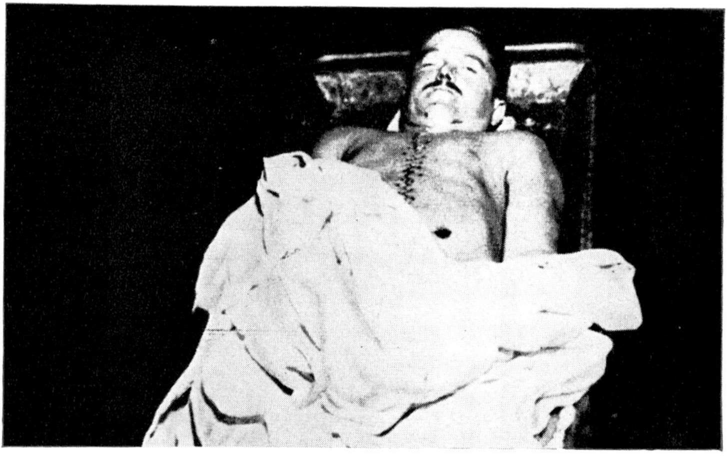

companion. He rarely tried to conceal his identity and often introduced himself to his victims. When leaving the scene of a robbery, he forced bank officials to ride on the running boards of his getaway car. It made bloodless, almost leisurely departures possible.

Of course there was always some damn fool who wanted to trade shots with him anyway. That was what put ten notches in the lucky piece he carried on his watch fob.

Floyd was a highly skilled gunfighter. His first love was the Thompson, but he was equally good with the smaller stuff. Kansas City's Chief of Detectives, B. H. Thurman, characterized him as "one of the quickest men on the draw, and the surest pistol shot I have ever known."

So great was the power of Floyd's name in Oklahoma in the early '30s that he passed unmolested in repeated public appearances. Once he even attended church in Earlsboro, a town in the eastern oil fields, and left a large bill on the collection plate—all without so much as a peep to police from either the congregation or the minister.

The newspapers called him the "Robin Hood of the Cookson Hills." Floyd liked that. He did, in fact, have a kind of rudimentary instinct for social justice. "I have robbed no one but moneyed men," he once wrote indignantly to the acting governor of Oklahoma.

When robbing country banks, Floyd delighted in tearing up first mortgages, just in case they weren't recorded. Everybody in the hills knew that bankers enjoyed foreclosing on destitute widows, and this was a kind of bonus, the satisfaction he got from saving someone's farm.

There are many stories of Floyd's generosity to the hill folk, but what isn't so well known is that he also paid his way outside the hills. He was as apt to offer a man ten dollars to take him somewhere as he was to pull a gun on him. As a relative of his put it years later: "Chock never suffered no man's charity."

Floyd was reared at Akins, on the southern edge of the Cookson Hills, but spent his teens in nearby Sallisaw. He worked hard on his father's farm by day and was a "heller" by night. That was a tradition in the hills. He was no worse than any other "good old boy" that way.

He was a tall, chunky youth with powerful shoulders. His nickname, Chock, came from his weakness for Choctaw beer, a home brew made in the hills since the Indian Territory days. When "likkered up" with it, he was apt to go tomcatting over half the ridges and up half the hoot-owl hollows from Siloam Springs to the South Canadian River and as far over as Fort Smith, Arkansas.

Reporters who trooped into Sallisaw and Akins years later,

looking for the usual "Public Enemy copy" about a youth who tore wings off flies and scalded cats, found themselves out of luck. Nobody could remember a bad story about Chock. One uncle of his said that he "never thought of nothin' but girls and engines"—but even that was said admiringly, with a wink.

Ma Joad probably summed up Floyd's early years best, and the later ones, too. Steinbeck heard the story from her real-life counterpart in California in the late '30s. It was still being passed from mother to son as a cautionary tale, an example of what happened to an Okie who went up against the system.

"I knowed Purty Boy Floyd," Ma said in *The Grapes of Wrath.* "I knowed his Ma. They was good folks. He was full of hell, sure, like a good boy oughta be. . . . He done a little bad thing an' they hurt 'im, caught 'im an' hurt him so he was mad, an' the next bad thing he done was mad, an' they hurt 'im again. An' purty soon he was mean-mad. They shot at him like a varmint, an' he shot back, an' then they run him like a coyote, an' him a-snappin' an' a-snarlin', mean as a lobo. An' he was mad. He wasn't no boy or no man no more, he was jus' a walkin' chunk a mean-mad. But the folks that knowed him didn't hurt 'im. He wasn't mad at them. Finally they run him down an' killed 'im. No matter how they say it in the paper how he was bad—that's how it was."

Floyd got the worst press, thanks to the Kansas City Massacre, of any gunman of the Public Enemy Era. The editorials that appeared after his death commended G-men for their "extermination of this mad dog."

Time hasn't really softened the image, either. Columnist Earl Wilson wrote in his column on October 5, 1967, "that I was as poor as anybody in the 1930s when Pretty Boy was killed. I saw him stretched out on a slab in East Liverpool (Ohio). He was never a folk hero to me."

Nor to anyone else outside the Cookson Hills, apparently.

Yet Floyd is a peculiarly sympathetic figure. He was a killer, true, but he killed only in the heat of combat or when avenging the murder of his father. And even during this time a bit of ethics still clung to him. He was an honest man; his word was reliable. He revered his father, loved his mother, and was protective of his brothers and sisters. His affection for his son was touching. He was a God-fearing man who, even at the height of his criminal career, took chances in order to attend church.

Yet at the same time there was a deep anger in him, and he could indeed be dangerous. He had a lot of friends, some of them close, but there was a wall over which they were never allowed to peek.

Floyd first ran afoul of the law after his marriage, in 1925, to Wilma Hargrove, a sixteen-year-old farm girl. She was pregnant and they needed money. There was none to be earned around Sallisaw. So Floyd took off to "follow the harvest" that fall. He trailed the threshing machines north as the wheat ripened, going from farm to farm to find work.

Somewhere in Missouri he got to talking with other migrant workers. They talked about how hard times were and how impossible it was to put money aside to send home, and as they talked an idea developed: they could get their hands on some extra cash by pulling a holdup.

When Floyd returned to Sallisaw that winter, lawmen followed him. They arrested him at home and recovered several hundred dollars, which had been stolen in a payroll robbery in St. Louis. Floyd was sentenced to five years in the Missouri State Penitentiary.

Jeff City was a tough pen. Repeaters, incorrigibles, and chronic troublemakers went there, and anybody else that the state's prison farms couldn't handle. "Rehabilitation" was just a fancy word back in the '20s. Jeff City's staff were first proponents of the treat-'em-rough school of penology. That meant the leather lash and cold baths, the sweatbox, and the ball and chain. Floyd went in a young roustabout. He came out, three years later, mature and dangerous.

He returned home to find his father dead, the victim of one of those bone-deep mountain feuds brought west from Kentucky. Floyd sat in the Sallisaw courthouse and listened while Jim Mills was tried for the murder and acquitted. Then he loaded up his rifle and headed into the hills. Mills vanished from his cabin a few weeks later. He was never heard from again. The folks around Akins and Sallisaw nodded solemnly. "Chock done what he had to," they agreed.

He couldn't stay in Oklahoma, though. After visiting briefly with his wife and infant son, Floyd set out for Kansas City.

"Tom's Town" (for Tom Pendergast, the Borgia of Mafia politics) was a rip-roaring, free-wheeling place in 1929. A city full of blowsy milk-fed whores, fences, buyers of hot money, tailors who made clothes with concealed pistol pockets, mob markers who advised which places to rob. Floyd's friends at Jeff City had all said the same thing: "When you get out, head for K. C."

Floyd vanished into the underworld there. Little is known about his daytime activities, but he was still a "heller" by night. The girls in the sporting houses up around Thirteenth and Cherry all loved him. It was a madam in one (some say Ann Chambers) who first saddled him with the famous nickname. "I want you for myself, pretty boy," she said to him one night, smiling. The name caught on. He loathed it. But there was no getting rid of it.

And no getting rid of the cops, either. They were on his back from the start. "i'm not as bad as they say i am," he wrote to a newspaper later. "they just wouldn't let me alone after i got out."

The Kansas City police said they had good reason for not leaving him alone. "I found this youthful ex-convict living among thieves," said Captain of Detectives Thomas J. Higgins, "and I tried to turn him aside from the ways of crime." Bringing Floyd in was fairly easy at first, but Higgins admitted that the job got tougher with each arrest.

The harassment got so bad that he finally decided to pull up stakes. Floyd had met a couple of experienced boxmen through Red Lovett, a Jeff City graduate. The two, Tom Bradley and Jack Atkins, were planning to bust open a whole flock of small country banks up in northern Ohio. Floyd traveled with them to Akron. There the three men rented a bungalow. Marie Maxwell, a Kansas City shoplifter who had come with them, cooked their meals and kept the place neat while they methodically worked their way through the list of targets.

For a while everything was fine. Then, on March 11, 1930, as the three men were returning from a bank robbery in Sylvania, Ohio, they jumped a light outside Akron. Patrolman Harlan F. Manes blew his whistle, kicked the starter on his cycle, and took off after them. A hail of bullets sent him sprawling all over the highway.

Bradley, who was driving, lost control of the car on a tight turn. It ploughed into a telephone pole. When the three of them were extricated from the wreckage, they were tried for murder. Bradley got the chair, Atkins life imprisonment—but Floyd was acquitted.

Not that it mattered. He'd been identified as one of the gunmen on the Sylvania job, so he was sentenced to fifteen years in the Ohio state pen anyway.

Floyd had no intention of going back to jail. He sat passively next to the window on the train taking him to Columbus on the night of May 25. He was surrounded by guards. He waited until they were dozing, then made his move. There was a sudden crash of glass, a muffled curse—and his seat was vacant.

Floyd rolled down an embankment and came up running. By the time the train could be brought to a halt, he was half a mile away. He was never arrested again.

He made his way to Toledo, where he joined forces with William (Bill-the-Kill) Miller, a Columbus escapee who was planning to hit a series of small-town banks in northern Michigan.

The two of them worked their way through Miller's list, then went to Kansas City to spend some of their loot. They stayed at Floyd's old hideout there—a cooling-off joint run by Mrs Sadie Ash on Holmes Street.

Mother Ash, as she was called, had two sons, Wallace and William, narcotics peddlers who also doubled as pimps, go-betweens, and general handymen for the North End combine. They lived with a couple of women in the house: pretty, blondined Beulah Baird and dark, smiling Rose Ash.

Floyd had already had a brief fling with Beulah and he now took up with her again. Miller found Rose entrancing, and vice versa. Mother Ash was not happy. "Them's Wally and Will's girls," she declared angrily.

"We're only borrowin' them," said Floyd. "The boys won't mind if we take 'em out, spend some money on them."

But the boys apparently did. Everywhere the four of them went there was heat. Whistles blew, windows were smashed, fists pounded on doors as voices shouted, "Open up! It's the law!" Speakeasies that hadn't been raided since 1919 seemed to be on the D.A.'s list the moment Floyd and Miller stepped into them.

Things finally came to a head on the night of March 23. Floyd went to a speakasy on Linwood Boulevard. As he placed his two .45 automatics on the shelf of a closet in the private room he had rented, he was suddenly braced by three Kansas City detectives. "Can't a fellow even put his hat away?" he asked plaintively as he stood there, hands still gripping the edge of the closet shelf.

They frisked him, and one of them said, "Okay, turn around."

Floyd did—both .45's blazing.

The detectives' wounds weren't fatal, but Floyd didn't know that. He was afraid he had killed one of them. He blamed Wally and Will. On the morning of March 25 the Ash brothers' riddled bodies were found sprawled along the highway outside Kansas City. Mother Ash ran screaming to the police. It was too late, though. Floyd and Miller had already flown the coop, taking Rose and Beulah with them.

The quartet rolled through Kentucky on a bank-robbing spree, hitting the Mount Zion Trust Company for $4,000 and a bank in Elliston the following day for $2,700. They crossed the Ohio River at Ironton and moved north, busting open another bank at Whitehouse for $3,600. Then, tired from several days of intensive driving, they pulled up to a hotel in Bowling Green, Ohio, and slept.

They stayed in town a couple of days—long enough for Police Chief Galliher to get interested in them. He checked their licence plates against his list. They were super hot. He summoned Patrolman Ralph Castner, and the two men moved in on the gang as they were about to enter a store on Prospect Street. "Hold on there," Chief Galliher called out.

Miller turned. The two girls were with him. Galliher didn't see Floyd, who was staked out across the street, watching for just such an eventuality. Floyd whipped out his .45's. "Bill!" he yelled. "Duck!"

As Miller threw himself to the pavement Floyd cut loose. Patrolman Castner fell, mortally wounded. Galliher dodged behind a car and returned Floyd's fire. Miller, crawling along the sidewalk on his belly, unlimbered his automatic.

For a minute it was a scene straight out of *High Noon*: Floyd standing in the middle of the main street, legs planted wide apart, both guns blazing.

The air was filled with the crackle of gunfire. Bullets ricocheted from buildings. Screaming pedestrians scurried for cover.

Miller had reached the curb. He leaped to his feet and dashed into the street. A well-placed shot from Chief Galliher's gun sent him sprawling, half his neck ripped away. Beulah Baird screamed and ran out after him. She reached for the automatic that had fallen from his hand, then suddenly toppled forward, shot through the head.

Floyd dashed down Prospect Street, crouching low, moving like a broken field runner. Chief Galliher shoved Rose Ash into the arms of Elmer Bowers, a startled City Councilman. "Hold this girl for me!" he shouted, and took off after Floyd.

Floyd was already behind the wheel of the gang's car. Chief Galliher sprang for the running board as it pulled away—but missed. He got the car's license number, though, and rushed to a phone.

Rose Ash refused to talk. Bill Miller was dead. Beulah Baird, with a bullet in her brain, was way beyond talking. But the car was registered in Rose's name, and Kansas City authorities were able to identify all four occupants. When Mother Ash heard the news, she was delighted. "Did they get Pretty Boy?" she asked eagerly.

It was the first time reporters had heard the name. They rushed to telephones. By morning it was plastered across headlines throughout the Midwest. The spectacular Ohio gun battle coupled with the name and with Floyd's two-gunned, straddle-legged image did the rest.

Suddenly he was "the deadliest gunman to ever stalk the nation." And just as suddenly he was everywhere at once: "Pretty Boy Robs Bank Here," "Pretty Boy Holds Up Cab-driver," "Pretty Boy Seen at Marathon Dance." Overnight he had become a household word, the bandit that everybody loved to fear.

Actually, Floyd was holed up in the Toledo area during most of May and June 1931. He had met some members of the Licavoli mob through Bill Miller the previous winter and was now feeding them the Elliston and Whitehouse loot in exchange for protection.

By July he was tapped out. He returned to Kansas City. According to some accounts, he became a "contract killer" for the mobs at this point. Not so, says Blackie Audett, who should know. Floyd was not a hoodlum; he was a bandit, and that's how he continued to make his living.

"Charlie Floyd played a lone hand most of the time," Audett wrote in *Rap Sheet*, "but once in a while he would tie up with some of the other boys on a big job. Him and Maurice Denning worked together quite a lot. And me and Maurice worked some jobs together. It was through Maurice that I met Charlie Floyd. Floyd was with us on a couple of smaller capers, but nothing that amounted to much."

As usual, he was spending most of what he earned on protection. His hideout in Kansas City was a two-story brick warehouse at 1039 Independence Avenue. It was owned by the mob. They leased the first floor to the Lusco-Noto Flower Shop; the second floor was the headquarters for the liquor syndicate.

Floyd lived in a special walled-off room that the mob rented to men on the run. The price, now that he had become so famous, was an exhorbitant $100 a night.

On July 21 Federal prohibition agents decided to raid the place. At 8 P.M. a dozen cars screeched to a halt out front. Axes flashed, wood splintered. Agents raced through the darkened interior, raking the walls with their flashlight beams.

They were on the lookout for secret partitions, so the one shielding Floyd was quickly located. Ax blades flashed once again, and the agents poured in. The room reeked of whiskey. A man lay with his head on the table. A half-filled bottle and a glass stood in front of him. He raised his head slowly as the lights converged on him. "What are you fellows looking for, whiskey?" he muttered indistinctly.

An agent named Curtis C. Burks moved toward him. "Hey, you know who this is?" he said. "It's Pretty Boy—"

"Watch out!" shouted Agent Glenn Havens. "He's got a gun!"

Floyd had two of them. Big, ugly, black .45's that blew the top half of Curtis C. Burks all over the room.

Before the agents knew what was happening, Floyd had charged through their midst. He ran the length of the building and down the front stairway into Independence Avenue, then wheeled around and fired as the agents reached the stairwell. They fired back. An overly curious bystander, E. J. Wilson, got caught in the cross fire. He dropped to the sidewalk, a bullet through his head.

Floyd got away, but he was red hot. Johnny Lazia, the North End boss for the Kansas City combine, was furious. A Federal agent had been killed—and on the mob's property. The word went out: Let the Feds have Floyd. It might smooth things over.

Floyd ran and didn't stop until he hit the Cookson Hills.

He operated solo for the next few months: a lone bandit with a submachine gun and a bulletproof vest who invaded small country banks in Muskogee and Cherokee counties.

In October 1931 he teamed up with George Birdwell. Birdwell was forty years old, a tall, bony man, tight of skin, with a beak-nosed, Lincolnesque sort of face. He had no criminal record. He was a former hill country preacher, a "Burning Busher" who used to howl out the name of Jesus to glory. Then he lost the call and "took to likker." Birdwell had a wife and kids and, until September of that year, a job in the oil fields at Earlsboro. The job was gone now, and his family was hungry. It's said that he traveled into the Cookson Hills, sought Floyd out, and begged to be taken on.

Birdwell had no experience, but Floyd patiently showed him the ropes.

The effort paid off. The Floyd-Birdwell combination was an extremely effective one. They developed a regular formula. They would steal a car minutes before the robbery, then go barreling into town. Unmasked, they would enter the bank. Floyd was always the "hot man"—the one with the heater. Birdwell would take the cages and scoop up the cash. Then they would select two of the bank employees, place one on each running board to protect themselves from gunfire, and roll smoothly out of town, dropping the bankers off a few miles away. They hit banks at Shamrock, Morris, Konawa, Maud, Earlsboro, Paden, Castle, and Tahlequah this way, then moved further afield.

Bankers began to froth at the mouth. They went to the state capital, and demanded action. The lieutenant-governor, Robert Burns, ordered the Oklahoma national guard to issue machine guns and tear gas bombs to lawmen. Then he added a reward of $1,000 to the $5,000 already offered by banks for Floyd's capture.

A few days later Burns received a postcard from Altus, Oklahoma. It read: "You either withdraw that one thousand at once or suffer the consequences. No kidding. I have robbed no one but moneyed men. Floyd."

Handwriting analysts checked it out. The signature was Floyd's all right. The lieutenant-governor took to the airwaves. "This is a desperate case," he thundered. "Floyd has terrorized the entire east-central section of Oklahoma with his outlawry. Already six killings and ten bank robberies have been charged to him. He must be stopped."

Burns was fudging a bit. The six killings were unconnected with the bank robberies. He was counting Jim Mills, the two Ash brothers, the Bowling Green patrolman, the Kansas City prohibition agent, and that innocent bystander, who may or may not have been killed by Floyd. As for the supposed terror he had aroused, it was felt only by the Oklahoma Bankers' Association, not by the population at large.

In early February 1932 Tulsa police learned that Floyd and Birdwell were in town. Five heavily armed officers were sent out in an unmarked car to scour the section in which they had been seen. Shortly after midnight, on February 7, they spotted the outlaw's Ford coupe on Admiral Street. They drove up beside it and ordered the two occupants to surrender.

The answer was a rain of machine gun bullets. Policeman Wilbur Wilson fell wounded. The coupe roared away through withering police fire. One patrolman, Wade Foor, said that he had pumped six bullets into Floyd's back, but they had all bounced off him. It was the work of a bulletproof vest, undoubtedly, but Foor's comment started some people to wondering if Floyd wasn't actually impervious to gunfire.

The coupe was found on a side street the next day. Its owner was located through a tag on its recently recharged battery. He was Jack Hamilton of 513 Young Street, Tulsa. The officers guessed correctly that Hamilton was Floyd.

The bungalow at that address was placed under observation. A woman was seen coming and going, accompanied by a seven-year-old boy. She was identified from photographs as Floyd's wife. The boy was his son, Jackie.

On the night of February 11 twenty police officers swung down Young Street in two armored cars equipped with two-way radios, machine guns, and high-powered rifles. They surrounded the bungalow and opened hostilities by hurling tear gas bombs through the windows.

There was no sound, no movement from inside. Police waited a few minutes, then decided that the gang had already flown the coop. They relaxed. Cigarettes were broken out. Somebody went for sandwiches and coffee.

Suddenly the bungalow's back door flew open. Two shadowy figures charged out, orange flame stabbing from the submachine guns they carried. The police hit the dirt. The men sprinted across the backyard, leaped into a car, and escaped in the usual "hail of bullets."

It was downright embarrassing. But the police had Mrs. Floyd and the boy anyway. They were taken down to headquarters and grilled. "I don't know anything about where Charlie hides," she said angrily, "and I don't know anything about his plans. All I know is you'll never catch him. He can outsmart every copper in Oklahoma, and the Federal men, too. I know it!"

Erv A. Kelley, ex-Sheriff of McIntosh County, shook his head.

He had been deputized by the State as a special investigator in the Floyd manhunt. "I'm sorry, ma'am," he drawled, "but my job is to capture your husband, and I am to bring him in, dead or alive. It'll be either him or me and I'm not worrying about myself."

When Mrs. Floyd was released, she went straight to her father's farm near Bixby, eighteen miles south of Tulsa. Sheriff Kelley and a posse of men followed her. They were sure that Floyd would try to visit her.

Kelley grilled neighbors, finally getting the information he needed. Floyd was planning to visit his wife and boy on the night of April 7.

He set his trap: four machine-gunners spotted along both sides of the road, with Kelley and two deputies acting as the cork in the bottle.

They took up their positions and waited. It was bitterly cold. The hours dragged past. The men grew restive. The two deputies with Kelley wanted to get some hot coffee. "Okay," said the sheriff. "Go get warmed up. I'll stay here alone—just to cover up."

As soon as they were gone, Kelley heard a car approaching. It was traveling at high speed, its lights off. He unlimbered his submachine gun and ran out into the middle of the road. Before he could squeeze off a shot, the car's headlights flashed on. Guns blazed—and down went Kelley, five slugs in his skull.

The car made a screeching U-turn. The other possemen rushed forward, firing, but it was too late, of course. The car vanished in the direction from which it had come.

In May George Birdwell's father died. Oklahoma authorities figured the son would try to pay his last respects. Plainclothesmen were spotted around the undertaker's establishment. They dozed in the thick spring heat, though. When they woke, Floyd was covering them with a Tommy gun. He kept it pointed at them while Birdwell stood with bowed head beside his father's coffin.

When the two left town, a posse followed them, so they grabbed a boy on a motorcycle and took him along with them as a shield against bullets. He was released thirteen hours later.

In early June lawmen thought they had Floyd and Birdwell trapped on the farm of A. W. Echols, twelve miles southeast of Ada, Oklahoma.

Nine heavily armed officers poured round after round into their green sedan as it slithered slowly up a muddy hill. Pontotoc County Sheriff L. E. Franklin estimated later that they had fired more than one hundred rounds at the car. He concluded that Floyd and Birdwell had worn not only bullet-proof vests, but also "steel plates in their sleeves and around the tops of their heads under their hats."

That was one explanation, anyway.

The state's law enforcement machinery moved into high gear. Sheriffs, marshals, and detectives employed by the Bankers' Association were all on the outlaws' trail. The highways of Pontotoc and Hughes counties were filled with man hunters and still more were coming; there were 500 after the two of them.

The lawmen knew they would head east toward the Cookson Hills, so men were rushed ahead to block their escape. Floyd and Birdwell slipped past them in the darkness. The Feds came and joined in, accomplishing nothing. In all their months of trailing Floyd they hadn't even seen him.

The trail petered out in Seminole County. The lawmen were still getting cooperation from the citizenry as far in as Hazel and Dewright, but at Bowlegs they entered enemy territory. A wall of silence seemed to close around them. Reporter Hubert Dail, who accompanied one of the posses, described what it was like to the readers of *True Detective* Magazine:

"Everywhere (we) received word that Floyd had been seen—a day, a week, or a month before. But in each case the inhabitants of the hillbilly country didn't know where the famous bandit was at that particular moment.

"At one house, in a hollow, about two miles off the road, a posse advanced in a semicircle to confront a woman chopping wood. She paused, stared at the officers with hostile eyes. 'What-dya want?' she demanded.

The deputies said they were looking for 'Pretty Boy.' A crafty glint came into the woman's eyes. 'I reckon he's been here a hundred times,' she said, 'but I ain't seen him recently.' She brought her ax down with a crash. 'I'm scared of him.'

"This was a typical instance," reported Dail. "Everywhere, the officers believed, people of the hills were refusing information about the outlaw, protecting him and his companions with tips as to the officers' movements."

The possemen finally gave up and went home.

Floyd remained holed up in the hills the rest of that summer. In early October, Aussie Elliott came looking for him. Aussie was a good old boy from Sapulpa. He had been a crack shortstop in the minor leagues but had switched to center-fielding on bank jobs sometime in 1930. He had been caught cracking open a Fort Gibson bank, had been sent to the state pen, had escaped, and was now looking for work.

Floyd had some for him.

On November 1 the two of them, plus Birdwell, pulled up in front of the State Bank in Sallisaw. Floyd climbed out of the car, a submachine gun under his arm, and waved good-naturedly to a group of men lounging in front of the barbershop. "How you, Newt? Jimbo?"

"Well now, hydee, Chock. What you-all doin' in town?"

"Goin' to rob the bank," said Floyd, grinning.

He ambled across the sidewalk, tipping his hat politely to a lady who was just coming out. "Better come back in with us, ma'am," he said, and took her by the arm. Birdwell followed them inside. Aussie Elliott remained behind the wheel of the car.

"Okay, everybody, hands up," Floyd said casually as he crossed the lobby. "Line up against the wall over there." He turned to cashier Bob Riggs. "Howdy, Bob. This man here will tell you what we want."

"Everythin'," said Birdwell, "startin' with the big bills. Just put it all in this here bag."

A farmer named Fitzsimmons moved suddenly, and Birdwell spun toward him, drawing his automatic. Floyd laughed. "Don't hurt him, Bird. He's a friend of mine. How you, Fitz?'"

When Riggs had filled the bag, Birdwell said, "Okay, come on out of there. You're coming with us."

A huge crowd had gathered outside. As the three men pushed their way through it to the car, Floyd waved to friends and acquaintances and called out, "Yep, it's a holdup, all right."

The car pulled away and headed out State 64 toward Fort Smith, Arkansas, with Riggs on the running board. A mile out of town they slowed down, and the cashier was told to jump off. Floyd leaned out the window and waved to him. "So long, Bob," he called out. "Take care of yourself."

One reporter summed the Sallisaw job up this way: "It was like the hometown performance of a great actor who has made good on Broadway."

The gate was lousy, though—a measly $2,530. And all at once Floyd needed money. Big money. His wife had been rushed to a Tulsa hospital on the morning of November 7 with acute appendicitis.

That afternoon he, Birdwell, and Elliott hit the American State Bank in Henryetta, Oklahoma. Birdwell was the center fielder this time: Floyd took the cages.

It was the best take of Floyd's career: $11,252.

The next day his wife was moved to a private room at the hospital and began to receive round-the-clock nursing care.

The Henryetta job was the final straw for Oklahoma bankers. They shifted their attack from "inept law enforcement officials" to the administration itself. Governor "Alfalfa Bill" Murray hurriedly took to the stump. "We would have had Floyd and Birdwell long ago," he said heatedly, "if sheriffs and other officials in the hill country were not protecting them. Floyd has lots of friends in the Cherokee Hills. He has sent me word twice by relatives that if I would save him from the electric chair he would come in and surrender. I sent word back that I would not do it."

Members of the Oklahoma Bankers' Association—more interested at the moment in their property than in vengeance—suggested privately that maybe two or three hundred years in prison would be just as effective as electrocution. The governor wouldn't budge. There was bitter behind-the-scenes wrangling.

Publicly all was optimism, though. Eugene P. Gum, the Association's Secretary, told the press: "Floyd has been the luckiest bandit that ever lived. Do not be surprised if you read, almost any day now, that Floyd and Birdwell have been slain."

The Chief of Oklahoma's Bureau of Identification and Investigation wasn't quite as optimistic. "This fellow Floyd is shrewd and slippery as an eel," said Charles Burns. "In a general way we know where he is all the time. He never leaves the hill country except for a robbery. He and Birdwell are heavy drinkers. They go to a speakeasy and stay for hours, keeping everyone in there until they are ready to go. When they leave, it is Floyd's custom to say: 'Now you fellows scatter and tell Governor Murray that I've been here. Maybe you can get that reward they have on my head.' "

Burns was right about the drinking. Both men loved the sauce and lapped it up freely. But Floyd drank only between jobs. A week before a scheduled robbery he would lay off the stuff and start getting himself into shape.

Birdwell couldn't do that anymore. The strain of being a fugitive had finally gotten to him. He was drinking around the clock. Floyd warned him about it, told him he would stop using him if he didn't shape up. Birdwell promised he would.

In mid-November Floyd heard about a fat goose in Boley, a Negro community in Okfuskee County, and decided to head over there and pluck it. Birdwell continued to hit the bottle, though. He was drunk nearly all that week. Floyd finally bowed out of the job. He wouldn't work with a man who was drunk.

Birdwell decided to pull the job with two other men. Floyd pleaded with his old partner, but Birdwell, muddle-headed and obstinate, insisted on going through with it. They parted at Okemah on the morning of November 23. Floyd returned to Tulsa; Birdwell and C. C. Paterson, a Kiowa bank bandit, and Charles Glass, a Negro wheelman, headed toward Boley—and disaster.

It was an Old West shoot-'em-up, with the town's Vigilance Committee doing most of the shooting. When the cordite fumes cleared, Birdwell and Glass were dead, and Patterson was crippled for life. The president of the Farmers & Mechanics Bank was dead, too—shot down by the bandits when he sounded the alarm.

Authorities were delighted at Birdwell's demise. The Secretary of the Oklahoma Bankers' Association sent the man who killed him five hundred dollars. Another five hundred was distributed among the members of the Boley Vigilance Committee for killing Glass. Governor Murray announced that in future the state would match the O.B.A.'s rewards. The going rate would be five hundred dollars to anyone who killed a bank bandit, two hundred and fifty dollars for anyone who killed the driver of a bandit car.

The really big money was still on Floyd's head, though—six thousand dollars altogether.

It's a measure of the hill people's devotion to him that none of them ever tried to claim that reward—and in a time when their kids were walking around in rags, bellies puffed up with hunger.

Outside the hills there was only one bank bandit in the entire United States as far as the public was concerned—Pretty Boy. He was identified as the leader of every gang to hit banks between Stockton, California, and Caribou, Maine.

Few of these sightings were taken seriously. But lawmen reacted with interest when witnesses in Tupelo, Mississippi, identified Floyd as the leader of a gang who hit the Citizens' State Bank there for $50,000 on November 30. At least twenty people, many of them leading citizens, swore they recognized Floyd.

Federal agents immediately moved into the area.

On December 3 the Memphis *Commercial Appeal* received and published a letter signed "Charles Floyd." It indignantly denied that he or any of his men had taken part in the Tupelo kick-in. Floyd was like Cole Younger that way. If he was innocent, he shouted at the top of his lungs; if guilty, he kept quiet.

Floyd stayed holed up in the hills the rest of that winter. In the spring he went shopping for a new partner. He found him in Boliver, Missouri. His name was Adam Richetti. He was a small, wispy man with liquid brown eyes and dark hair thinning at the crown. Before he met Floyd, "Eddie" Richetti had never stuck up anything bigger than a gas station. But inexperience never bothered Floyd. He preferred to train his own partners.

He started Richetti off easy, hitting a dance hall near Wewoka, Oklahoma, in April 1933. While Floyd held his submachine gun on three police officers, Eddie scooped up the cash in the ticket seller's booth. Then both men vanished into the darkness.

A string of bank jobs followed in Oklahoma, Arkansas, and Missouri.

The William J. Burns International Detective Agency had been assigned to Floyd now. With bank insurance rates up double in Oklahoma, the American Bankers' Association had decided to call in the big guns. Detective A. B. Cooper of the Burns Agency took after Floyd; he would soon have him pushing up daisies, he announced. That was the end of it. He trailed him to the edge of the Cookson Hills, and there the trail ended.

Floyd's mother was the one to watch, Cooper decided. Burns's men were staked out across the street from her house in Sallisaw. Friends warned Floyd, though, and he stayed away from the house while they were there.

On June 16 Floyd and Richetti surfaced briefly at Bolivar, Missouri. Their car had broken down along the highway, and they had phoned Richetti's brother, Joe, who had towed it into his garage. The repair job drew a sizable crowd—an indication of how much ever happened in Bolivar.

Sheriff Jack Killingsworth noticed the excitement and strolled over. Now things got really exciting. Floyd whipped out an automatic and demanded his gun. Killingsworth handed it over.

"Never mind fixing the car," Floyd called out to Joe Richetti. "Give us that one"—he pointed to the fastest car in the shop, a brand-new Ford V-8.

Killingsworth was forced into the front seat between Floyd and Richetti, and away they sped. The stunned citizens stood for some minutes, shaking the water out of their eyes; then they got on the phone to the cops in nearby Springfield and Joplin. Posses immediately set out after them.

It was the standard chase of the day: guns roaring, cars screeching around curves. Only a new element had now been added: airplanes. Floyd's reputation demanded the latest technological wrinkle—observation planes equipped with two-way radios.

Floyd decided that they had better switch cars. He forced Sheriff Killingsworth to flag down a motorist—Walter L. Griffith, a real estate man from Clinton, Missouri. "We'll have to use you and your car for a while," Floyd explained to him.

The four of them roared west now, across the Kansas line. A few miles outside Ottawa, they pulled off the highway and into a wooded ravine along the banks of the Osage River. Here, with pursuers on all sides and planes crisscrossing the sky overhead, Floyd sat back and relaxed, his submachine gun lying across his knees.

He talked quietly about his past life while Killingsworth and Griffith marveled at his calm. He told them of his hatred for the police, of his affection for his son, Jackie, of his fatalistic belief that he would some day "go down full of lead."

When darkness fell, the four men got back into Griffith's car and resumed their journey to Kansas City.

At that moment, many miles to the southeast, someone else was traveling towards Kansas City: Frank Nash, the veteran bank bandit.

Nash had been arrested that afternoon in Hot Springs, Arkansas, by two FBI agents and the police chief of McAlester, Oklahoma.

Since busting out of Leavenworth in 1930, Nash had worked with the Holden-Keating gang and the Barker-Karpis outfit. When the Barkers had gotten mixed up in the Hamm kidnapping, Nash had lit out for Hot Springs with his wife.

Now he was on his way back to Leavenworth to finish the twenty-five-year sentence that he had run out on. Nash was past fifty. He knew there was only one way he would ever leave prison again—toes up.

He hoped Dick Galatas had caught his hand signal and had called his wife. She would know what to do.

Galatas, who ran a horse-racing book inside the White Front Pool Hall in Hot Springs, had seen the Feds close in on Nash and had caught the signal. He had phoned Frances Nash immediately, and a series of long-distance calls were now spreading word of Nash's arrest through the underworld.

Verne Miller received one of these calls in his Edgevale Road home in Kansas City around seven o'clock that night. The former South Dakota sheriff had worked a number of jobs with Nash. He liked and admired the older man. Miller had also worked as a torpedo for the Barkers. He had plenty of mob connections in Kansas City and elsewhere. If anyone could organize Nash's delivery, it was Miller.

He listened to the voice at the other end of the line, then said: "Have Frances call me as soon as she finds out what route they'll be taking to Leavenworth."

Galatas called the Hot Springs police a little after seven and asked them what highway the Feds were traveling. The Joplin road, he was told. Galatas immediately phoned Herb Farmer in Joplin and filled him in on what had happened.

Farmer, an old friend of the Barkers and of Frank Nash, ran a cooling-off joint in the Joplin area. Southwest Missouri was his "turf"; nothing happened in that section without his knowledge. "We're flying up there," Galatas told him. "Meet us."

He and Frances Nash chartered a private plane for the two-hundred-mile trip. Farmer was waiting for them at the Webb City field. The Joplin road bit had been a feint, he told them; the Federal agents had doubled back onto U.S. 64 and were now heading toward Fort Smith, Arkansas.

The three lawmen were sure they had thrown off their pursuers. They stopped for dinner at Russellville, Arkansas, then drove on to Fort Smith, arriving in time to catch the Missouri Pacific Flyer.

With their prisoner safely installed in a stateroom, the three men finally relaxed.

"You've changed a bit," chuckled Special Agent Frank Smith as he pulled at Nash's hair. It came away in his hand, revealing a bald pate.

"Don't pull the mustache," said Nash. "It's real."

"What's with the toupee, Frank?" Police Chief Otto Reed of McAlester, Oklahoma, wanted to know.

"I gave a hundred dollars for it in Chicago," Nash said. "I've been making some good money there in beer and slot machines."

"The nose seems straighter now, too," said Special Agent F. J. Lackey. "And those cheeks—they used to be sunk in. Now they're nice and plump."

"A little face lifting," said Nash, grinning. "You do what you can." He reached into his pocket and pulled out a Blue Lodge Masonic card. "Here, I've humbugged enough people with this," he said. "You boys might as well have it."

It was a few minutes past nine now. As Nash and his captors roared through the night toward Kansas City, Floyd and Richetti were continuing to jounce along the back roads of eastern Kansas with their own prisoners. At Bonner Springs they swung east, slowly circling the city so as to enter it from the north. Overhead, amid the humming telephone wires, Verne Miller's voice was saying, "The train gets in at 7:15 in the morning. Union Station might be the place to spring him. They'll only have shotguns and pistols. We'll have choppers—"

"Do you have anybody yet?"

Miller said that he had tried to get the Barker boys but that they were "tied up." He said: "I'll have to borrow a couple of typers (machine gunners) from the North Side crowd."

Floyd and Richetti arrived in Kansas City's Central Industrial district around ten. Sheriff Killingsworth and Walter Griffith were still with them. Floyd had phoned ahead, they would later say, and seemed to be looking for someone. Suddenly he swung over to the curb and parked. "Watch these two," he told Richetti, and walked up the street to where a car was parked. Killingsworth saw two men get out of the car and confer with him. Then Floyd came back. "Come on," he told Richetti. "Get the guns, we change cars."

He leaned in the window. "You two watch your step," he told Killingsworth and Griffith. "Do as I tell you and you'll be okay. Drive to Lee's Summit and eat dinner there. Don't tell anyone you've seen us. Then head home."

The two men did as they were told.

The next morning, June 17, was clear and pleasant. Only 71 degrees. Cool for Kansas City in June. Mrs. Lottie West, a caseworker for the Traveler's Aid Society, arrived at her booth in the lobby of Union Station around seven o'clock. She found a man sitting at her desk—"round-faced," she would later describe him, "rather fleshy, weighing about two hundred pounds." He got up, yielding the chair to her. She saw him a few minutes later, loitering near the entrance. He seemed to be waiting for someone.

Outside the station, taxicabs were loading and unloading passengers. The sidewalks were crowded with people hurrying to work. At 7:10 a green Chevrolet coach with a Nebraska license pulled into the parking area directly opposite the station's east entrance. Special Agent Raymond Caffrey and R. E. Vetterli, agent in charge of the FBI's Kansas City office, got out. This was the car that was to carry Frank Nash to Leavenworth.

A few minutes later an armored police car stopped at the station's west entrance. Two city detectives, W. J. "Red" Grooms, only a year on the force, and Frank Hermanson, a veteran of thirteen years, got out and joined the FBI men inside the lobby. The four men went downstairs to meet Missouri Pacific Train No. 116 from Fort Smith, Arkansas.

The hands of the big clock in the archway between the lobby and the waiting room stood at 7:18. Mrs. West, who had just found lodging for six Sisters of Mercy at St. Benedict's Church, walked over and chatted with the manager of Harvey's restaurant.

It was an ordinary June morning in the station: heels clicking on the marble floors, an amplified voice announcing train arrivals, the clatter of dishes coming from inside the restaurant. The manager pointed to a group of eight men coming up the stairs from the train platform. "A pinch," he said.

Mrs. West looked. Frank Nash was in the center of the group wearing an open white shirt, his handcuffs poorly concealed by a handkerchief. He was having trouble with his toupee, which kept sliding off to one side. Two of his captors carried shotguns, the others pistols. "That must be Pretty Boy Floyd," said Mrs. West. Floyd was on everybody's mind that June; his picture was in every paper.

She turned in time to see the heavyset man who'd been loitering at the east gate go darting out ahead of the group. There was no time to wonder about it, though. The nuns were back, wanting to be directed to the taxicab ramp. "Come along. I'll show you," she said, and walked with them toward the east entrance.

The seven lawmen marched Nash across the plaza toward the waiting Chevrolet. Caffrey unlocked the right door. "Get in front," he said. Nash slid in, sitting for a moment behind the steering wheel while Lackey, Smith, and Chief Reed climbed in the back. The two Kansas City detectives, Grooms and Hermanson, stood at the right of the car with Vetterli, who was waiting to get in.

Caffey walked around the back of the car to the driver's door and was about to open it.

"Up, up! Get 'em up!" a voice shouted. The officers whirled. Three men were standing on the running boards of nearby cars. Each held a Thompson submachine gun.

The lawmen stood motionless for a split second, stunned. Then Detective Grooms whipped out his automatic and fired two quick shots at the heavyset man on the right, winging him in the arm. "Let 'em have it!" the man shouted.

The three submachine guns roared. A blizzard of lead sent Grooms, Hermanson, and Caffrey sprawling to the pavement. The car's windshield shattered. Chief Reed crumpled to the floor, dead. Agent Lackey, sitting next to him, tried to return the fire with his service revolver. It was shot from his hand, the grip smashed and splintered by bullets. He toppled forward with a half dozen slugs in him. Special Agent Smith heard Nash shout, "For God's sake, don't kill *me*!" Then Nash's head whipped back as if clipped by a sharp uppercut to the chin. His toupee went sailing—the top of his head still inside it.

Smith saw the barrel of a machine gun spitting flame at him. He could feel the heat of the firing, hear the thuds of the bullets. Shattered glass spurted in all directions. He crumpled to the floor, pretending to have been hit.

Out on the plaza two taxicabs collided. Drivers, petrified with fear, piled into one another along Broadway. Bystanders crawled under parked cars, seeking safety.

Mrs. West watched from the sidewalk, open-mouthed with horror. One of the machine-gunners was the heavyset man who had been sitting at her desk earlier. "Everyone into the station!" she screamed. "They're killing everybody!"

Patrolman Mike Fanning came running out the east entrance, his gun drawn. "I saw a Chevrolet coach with a Nebraska license straight across from me," he recollected later. "Two machine gunners were shooting into it. The confusion was awful. Traffic was in a terrible snarl. Men and women were running around like scared rabbits. Bullets were whistling everywhere. . . . I saw Grooms and Hermanson fall. 'Shoot the fat man, Mike! Shoot the fat man!' The voice of Mrs. West came to me in frantic, high-pitched tones from her refuge behind a taxicab.

"I knew she meant the big man whose machine gun was doing such bloody work. I aimed at him and fired. He whirled around and dropped to the ground. I don't know whether I hit him or whether he fell to escape. In any event he got up, fired another volley into the car, and ran toward a light Oldsmobile car, which roared west toward Broadway. As the car raced out of the parking lot I saw three men in it and there may have been more.

"A nineteen thirty-three Chevrolet car with more gunners swooped past the parked car and riddled it from the rear. I ran into the street, fired two shots into the back of that car, and rushed to the parked Chevrolet. I still didn't know the men in it were officers.

"With my revolver pushed ahead of me, I looked into the car. It was a shambles. In the front seat a man was dead under the steering wheel. On the left of the rear seat was another dead man. On the right was an unconscious man, but he was groaning. A third man lay face down on the floor. I could see that he was alive."

This was Agent Frank Smith, the only man to escape unhurt. Agent Lackey was seriously injured. Vetterli had been shot in the arm. The others—Caffrey, Grooms, Hermanson, Chief Reed, and, of course, Nash—were dead.

It was a shocking scene. People milled about, staring at the car and its grisly occupants. They seemed stunned. The whole city seemed stunned. "My God, it's like Chicago!" somebody said.

Newspapers called it the "Kansas City Massacre." The gunmen, still unidentified, were referrred to as the "Mad Dog Killers of KC."

It was the most traumatic criminal event since the Lindbergh kidnapping. People simply couldn't believe it—four law officers murdered in the open plaza of a great railroad station. Angry editorials appeared across the country, demanding new laws, stronger police measures. Crime was everybody's business, the editorials said. Something had to be done.

Federal agents poured into Kansas City. An exhaustive check was made of all long-distance calls logged through the Southwestern Bell Telephone Company's regional offices. The records of a call made from Herb Farmer's Joplin home to Verne Miller were found. Farmer, Frances Nash, and Richard Galatas were quickly flushed from cover.

The Feds and the Kansas City police rushed to Miller's home on Edgevale Road. He had already fled, though, taking his wife and daughter with him. They found blood-soaked rags in the bathroom, which had apparently been used as bandages.

The lawmen left everything as it was but told a neighbor to keep the house under observation. The next day a moving truck appeared. A large, heavyset man pulled up behind it in a Packard. Under his direction the movers carried all the furniture out of the house, loaded it aboard the truck, and drove away. So did the big, heavyset man. The neighbor had gotten his licence number, though. He gave it to the police. The man was identified from it as William (Solly) Weisman, a St. Louis torpedo wanted for the murder of a prohibition agent in Elizabeth, New Jersey, in 1930.

Before this promising lead could be followed, Sheriff Thomas B. Bash of Jackson County, Missouri, came up with another one. Bash was convinced that Pretty Boy Floyd and Richetti were mixed up in the Union Station killings. They had arrived in Kansas City the night before; their hostage, Sheriff Killingsworth, had seen them meet with two other men and had seen them drive off in their car.

Kansas City's Captain of Detectives, Thomas J. Higgins, scoffed at the idea. He had been trailing Floyd for four years now; he knew his prey intimately. It wasn't Floyd's kind of job, he pointed out. Besides, Richetti was just a small-timer. Nobody in his right mind would have used him on a job like this.

Bash refused to be deterred. He sent for Mrs. Lottie West and showed her a group of photos. She immediately picked Floyd's out of the bunch. "That's the man who was sitting in my chair," she said, "the one I later saw across the street, operating a machine gun."

That did it. The press got the story and by morning every newspaper in the country had convicted Floyd of the Kansas City Massacre.

In the midst of all the screaming and excitement Captain Higgins received a plain business postcard in the mail. It was postmarked Springfield, Missouri, and read:

Dear Sirs:

I—Charles Floyd—want it made known that I did not participate in the massacre of officers at Kansas City.

Charles Floyd

Lieutenant William Gordon, head of the Bureau of Identification, studied the handwriting and announced that it was definitely Floyd's.

The disclaimer was ignored, of course. To this day, Floyd and his pal, Richetti, stand accused of having participated in the Union Station massacre.

The underworld knew it was a lot of hooey, though. Blackie Audett wrote in *Rap Sheet:* "One of the officers that was killed was a federal agent. The FBI was on the case in a matter of minutes. They got a bum steer somehow or other, because later they killed Charlie Floyd and hanged Adam Richetti as being the two men that was in the second car.

"I knowed better, because I seen with my own eyes who was in that car. Both of them that was in it got clean away."

And Blackie named the actual killers: Verne Miller, Maurice Denning, and Solly Weisman.

According to Audett, Johnny Lazia—the Combine's North End boss—personally recruited Denning and Weisman. And Blackie should know. He was Lazia's right-hand man in 1933.

Blackie said that he had also witnessed the massacre. City Manager Henry McElroy, "Tom's front man," had a daughter named Mary. Mary got advance notice of the delivery attempt and drove down to the Union Station plaza with Blackie. "Me and Mary McElroy watched the whole thing from less than fifty yards away," he wrote.

There were four gunmen altogether, according to Blackie, and they arrived in two cars. He refused to name the fourth man, who had remained behind the wheel of the second car, a Chevrolet, since Blackie thought (in 1954) that he might still be alive.

Miller, Denning, and Weisman had been paid in advance, Blackie said. When they botched the job, the mob hunted the three of them down.

They reached Verne Miller first. His naked body was found in a drainage ditch outside Detroit on November 29, 1933. He had been trussed up like a turkey ready for roasting. His tongue and cheeks had been punctured with ice picks. Hot flatirons had left searing burn scars on his body. Some heavy object had finally bashed in the back of his skull.

Solly Weisman was found in similar condition outside Chicago a few weeks later. Maurice Denning's body never turned up at all. He's still among the missing.

Blackie Audett's story deserves serious consideration. For one thing, Solly Weisman and Floyd would have been easy to confuse. Both were large, fleshy men, weighing around two hundred pounds each. Both had massive, squared-off jaws. Both parted their hair similarly.

Furthermore, Blackie's version clears up a puzzler—why the mob never bothered to rub Floyd and Richetti out for their part in the botched-up massacre. They had plenty of opportunities. Yet a year after it happened Floyd and Richetti could be found living amicably among remnants of the Licavoli mob in Toledo.

It's something the FBI has never been able to explain.

Floyd's name was selling plenty of papers in 1933, and the Kansas City Massacre was selling plenty, so city editors and headline writers didn't exactly fight the idea of linking the two. It was neater that way, and the reading public liked their crime news neat.

It took a little tailoring, of course. That second Chevrolet had to disappear—the one that swooped past, riddling the lawmen's car with more bullets. And poor little Eddie Richetti of Bolivar, Missouri, had to become a "top Kansas City torpedo." But the newspapers received plenty of cooperation from the lawmen on all counts.

There wasn't much that Floyd and Richetti could do, aside

from writing letters to the editor. So they ran—to Cleveland first, where they were denied help. Then to Akron, where more doors were slammed in their faces. The underworld knew they were riding a bum beef, but they were hotter than fire. No one dared help them.

So they headed south to the only friend they had left—the Cookson Hills.

They vanished so far into the hills that even the local inhabitants lost track of them for a couple of months. They literally "took to the brush," living on ears of field corn and stalks of sorghum, sleeping in abandoned farmhouses.

During the summer of 1933 Floyd was a gray wolf, seen only at night in the timber. He had good reason for living that way. A crowd of good old boys had busted out of the Kansas State Pen on Memorial Day and had headed straight for the hills, bringing plenty of heat in after them.

Reports poured in from settlements along the edge of the wilderness: groups of strangers, on foot and carrying guns, had been seen at Titanic, at Bunch, at Box, and Addielee, and even as far in as Nicut and Short.

Finally, in September, the situation began to ease somewhat. Two members of Wilbur Underhill's escape party decided to run for it. Bob Brady and Jim Clark pushed off from the hills on September 28. Clark was captured at Tucumari, New Mexico, on October 7; Brady was gunned down by a posse at Paoloa, Kansas, on January 19, 1934.

Wilbur Underhill had teamed up with the Ford Bradshaw gang, meanwhile. Using the hills as their home base, they raided banks at Helena, Kansas; Stuttgart, Arkansas; and Coalgate, Oklahoma. On November 2 they hit the jackpot: the Citizens National Bank at Okmulgee. The take was an impressive $13,000—enough, Wilbur figured, to finally ask his girl, Hazel Hudson, to marry him. She said yes, and the "Tri-State Terror" sneaked out of the hills just before Christmas to tie the knot.

Poor Wilbur. He was not a thoughtful man. When he got hitched at Coalgate, he used his real name. Federal agents, led by R. H. Colvin, traced him to Shawnee, Oklahoma, where he was honeymooning with his bride. They surrounded the nuptial bungalow and demanded that he come out with his hands up.

A terrific gun battle ensued. Riddled with bullets, Underhill fled through the rain clad only in his underwear. The agents found him hiding in a Shawnee furniture store, and he was taken dying to a hospital.

They were afraid that Floyd would try to rescue him, though, so they got him up out of bed again and transported him in a heavily guarded ambulance to the state prison hospital at McAlester. "Tell the boys I'm coming home," said Wilbur. Nobody knew what he meant. He died at McAlester on January 6, 1934.

Ford Bradshaw didn't like the way the Feds had interrupted Wilbur's honeymoon. It was unsporting of them not to have waited a couple of days. He and his gang roared out of the hills the night after the Shawnee gun battle and "huzzah'd" the town of Vian in revenge.

While deputies frantically called Fort Smith, Muskogee, and other towns for help, three cars loaded with good old boys circled the business square, firing into windows and terrorizing citizens. When reinforcements arrived, the Bradshaw gang slipped back into the hills.

The authorities were hopping mad. A punitive raid was launched against a likely hideout near Marble City. It flushed Aussie Elliott and Raymond Moore from cover. They went down before officers' guns at Sapulpa in early February, taking the chief of police and a patrolman with them. Floyd attended Aussie's funeral on February 6. He made no attempt to disguise himself. Fellow mourners waited until he had a couple of hours' lead, then phoned the sheriff.

A few days later Ed Newt Clanton bought it at Chelsea, Oklahoma. Ed was one of Bradshaw's boys, a hero of the Battle of Braggs Mountain. He took Deputy Sheriff Earl Powell along with him in a fight so fierce that, as one witness put it, "you couldn't see the trees for the lead flying."

In mid-February Clyde Barrow's gang was sighted at Eldon, then at Bidding Springs. They were heading into the hills. They had just brought off the Eastham prison break and were hotter than a sheriff's pistol barrel.

Floyd sent a message to the hill people through Bradshaw: no supplies, no help. If they weren't gone in twenty-four hours, the sheriff at Tahlequah should be notified.

It was too late, though. The sheriff already knew they were in the hills. The two cars, as hot as their occupants, had been sighted turning off U.S. 69 at Muskogee.

On February 17 a thousand-man comb-out was launched from Tahlequah, Muskogee, Stilwell, and Sallisaw.

Most of the big-timers, including Floyd and Richetti, slipped across the Arkansas line under cover of darkness. The Barrows drove south through the Tenkiller country and crossed the Arkansas river at Gore unopposed. Only Ford Bradshaw came a cropper. He was recognized by lawmen at Arkoma, just across the Oklahoma line from Fort Smith. Deputy Sheriff Will Harper shot him fuller of holes than a colander.

Floyd and Richetti headed north.

In the past ten months Floyd's name had gradually faded from the news. There had been a spate of rumors in the summer of 1933: Pretty Boy had dyed his hair red, had died of bullet wounds, had lost a leg as a result of an injury, was in South America. Then, when the Dillinger gang had exploded into headlines that fall, even the rumors had stopped. Floyd was last year's bogeyman; the public had a new favorite.

Now his name began to appear once again. He was identified as the center fielder on bank holdups at Centralia, Illinois; Fort Dodge, Iowa; and Anderson, Indiana. He was also seen driving a car at Holland, Booth, and Winameg, Ohio—all towns in the Toledo area.

The sightings were probably accurate. Floyd was holding up banks once again so that he could earn the protection money that the Licavoli mob demanded for sheltering him. It was a vicious circle, but there was no other way to live outside the Cookson Hills.

In June 1934 the Chicago underworld buzzed with rumors of a Floyd-Dillinger merger. On June 30 five men hit the Merchants National Bank at South Bend, Indiana. Three were easy to identify: Dillinger, Baby Face Nelson, and Homer Van Meter. The fourth, a fat man, has never been identified. The fifth man, the center fielder, was identified by a number of people, including Perry Stahly, the director of the bank, as Pretty Boy Floyd.

It was a bloody raid. One policeman was killed, two bandits wounded, and a couple of bank officers and bystanders nicked by flying bullets. The gang got away, but the take was poor—only $4,800 apiece.

The protection demands kept mounting. Floyd couldn't keep up with the payments. In September 1934 he left Toledo to try and make it on his own.

Early in October Deputy Sheriff Will Owens of Howard County, Iowa, went to a lonely farmhouse to serve some papers. While there, he saw a man who looked strangely familiar. When he got back to his office, he went through his file of wanted posters. It was Pretty Boy Floyd!

Owens immediately got in touch with the State Bureau of Investigation at Des Moines. State Agent A. G. Haight was sent out to aid him.

The two men prowled the countryside around the farm. On October 11 they came across a car parked beside a cornfield. The man behind the wheel was Floyd—they were both sure of it. Haight stayed on the road while Owens, pretending to be an innocent pheasant hunter, entered the cornfield.

Suddenly another man came out of the field and got into the car with Floyd. The motor was started, and the two pulled away. Owens and Haight took after them. They pursued them up a blind road. Floyd swung around and started back, and this time he and his companion were shooting. Floyd opened the throttle, and the car came jolting along the rutted road, guns blazing from the front and rear windows. Haight and Owens returned the fire as long as they could, then hit the floor. They escaped injury, but Floyd got away.

He and his companion, identified as Richetti, were seen next in Minnesota, then—the following day, October 12—in the central part of Missouri. National Guard observation planes took to the air once again. The main bridges across the Mississippi were blocked. National Guardsmen and state troopers patrolled the back roads in armored cars. "This time we've got him," said the Director of Public Safety.

They didn't have him. Floyd got across the Cairo bridge and escaped into Kentucky. The Missouri heat had accomplished something important, though. It had cut him off from the Cookson Hills. Floyd drove north now—into an Ohio that was saturated with Feds investigating the recent kidnapping of Mrs. Alice Stoll.

On October 20 a farmer phoned J. H. Fultz, the Police Chief of Wellsville, Ohio, and told him that he'd seen a couple of men "acting suspiciously" near the intersection of State 7 and the Pennsylvania Railroad tracks. The Tiltonsville bank had been robbed the day before, so Fultz set out to investigate. Two friends who'd been visiting his office accompanied him.

They spotted the men lying on a couple of blankets near an old quarry. The two looked innocent enough, almost like picnickers. The police chief and his friends made no attempt to conceal their approach as they picked their way down through the rocks.

Halfway, Fultz paused and looked at the men. One of them was gone now. Suddenly a voice to his left barked, "Get 'em up!" He turned—and swallowed heavily. It was Pretty Boy Floyd, and he was holding a submachine gun on them.

One of Fultz's friends started to say something. The chief kicked him. He stared Floyd right in the eye and said, "You wouldn't hurt a working man, would you?"

Floyd looked the three men over carefully. They were in civilian clothes. Fultz had no holster; his pistol was in his coat pocket. "Where do you work?" he asked suspiciously.

"Down at the pottery plant."

Floyd said, "Okay, move down the hill ahead of me."

Adam Richetti lay on the blanket, watching them approach.

Chief Fultz smiled at him and said, "Hiya, friend. Takin' it easy?"

Richetti looked quizzically at Floyd. "Don't let him kid you, Eddie," Floyd suddenly rasped. "He's a cop. Kill him!"

Fultz saw an automatic appear in Richetti's hand. He whipped out his pistol as his two friends hit the dirt. Behind him, Floyd was already bringing his submachine gun up as he darted toward a stand of trees. Fultz swung toward him, pegged a couple of shots at him, then dived behind a nearby rock. Floyd and Richetti returned the fire.

Suddenly the chief saw Floyd's submachine gun come apart. The grip had broken. Floyd cursed and flung it to the ground. He whipped out an automatic, fired one shot, then plunged off into the woods.

Fultz took off after Richetti, who was now dashing across an open field, trying to reach the road. "Halt or I'll shoot," he yelled. Richetti kept running. The chief sent a bullet spanging past the gunman's ear. Richetti skidded to a stop, hands high. "Don't shoot," he yelled. "You've got me."

Fultz raced back to Wellsville with his prisoner and phoned the Feds. They came pouring into Columbiana County. Melvin Purvis, Agent in Charge of the Chicago office, set up headquarters at the Travelers Hotel in East Liverpool.

Sunday, October 21, passed with no word on Floyd's whereabouts. He was sticking to the woods.

Then, around noon on Monday, Floyd knocked at the door of a farmhouse on the East Liverpool RFD route. He asked directions for Youngstown, bought a sandwich for a dollar, and was permitted to wash his face and hands. "Do you have a car?" he asked the woman. She told him no, and he left right after that, walking north along the highway. The woman immediately notified Constable Clyde O. Birch, who passed the word along to the Feds.

Squads of heavily armed agents were thrown in a ring around the St. Claire section.

The next report came from a youth who had given Floyd a lift along State 7. The outlaw had offered him $10 for a ride to Youngstown. The car had run out of gas four miles south of Clarkson, though, and Floyd had taken to the fields once again.

As night fell, the Federal ring drew tighter.

Shortly after dawn, October 22, Floyd knocked at the kitchen door of Mrs. Ellen Conkle's farmhouse. He was haggard, disheveled, in need of a shave. He said he was lost and hungry but had money to pay for any food she could give him.

Mrs. Conkle felt sorry for him and asked him in. As he ate, Floyd noticed an old jalopy sitting out in front of the barn and asked about it. "It belongs to my brother," she said. "He's out in back, working."

"Do you think he'd drive me to Youngstown?"

Mrs. Conkle said she'd ask him. The brother, Stewart Dyke, came to the kitchen. "I got my chores to do," he told Floyd, "but I'll take you as far as Clarkson."

Floyd nodded. "All right."

He climbed into the jalopy's rear seat, and Dyke started the motor.

"I was backing up the car," Dyke said later, "when I saw the two automobile loads of officers coming. I saw them before Floyd did. When Floyd sighted them, he turned pale and ordered me to drive back of the corn crib.

"After I backed up, he said, 'Get going!' and called me a bad name. He pulled out his gun and jumped out of the car and crawled under the corn crib. An instant later he darted out and came toward the car. Then he started across a pasture."

The two cars full of FBI men screeched to a stop. Melvin Purvis leaped out of the second car and issued rapid-fire orders. The Feds, most of them armed with submachine guns, spread out in a long line. "Halt or we'll shoot!" Purvis yelled.

Floyd kept running, zigzagging diagonally up the open hill. A deafening roar filled the air as a dozen weapons fired at the sunlit target.

Floyd stumbled and fell, then rose again and seemed about to break into a run. He never made it. After one wobbly stride he crumpled to the ground.

Purvis was the first to reach him. "Are you Pretty Boy Floyd?" he demanded, as he snapped the handcuffs on him.

"I'm Charles Arthur Floyd," the outlaw whispered.

Purvis rushed away to phone J. Edgar Hoover in Washington. One of his assistants asked Floyd if he had taken part in the Kansas City Massacre.

"I didn't do it," he gasped. "I wasn't in on it."

His life was rapidly ebbing away. "Where's Eddie?" he muttered. Then suddenly his eyes flashed open, and he raised himself on one elbow. "Who in hell tipped you off?" he croaked. Then he fell back. "I'm Floyd, all right," he whispered. "You got me this time." And he died.

His body was shipped home to Akins in a cheap pine coffin. People came from fifteen states to attend his funeral. The crowd was estimated at 40,000. His mother, a gnarled woman with a lean, strong jaw, sat unweeping as the Baptist minister preached a sermon on the folly of crime, concluding with Christ's last words on the cross: "It is finished."

At Richetti's trial in Kansas City most of the witnesses refused to testify. Mrs. Lottie West was one of the few who agreed to take the stand. Richetti was convicted of murder in the first degree and was sentenced to hang. By the time he was finally executed (October 7, 1938), Missouri had switched from the noose to the lethal gas chamber, so that was how Eddie took his leave of this world.

CHAPTER FIVE

John Dillinger—the Fastest Mind and the Slowest Gun in the Midwest

If Dillinger actually did link up with Floyd to pull the South Bend job, as witnesses claim, it was against his better judgment. For John is on record as having said of the Oklahoma bandit: "That bird's too fast with the fireworks."

But then that was Dillinger's opinion of practically every major figure of the Public Enemy Era.

John was the slowest gun in the Midwest—by choice.

He carried a heater and he pointed it at people during hold-ups. But he used it as a persuader rather than a weapon. Shooting was a last resort with him. If there was any other way out of a "pickle," he went for it.

His driving skill got him out of plenty of situations that Clyde Barrow would have solved with lead. He also used his gun butt and his fists. And sometimes he talked his way out of tight spots. And when everything else failed, he ran.

He used his gun only when cornered. And even then he didn't shoot to kill. Of the eleven killings that are usually linked with his name, only one can personally be laid at his doorstep—and there are some who claim that he wasn't responsible for that one, either.

All this is pretty hard to square with the mythical picture of Dillinger, submachine gun in hand, mowing down scores of cops as he rasps, "Come an' get me, you dumb flatfoots."

That was a picture created by the lawmen who chased Dillinger. An Indiana policeman named Matt Leach started it, the press took it up, and the FBI completed it. Dillinger wasn't any "Prince of Desperadoes," and he certainly wasn't what the FBI said he was: "the most brazen killer this nation has ever known."

What Dillinger was was a tough, competent heist man of the old school. He robbed with imagination and flair. His hairbreadth escapes were daring and colorful. So was he, personally. He was a cocky man, sure of himself, an admirer of Douglas Fairbanks and Clark Gable. He thought of himself as a kind of latter-day

Jesse James and enjoyed living up to the role that lawmen had created for him. He had an innate sense of theater and a tough, rather sardonic view of things. Humphrey Bogart played him later under many different names: Duke Mantee in *The Petrified Forest*, Roy Earle in *High Sierra*. The two men even resembled each other physically. It would be interesting to know how much of Bogart's character was really Dillinger.

Dillinger was out of step with most of his lead-spewing contemporaries. He would have been more at home with the Harvey Bailey-Eddie Bentz crowd—those cool, calm artisans of bank robbery who rarely spilled blood. The Denver Mint caper, the $1-million Lincoln National Bank and Trust Company kick-in—those were jobs that would have tickled him.

It was Dillinger's misfortune to come along late in the game, however, after Bailey and Bentz had been locked up, and after banks had equipped themselves with alarms and safety devices, and after the big city police forces had been beefed up to meet the Depression crime wave. It was his misfortune, too, to work with some of the most violent men of the whole Public Enemy Era.

The Dillinger manhunt was the biggest, the most famous this country has ever experienced. Dillinger himself was the most publicized criminal in the nation's history, bar none. Even today he remains the FBI's most famous single case. A white plaster facsimile of his death mask hangs outside J. Edgar Hoover's office in Washington, staring empty-eyed at all who enter—the "prize scalp," as one critic has put it, in the Director's collection.

Because Dillinger is so central to the FBI's myth of infallibility, he has himself been a target of the Bureau's critics. Some of them have pictured him as a small-time gunsel inflated out of all proportion by FBI publicity flacks, a mere hanger-on of gangs actually led by other men.

This is as false a picture of him as the "mad dog" concept of the '30s.

The actual facts are these: There was no single "Dillinger gang." What there was was a constantly shifting coalition of forces as men were killed or arrested, or drifted away. It's true that Dillinger was not the leader of these forces. He was an equal partner in the sharing of loot and the making of decisions. There was no leader. Everyone had his say. What Dillinger was, however, was a unifying force. Many bandits who otherwise would not have worked together did so because they liked Dillinger and trusted him. In this sense there could have been no gang without him.

He was a lot like Butch Cassidy—that calm center of the stormy group known as the Wild Bunch. They too were a "coalition of forces" rather than a single gang. And it was Cassidy's judgment and calm good nature that held them together. Vicious gunmen like Kid Curry and the Sundance Kid would have been at each other's throats in a second if it hadn't been for Cassidy's presence.

That's how it was with Dillinger. He kept Homer Van Meter and Harry Pierpont from drilling each other on a number of occasions, and he even managed to get Homer and Baby Face Nelson to work together with some degree of efficiency.

In the end, however, Dillinger will be remembered because of something else. His own life. It's a classic of its kind—the clearest, best documented, step-by-step example that we have of how a society goes about creating its own worst enemies.

He was born in Indianapolis in 1903, the son of a grocery store owner. His mother died when he was three. The father remarried shortly after that, and in 1920 the family moved to a farm outside Mooresville, Indiana.

Young Dillinger (the family pronounced it with a hard g) was really an admirable sort of boy, normal in every way. As typically Hoosier as Penrod or Sam. He hunted and fished and was mighty with a rifle, as were all boys in the American heartland in this period. He was strong, popular, and interested in mechanical things; and he was a first-rate baseball player.

His first brush with the law, at age seventeen, was a typical Andy Hardy scrape. He was arrested for speeding and paid an eleven-dollar fine. His second brush, in 1923, was a little more serious. He was refused permission to marry his uncle's pretty stepdaughter (the uncle favored a well-to-do Greencastle boy). Young Dillinger brooded about it. He got drunk, stole a car, and went for a joyride. The owner refused to press charges, but Dillinger was embarrassed about the whole thing and ran away to join the Navy.

He hated Navy life, went AWOL, and was thrown in the brig. It was his first taste of prison: ten days' solitary on bread and water with full ration every third day. Dillinger jumped ship and came home. He got married. At the same time he fell in with Ed Singleton, an older man with a criminal record. Needing money, he agreed to join Singleton in the stickup of a neighborhood grocer.

The two men were caught. Dillinger's father advised his son to plead guilty. He did—and received a sentence of *10-20 years* on charges of conspiracy to commit a felony and asault with intent to rob. Singleton, whose idea the robbery had been, got off with only a two-year sentence. As Indiana Governor Paul V. McNutt wrote years later: "There is no question whatever that this obvious injustice had much to do with the bitterness which

Dillinger developed. . . . A mistake by a court probably made Dillinger what he was."

He was an obstreperous prisoner at the Pendleton Reformatory and tried repeatedly to escape. Caught each time, he had additional months added to his sentence. In 1929 his wife was granted a divorce. This increased his bitterness. He requested a transfer to the state penitentiary at Michigan City, an odd sort of request. The reason he gave was that he wanted to play on their baseball team.

The request was granted. But Dillinger played no ball at the Big House. He was too busy getting an education—in crime.

His job at the pen was working a "tomcat" in the prison shirt factory. The men who worked alongside him were a type penologists have since labeled "Elders of the Tribe"—hardened repeaters who form the aristocracy of a prison's population. They are the custodians of underworld culture, heroes to the young apprentices, the teachers who shape their minds.

Two of the most powerful influences on Dillinger at Michigan City were John ("Three-Finger Jack") Hamilton, a stocky, muscular con with an irregular scar running down his forehead, and Charles Makley, a veteran Ohio bank bandit serving a 10-20 set for armed robbery.

"Fat Charlie" shared the same cell with Dillinger for some time. His influence on the younger man was incalculable. A "prison library intellectual," he resembled Major Hoople of the comic strips, and he strengthened that impression with his "gadzooks, kaf, kaf" style of delivery. But his easygoing exterior masked a cold, ruthless personality. The prison classification director described him as "dangerous, with strong antisocial tendencies."

The course he taught was the standard prison one. First lesson: "If you're not a bull, then you'd better be a fox. Wise up, Johnnie. This world is a joint where the bulls and the foxes live well and the lambs wind up head-down from the hook." And Lesson No. 2: "Take any official, any policeman, anybody else that's doing everything in the book and getting by with it, then take your square john working his heart and soul out, and if he misses three days at work, he's three months behind—it's so foolish."

John Hamilton's course was a postgraduate one. He was convinced that there was still time to organize one last unbeatable gang before the two-way radio and the airplane ended the old style of bank "kick-in'" once and for all. J. Edgar Hoover would later credit him with originating the idea of an interstate network of parolees and hideouts, and would call him "Dillinger's tutor, the most cunning crook in the gang."

There was only one hitch to Hamilton's ambitious plans. He

was serving twenty-five years for automobile banditry and wouldn't be up for parole until 1950. Dillinger's case, on the other hand, would be reviewed in 1933. Now if Johnnie kept his nose clean, he would be released on schedule and could get things organized on the outside . . .

Dillinger had already decided to pursue a criminal life. As he told a reporter later: "They took away nine years of my life, and I decided to do some taking of my own when I got out." The idea of working with Hamilton and Makley in a "super gang" impressed him. So he took the older man's advice and started doing "his own time."

He stayed away from two former Pendleton buddies in particular—Harry Pierpont and Homer Van Meter. Prison officials had labeled the two "confirmed criminals of the most dangerous type." Their records were filled with disobedience, insolence, refusal to work. Most of their stay, both at the Reformatory and Michigan City, had been spent in "the hole." Their ability to endure hunger and to absorb beatings was so exceptional that they had won the awed respect of every con at the State Pen.

Pierpont was the more openly defiant of the two. He was a slender, good-looking man in his late twenties. His clear blue eyes, wavy chestnut hair, and fair complexion gave him the handsome collegiate look of an F. Scott Fitzgerald hero. He was a highly dangerous man, however, with an almost pathological hatred for authority of any kind. If he could get his hands on a prison guard, Pierpont would try to kill him. So most of the time he was kept in the segregation block on Red Card, the maximum security classification.

Van Meter, almost six feet tall but weighing only 125 pounds, had a sleepy-lidded clown's face. He was the prison "comedian." His specialty was mimicking the guards. He spent months at a time in "the hole," where he received nightly beatings with a blackjack. He would come back with half his teeth missing and his body covered with bruises—but still joking. Pendleton's Director of Research examined him and reported: "Moral sense is perverted and he has no intention of following anything but a life of crime. . . . He is a murderer at heart and if society is to be safeguarded, his type must be confined throughout their natural lives."

Pierpont and Van Meter hated each other. Rivalry had something to do with it, of course. They were the two leading contenders for the "toughest-con-in-stir" award. But their personalities clashed, too. They were opposite types. Pierpont believed in open, naked aggression; Van Meter preferred the sly dig, the innuendo. Each man thought the other a fool.

The only friend they had in common was Dillinger, who

thought Homer was very funny and who respected Pierpont's criminal record—an extensive one that already included several bank robberies.

Sometime around 1931 Van Meter decided to get a parole. He had a sharp mind. He knew how to make the system work for himself, and he knew the poses he would have to adopt in order to exploit that system. He spent every available hour in the prison library. He volunteered for extra duties. He stopped ridiculing the guards. And he wrote letters to the parole board, each one a masterpiece. The one that finally got him sprung concluded: "My plea is—be big enough to cast aside the musty archives dealing with the follies of an unthinking boy before the needs of a clean matured man. . . . This is the age of the new deal. I place my destiny in your hands. You can restore a sterling citizen and a sound matured man to freedom."

The parole board rose to the occasion. Van Meter was restored to freedom on May 19, 1933. Dillinger followed him out three days later. The two men had talked frequently in the past few months. Homer had promised to show Dillinger how to make "the big money" on the outside. Pierpont had talked to Dillinger, too, and had given him a list of banks to rob plus the names and addresses of some reliable accomplices. The understanding was that Dillinger would put some of the money to work on a crashout by buying guns, arranging hideouts, and bribing guards.

Dillinger went home to Mooresville first to see his family. They barely recognized him. Prison had changed everything about him, even his face. It was a stranger's face, smooth and hard, trained to indicate nothing to a prison guard, neither resistance nor slavishness. He said little to them and when he joked at all, he had a "twisted smile."

A few days later he left for Indianapolis, where he looked up some of Pierpont's contacts. The first jobs he worked with them were minor—supermarkets, sandwich shops, gas stations. There were lots of things he still had to get used to. The new cars, for instance. And the feel of a gun in his hand.

Finally he felt ready for Pierpont's list. But when he checked it out, he found half the targets boarded up, gone out of business. It was 1933, and the Depression had hit bottom. There were breadlines everywhere, Hoovervilles, untenanted shops, and closed-down banks.

He hit the targets that were still open, then swung over to Ohio and raided a bank fingered by Homer Van Meter—the New Carlisle National. The bookkeeper was so unnerved by the sight of the three men, their faces masked by handkerchiefs, that he couldn't get the safe open. "Let me drill him," growled one of Dillinger's companions. "He's stalling."

Dillinger ignored him. "Take your time, Pop," he said soothingly.

While the bookkeeper was struggling with the safe, a woman bank clerk entered. Dillinger spread a banker's smock on the floor for her and apologized as he trussed up her hands and feet with wire. "I hope this doesn't hurt you," he said.

When the bookkeeper finally got the safe open, the trio removed $10,600 from it and fled, leaving a trail of roofing nails along the highway to discourage pursuit.

During the next three weeks the gang looted some ten banks in five states. Then, in mid-July, the police trapped them in Muncie. Dillinger, who was driving, reversed gears and shot backward out of the trap—faster, according to one of the gang members, "than some people drive forward." He had apparently got the hang of the new '33 cars.

On July 17 Dillinger and another man strolled into the Daleville, Indiana, bank. "Honey, this is a holdup," Dillinger told teller Margaret Good. And using the ledge of her cage as a step, he vaulted smoothly over the six-foot barrier while his companion covered the customers in the lobby.

The take was small—$3,500—but that Douglas Fairbanks-like leap over the barrier was to put Dillinger into the big time. It marked him as a bandit with a certain distinctive flair—and that was exactly the kind of bandit that Captain Matt Leach of the Indiana State Police was looking for at that moment.

Leach was a remarkable man—shrewd, self-educated, desperately ambitious. He had a carnival advance man's instinct for publicity. The press loved him. He could always be depended on for colorful angles, exciting copy. Fellow lawmen detested him. "To disclose confidential information to (Leach)," wrote one disillusioned detective, "is to jeopardize the success of any important investigation."

Leach's discovery of Dillinger was almost as great a moment in the history of press agentry as of crime. Dr. Charles R. Bird, the Indiana State Police Surgeon who was present when it happened, remembered Leach's saying: "John Dillinger's methods are unique and something new in the criminal world. He stands out as a unique character. I am going to publicize him—watch him go!" Then he added: "I'll wager you police stations themselves won't be safe in the future."

"Which proved to be true," Dr. Bird added, "as a prophecy."

The beginnings were small—limited to the Muncie area, where Dillinger appeared in the local headlines as "Desperate Dan, the Bandit Man." But bigger things were on the way.

One was a press agent's dream. Dillinger and Van Meter cooked it up between them that summer. It was based on an original idea by John Hamilton and it featured three gangs operating separately in Indiana, Ohio, and Kentucky under a centralized command based in East Chicago.

A tristate network of parolees were ready to shield them, act as fences, use their homes as drops, refueling stations, and hideouts. The three gangs operated along this network like trains, shuttling between hideouts, robbing banks along the way, working in small, separate bands, converging only when a job needed a large force or when an expected clash with police called for more strength.

It was John Hamilton's dream of a "super gang" come to life, and, if all went well, he, Pierpont, and Makley would soon be joining it.

Between bank jobs Dillinger and Van Meter drove the back-country roads of northern Indiana, mapping out an isolated route from the pen to a hideout in Indianapolis. They made a 14-page "crawl" of the route, noting down every curve, bump, and landmark along its 155-mile length. It was timed to the second and so detailed that it even included such night-driving details as reminders to douse the car's headlights 800 yards before coming to main highways.

Before the crashout itself could be rigged, however, money would be needed for guns, bribes, and additional hideouts. Lots of money. So Dillinger looked around, searching for a nice, fat target.

On the morning of September 6 the assistant manager of the State Bank of Massachusetts Avenue in Indianapolis was talking on the telephone when he heard someone say quietly, "This is a stickup." He glanced up to see John Dillinger sitting cross-legged on the seven-foot high barrier. A straw hat was tilted cockily on his head. An automatic was pointed at him. "Hang up," said the outlaw, "and raise your hands."

The assistant manager did just that. Dillinger leaped down and went swiftly from cage to cage, sweeping money—including $500 in half dollars—into a white sack while the second man, a handkerchief over his face, covered the staff and the customers with a machine gun in the lobby.

When Dillinger was finished, the two men backed out and got into a waiting car. It roared away. The story about Dillinger pausing in the doorway to shout, "Tell the home folks little Johnnie Dillinger staged this," is just that—a story. It was a Matt Leach invention. Another brick added to the growing Dillinger legend.

The bandits had struck the bank on the Real Silk Hosiery payroll day, so the take was lush: $24,800—the second largest holdup in Indianapolis history.

Dillinger took his share of the loot and got down to work on the crashout.

He was in communication with the boys on the inside through a former cellmate, James Jenkins. Jenkins, a Floyd County hillbilly serving life for murder, had a sister named Mary who lived in Dayton, Ohio, and Mary was Dillinger's present girlfriend. She visited her brother frequently and interspersed a lot of harmless chitchat about their Pentecostal Preacher Dad and the family dog with such terse instructions as "Give Blue Eye a C," and "Ray is in crock," and "Sit tight."

Dillinger wanted Jenkins included in the crashout party. Pierpont, now in command on the inside, vetoed the idea. Jenkins was a small-timer. There were also rumors that he had been Dillinger's "old lady."

To Pierpont, this indicated a weakness of character. It was like Homer Van Meter's propensity for "kidding around." There was no room for sex or levity in Pierpont's list of priorities. He was all business—and the business at hand was busting out, then hitting every bank in sight. The fun and games could come later. Maybe.

Pierpont was an ascetic at heart. He mistrusted anyone who suffered from weaknesses of the flesh. And that included Dillinger, as infirm a vessel of clay as one could find. Dillinger was not homosexual, just oversexed. When he had to go a day "without it," he once confided to a fellow prisoner, he felt as if there were an iron band around his head, "squeezing" his brains out. When he couldn't get women, Dillinger sought relief with men. When he could get women, that's all he went for—and no risk was too great if it ended in satisfaction. Pierpont had often prophesied that his strong sex drive would be his undoing. And he was right, of course. It would be.

Dillinger's demand that Jenkins be included in the escape party had nothing to do with sex, however. He had given his former cellmate his word and he intended to abide by it. As he told reporters later: "I stick to my friends, and they stick to me." He refused to rig the crashout unless Jenkins was in on the play. So Pierpont was finally forced to give in.

The crashout party continued to grow. Another friend of Pierpont's was now added to it—Russell Lee Clark, a big, powerful, sleepy-lidded Detroit bank bandit. Clark's prison record was a bad one. It included participation in the strike of '29, refusal to work, trying to foment a revolt, trying to escape, trying to kill his guards en route to prison.

Ed Shouse, a former dirt track racer with twenty-two years left of a robbery term, was also included. There was always room for a good wheelman, and Shouse could make a car do everything but sit up and beg.

On September 11 Dillinger visited Mary Kinder in Indianapolis. Mary, a tiny, twenty-two-year-old redhead, was an old friend of Pierpont's. She agreed to help with the crashout if her brother, Earl Northern, was added to the list of escapees. Dillinger said he would arrange it, and Mary agreed to find a hideout for the boys.

A week later Dillinger visited her again and gave her $150, saying that the group would arrive on September 26. Then he drove to Chicago, bought four guns, and turned them over to another conspirator. This man went to a factory in Indianapolis, where he bribed an employee to open a box of thread addressed to the prison shirt shop. The two men hid the guns under the thread, resealed the box, and marked a big *X* on it in stencil ink.

The trusty in charge of incoming goods at the prison had agreed to get the weapons to the gang if he and three of his buddies were included in the crashout group. This added four lifers to the party: Walter Detrich, serving it for bank robbery, Joe Fox for the same, James Clark for automobile banditry, and Joe Burns for murder.

Dillinger's part was finished. He headed to Dayton for a little relaxation with his "sweetie pie," Mary Jenkins Longnaker. Ohio authorities had learned of his frequent visits from a stoolie, however, and had placed Mary's West First Street rooming house under 24-hour observation. Within minutes of Dillinger's arrival on the morning of September 22, a force of thirty cops had the place surrounded.

Four detectives, carrying rifles and submachine guns and wearing bulletproof vests, moved cautiously up the stairs and kicked in the door. Dillinger was in bed. He just shrugged as the cops came pouring into the room. "I'd have been pretty stupid to go for my gun," he told reporters later.

On the afternoon of September 26 the escape party gathered in the basement of the shirt factory at Michigan City. There were ten cons in the group altogether. (Earl Northern wasn't among them. He was in the prison hospital, dying of tuberculosis.)

They subdued and gagged the shop foreman, then turned their guns on Superintendent G. H. Stevens and Day Captain Albert Evans. "We're going home," Pierpont snarled at Evans, "and you're leading us out. Try anything and you're dead. Get it, you big, brave man?"

Quickly they moved out, each con carrying a bundle of shirts to make the troop look like a routine work detail led by two officers. No one tumbled until the crashout brigade reached the front gate—twin barred doors ten yards apart. There the shirt bundles dropped. "Open up," rasped Jack Hamilton. Guard Guy Burklow gaped at the automatics pointed at him and obeyed. The cons swarmed through, slugged Fred Wellnitz, the outer gate turnkey, and grabbed his keys.

Four of the cons—Detrich, Fox, James Clark, and Burns—seized a sheriff who had just delivered a prisoner and fled in his car. These four never joined the Dillinger gang. All were subsequently recaptured.

The others—Hamilton, Makley, Pierpont, Russell Clark, Ed Shouse, and James Jenkins—raced across the prison grounds and flagged down a passing car. Two elderly women were hustled out of it. The driver, also elderly, was kept at the wheel. But minutes later, with the needle still under fifty and the car weaving erratically, he was forced out, too, and Shouse, the expert wheelman, took over.

Motorist Glenn Green, who sighted the car a few minutes later, told police that it was doing at least ninety and taking curves on two wheels.

At 6:45 that night millions of Americans heard H. V. Kaltenborn open his news broadcast with a tense, "Ladies and gentlemen, Indiana is in a virtual state of siege tonight."

In clipped, measured tones, he quickly filled in the picture: "State and local police, sheriffs, deputized citizens, and National Guard units are manning every highway, bridge, and crossroads in the northern part of the state after ten dangerous, long-term convicts shot and clubbed their way out of the Indiana State Penitentiary at Michigan City this afternoon."

In Indianapolis Matt Leach was busy linking Dillinger to the crashout. He told reporters that Ohio authorities had refused to let him examine the documents found in Dillinger's possession when he was arrested, and that these documents contained information connected with the break. It's true, the documents did—but Ohio authorities claimed that Leach had seen them and had refused to act on the information.

Leach's office, meanwhile, sprayed reporters with an unceasing rat-tat-tat-tat of items about Dillinger. The press used them all. His Ohio mug shot—a classic of its kind—was reproduced over and over in newspapers throughout the nation. Dillinger was wearing a double-breasted pinstripe suit and a pearl-gray fedora in it, and the smile on his puss was the smug, sardonic one of a man who knew he was going to be sprung.

Between September 26 and 29 the escaped cons dodged around Indiana and Ohio, engaging in numerous shoot-outs with lawmen.

James Jenkins split from the main group on September 29 and made his way south toward his native hills. At Beanblossom, in

Brown County, a posse braced him, then blew his head off when he tried to draw.

On September 29 Dillinger pleaded guilty to a Bluffton, Ohio, bank robbery, and was transferred to the Allen County Jail in Lima, a very flimsy institution.

Dayton authorities warned Sheriff Jess Sarber that Dillinger's friends would probably try and spring him and that he had better take some precautions. Sarber laughed, calling his new prisoner "just another punk."

At 6:20 P.M., October 12, Pierpont, Makley, and Clark entered the jail. "We're officers from Michigan City," Pierpont told the sheriff. "We want to see John Dillinger."

"Let me see your credentials," said Sarber.

"Here are our credentials," said Pierpont, pulling a gun. Sarber lunged at it, and Pierpont shot him twice. The sheriff tried to rise, and Makley slugged him with the butt of his pistol. The sheriff died.

Dillinger, who had been playing cards with another prisoner, got up when he heard the shots and put on his hat and coat. Pierpont entered, tossed the keys to a deputy, who unlocked the cell, and Dillinger walked out.

The nation's most famous crime wave had begun.

Two days later the gang descended on the Auburn, Indiana, police station. They got a submachine gun, two steel vests, and 1,000 rounds of ammunition.

On October 20 the gang hit the City Hall in Peru, Indiana. This time the take was two machine guns, six bulletproof vests, two sawed-off shotguns, four .38-caliber police specials, two .30–.30 Winchester rifles, three police badges, and another 1,000 rounds of ammunition.

Officials got hysterical. Several prominent ones stated that the escapees had declared "open warfare" on the state. The Marion County sheriff predicted that the gang would try to break *into* the state pen to enlist an army of desperadoes. The *Indianapolis Times* sent a telegram to U.S. Attorney General Homer S. Cummings, asking for help, saying that the situation was too much for state authorities to handle.

Leach, meanwhile, continued to grind out Dillinger material. His avowed purpose was to make Pierpont jealous, to stir up a battle for leadership that would destroy the gang.

In Chicago, where they were hiding out, the men laughed at his efforts. Pierpont was grateful to Dillinger for springing him and vice versa. There was no struggle for leadership. Decisions were reached democratically, with every man putting in his two bits and being listened to in respectful silence.

The gang's first order of business was money. They needed

some. Pierpont and the others had hit a bank in Makley's home town, St. Mary's, Ohio, on October 6. They had withdrawn $14,000, but they were heavy spenders and that money was already gone.

So, on October 23, they raided the Central National Bank in Greencastle, Indiana.

Pierpont had sketched its interior, laid out the escape route. Makley had fingered it, knew it would be plump that Monday because merchants had done brisk business over the weekend with homecoming alumni of DePauw University. Hamilton stayed outside the door as the "tiger"—the lookout. Dillinger and Pierpont took the cages; Makley held down center field with a submachine gun.

The take was lovely—$74,782.09 in cash and negotiable bonds. And not a shot fired. It was heady stuff.

Back in Chicago the gang relaxed. Dillinger had a new girl friend now—Evelyn (Billie) Frechette, a French-Indian beauty born on the Chippewa Reservation at Neopit, Wisconsin. Billie had raven-black hair and a trim figure. She had a husband, too, but he was in Leavenworth on a mail robbery rap. Dillinger asked her to move in with him. She did, quitting her job as a hatcheck girl in a Chicago nightclub.

The others had acquired girl friends, too. Mary Kinder was now keeping house for Harry Pierpont. Makley was living with Pat Cherrington. Her sister, Opal Long, was paired off with Russell Clark. John Hamilton had a girl with a name that sounded like a tin can rolling down a flight of stairs—Elaine Sullivan Dent Burton DeKant. And Homer Van Meter was on the scene, too, with his girl, pretty Marie Conforti.

The men didn't hide in their apartments but moved freely around Chicago, looking like prosperous businessmen out on the town. They went to nightclubs and to movies (Dillinger's favorite was *The Three Little Pigs*), and they ate at the best restaurants.

They had to keep on the move, though, for Chicago was full of cops looking for them. Matt Leach was there with a group of Indiana State Police detectives, and Forrest Huntington, a former Pinkerton agent now working for the American Surety Company, had come to town with his extensive army of stool pigeons. The Chicago police had also formed a special "Dillinger Squad." It was made up of forty hand-picked men, the toughest on the force, armed with machine guns, bulletproof vests, and tear gas bombs. They were on round-the-clock duty and divided into two watches—one led by Captain John Stege, the other by Lieutenant Frank Reynolds.

"Those were exciting times," Dillinger reminisced later to reporters. "We moved from house to house, rented one, stayed a few days, and moved on when the neighborhood got too hot. Stege and Reynolds and the rest of the police were sure hot on our trail. Just about a day behind, I guess. They almost got me once, out on Irving Park Boulevard. That was because a stool pigeon turned me up to the police. His name is Art McGinnis. I fed him and clothed him when he was broke, but he squealed on me. The police found me in a doctor's office where Art had sent them. They shot at me and I shot at them, but my car was too fast and I got away."

It was a rather modest description of what was actually a classic auto chase across half of Chicago, with Dillinger gunning his Terraplane between two converging trolley cars at one point, and vanishing down a nearly invisible alleyway on a dead end street at another. "That bird can sure drive," said the man who did the chasing—ace police driver, John Artery.

A few days later the gang hit the American Bank and Trust Company in Racine, Wisconsin. Things didn't go as well as at Greencastle. A teller kicked an alarm. Cops came, and a crowd gathered outside. The money gatherers—Dillinger, Pierpont, and a Lebanon, Indiana, gunman named Leslie Homer—neither bolted nor panicked. They kept right on stuffing the loot into bags.

When they had it all, they started out. Makley, the center fielder, and Russell Clark, holding down the door, herded the bank president and two women employees ahead of the group as shields.

There was some shooting anyway, and a policeman named Wilbur Hansen was wounded. The group headed around the corner to where John Hamilton sat waiting in the getaway car. They got in and drove slowly out of town with the hostages on the running boards. The take was disappointing: $27,789 plus securities. Dillinger was philosophical about it, though. "You can't strike twelve every time," he observed.

It was around this time that Ed Shouse left the gang—by invitation. Shouse had made a couple of serious mistakes. He had made a play for Billie Frechette and he had tried to talk Hamilton into pulling some private jobs on the side. "There's your money," Dillinger told him, throwing down a roll of bills. "Now get your ass out."

Shouse left, taking Russell Clark's car with him.

Now it was Hamilton's turn to pull a boner. On December 14 he took his car to a North Side repair shop to have a fender straightened. The repairmen recognized him and called the police. Sergeant William T. Shanley and two patrolmen staked the place out. Hamilton returned that night. Elaine Sullivan Dent Burton DeKant was with him. Shanley braced them. Hamilton didn't fool around. He drew fast, shot Shanley dead and bolted. Mrs. Dent Sullivan, etc., was caught. She was all outraged innocence.

"He certainly deceived me," she told police. "I thought he was a rich man's son. Why I never heard him say 'damn.' And clean! He'd take two baths a day."

Shanley's killing caused a big flareup. The "Dillinger Squad's" new instructions were "shoot to kill—shoot first." Captain Stege said: "We'll either drive the Dillinger mob out of town or bury them. We'd prefer the latter."

The gang got the message and left Chicago, heading to Florida for an extended vacation.

The day they left, Ed Shouse was bagged at Paris, Illinois. There was a gun battle and a cop was killed—not by Shouse, but accidentally by another policeman.

Shouse was eager to talk, and Matt Leach brought the reporters in to listen. The tale Shouse told was worthy of the old maestro himself. The Dillinger gang was constantly on the alert, he said. They slept in their bulletproof vests. They held nightly drills in preparation for a police attack. "They're a kill-crazy mob," he warned solemnly. "Every man knows just what to do when the police come to the door. They'll shoot it out to the last bullet."

In Florida the gang relaxed in the sun. Dillinger had rented a two-story house at Daytona Beach from a Chicago agency. He and Billie shared it with Russell Clark and his girl, Opal "Mack Truck" Long. Pierpont and Mary Kinder stayed at a nearby hotel, and on December 21 Homer Van Meter and Charlie Makley arrived to join the fun.

The eight of them swam a lot, and went down to Miami to view the air races, and on Christmas Day gifts were exchanged. Johnnie gave Billie a diamond ring.

On New Year's Eve, as they sat listening to the radio in the living room, they heard a newscaster announce that John Dillinger and his gang had struck again. They had raided the Beverly Gardens, a roadhouse near Chicago, slugged the doorman, and ruthlessly shot two policemen in a gun battle.

"That goddamn Leach," seethed Pierpont.

Dillinger merely shrugged. "Now they'll blame everything on me," he said.

Leach's incessant hammering had already done its work. The name Dillinger was on everybody's lips. Every crime in the U.S., and even a couple in Europe, were being blamed on the gang. Any criminal who had ever served time at Michigan City was labeled a "Dillinger mobster."

On January 15 the First National Bank in East Chicago, Indiana, was held up by two bandits wearing bulletproof vests under their bulky overcoats. The bank's customers and staff later identified the men as Hamilton and Dillinger.

Hamilton took the cages, they said, while Dillinger covered

everyone from the lobby with a submachine gun. As Hamilton was scooping $20,376 into a Federal Reserve sack, the bank's vice-president sounded the alarm. Dillinger looked casually out the window and saw policemen hurrying down the street with drawn guns.

"There's some cops outside," he called to Hamilton. "But don't hurry. Get all that dough."

When the two were ready to leave, they took a couple of bank officials along as hostages. As they emerged from the bank, one of the hostages leaped aside, giving Patrolman William Patrick O'Malley a clear shot at the man later identified as Dillinger. He fired. The bullets rattled off Dillinger's bulletproof vest. Dillinger pushed the other hostage aside and fired a short burst at O'Malley's legs. O'Malley fell—*into* the line of fire. A bullet tore through his heart, killing him instantly.

With the hostages out of the way, the other officers opened fire. One slug ripped through a weak spot in Hamilton's vest. He fell. Dillinger turned around and came back for him. He helped him to his feet, picked up the money bag with his other hand, and the two men ran toward a car parked in the middle of Chicago Avenue. They climbed into it and managed to get it started despite bullets slamming into them from three directions. The car roared away.

Dillinger had killed his first man.

If he actually *was* the second bandit.

Dillinger always maintained that he wasn't. "They can't hold me for that," he told reporters later. "When that job was pulled, I was in Florida. I never had anything to do with that East Chicago stickup."

He told his family the same thing. Today, thirty-five years later, Mary Kinder still swears that Dillinger heard the news of the holdup over the radio in Daytona Beach. And Mrs. Emmett Hancock, Dillinger's sister, maintains just as firmly that she was once told by an FBI man that her brother had never killed anyone.

Against this, we have the sworn statements of police officers and bank officials in East Chicago, plus the fact that some cash from the robbery was later found in Dillinger's possession.

On January 17 Dillinger and Billie Frechette showed up at his father's Mooresville farm. John said that he had just returned from Florida and that they were headed west. They visited with friends and neighbors, and Dillinger openly walked the streets of Mooresville, as was his custom, greeting the townspeople.

A few days later they left for Tucson, Arizona, where they were to rendezvous with the rest of the gang.

Makley and Clark had gone on ahead of the others. Without

Pierpont or Dillinger to keep an eye on them, the two began to spend freely and drink too much.

On the night of January 22 the Congress Hotel in Tucson caught fire. Clark and Makley, who were registered there with Opal Long, tipped a couple of firemen fifty dollars to rescue their luggage. "If the saps had made it only a couple of bucks," Dillinger groused later, "we'd still be safe—and happy."

The firemen took a good long look at the generous strangers. The next day, while leafing through a copy of *True Detective* Magazine, they came across pictures of the two. They rushed to Police Chief C. A. "Gus" Wollard. He told them to keep the information to themselves for the time being. "Maybe we can get the whole gang," he said, "one at a time."

That's exactly what the Tucson police did, too—smoothly, quietly, without firing a shot. After a couple of days of discreet checking, they plucked Makley out of a downtown radio shop, curbed Pierpont in his car, and took Clark in his North Second Avenue bungalow.

Dillinger hadn't yet been spotted, but Chief Wollard had Clark's bungalow staked out as a precaution. Just after dark a car pulled up in front. Dillinger was at the wheel. Billie Frechette sat beside him, holding a Boston bull puppy on her lap. Dillinger got out and started up the walk—into leveled riot guns.

As he was being searched, his hands, only shoulder high, began to drop slowly. One of the policemen, "Swede" Walker, pulled the hammer back on his gun. "Reach for the moon," he said, "or I'll cut you in two." Dillinger grinned—and reached.

News of the gang's capture spread like wildfire. Lawmen from every state in the Midwest rushed to Tucson to share the spotlight. Matt Leach arrived, but the crush of reporters, photographers, and newsreel cameramen kept him from reaching the side of the celebrity that he had himself created.

He tried again the following morning and got through, but all he had time for was a quick handshake and a "How are you, John?" before he was pushed aside by jostling news photographers.

This was the first close-up look the press had had of "America's Number One gangster." They were frankly puzzled by the amiable, easygoing man who sat in his cell signing autographs and urging gawkers to vote for Pima County Sheriff John Belton. "Dillinger has none of the look of the conventional killer," wrote one reporter. "Given a little more time and a wider circle of acquaintances, one can see that he might presently become the central figure in a nationwide campaign, largely female, to prevent his frying in the electric chair."

Every state, county, and city wanted Dillinger for itself, but it was Lake County, Indiana, that finally got him. And they did it by practically kidnapping him out from under the other lawmen's noses.

Dillinger braced his feet against the bars of his cell and struggled against the combined efforts of five East Chicago policemen.

"Where's my mouthpiece?" he shouted. "He told me this was illegal! They can't take me East without a hearing!"

They did, though. They flew him by charter plane to Douglas, Arizona, and from there by American Airways. The plane touched down at Fort Worth, Dallas, Little Rock, and Memphis, and at each airfield there were large crowds waiting to catch a glimpse of the country's most famous outlaw.

Pandemonium reigned at Chicago's Midway Airport as he stepped from the plane. Sixty policemen tried to hold back the surging crowds. Dillinger blinked as a host of photographers set off flash powder. Thirty-two Chicago cops wearing bulletproof vests and carrying rifles and machine guns closed around him and rushed him through the crowd toward an unmarked sedan.

It was part of a thirteen-car cavalcade that would take him to Crown Point, Indiana, where he was to be held for the murder of Patrolman O'Malley. In addition to the Chicago police, there were twenty-nine heavily armed Indiana troopers in the escort party.

The motorcade pulled away. Lieutenant Frank Reynolds sat beside Dillinger, a submachine gun pointed at his heart throughout the trip. His orders were to kill the outlaw at the first sign of a rescue attempt.

There wasn't any, though. The small army reached the Lake County Jail in Crown Point without incident.

It was the airport scene all over again, with crowds pressing against the police barriers and reporters running alongside Dillinger as he was rushed past them. One of them pointed at the gangster's bare head and asked him if he was "going collegiate."

"Hell, no," said Dillinger, grinning. "Somebody swiped my hat in Tucson, just as they did my money."

Dillinger was taken into the sheriff's office. It was packed solid with reporters and photographers, all vying for his attention. Someone asked him what he thought of President Roosevelt. Dillinger said, "You can say that I'm for him all the way, and for the NRA—particularly the banks."

There was a roar of laughter. Then, as powerful lights flashed on, the newsreel cameramen began to film the impromptu press conference. Dillinger denied taking part in the East Chicago job. He said that John Hamilton was dead. "I wasn't with him when he got shot," he said, "but one of the boys told me about it.

Hamilton's got some kids. Before he died, he sent me some money to take to them. It was in one of the sacks that the Tucson police took away from me. I guess it was about sixty-eight hundred dollars."

Reporters were skeptical but had to admit that it was a neat explanation of how the East Chicago loot happened to be in his possession.

On Dillinger's right stood Robert Estill, the prosecuting attorney. On Estill's right was the Lake County Sheriff, Mrs. Lillian Holley, filling out the term of her late husband. A reporter asked Dillinger what he thought of them. "I like Mr. Estill," he said, "and Mrs. Holley seems like a fine lady."

One of the photographers shouted to Estill, "Bob, put your arm around him." Estill didn't hear him, but Dillinger did. He rested his right elbow on the prosecutor's shoulder. Estill automatically put his arm behind the gangster's back. Photographers snapped away as Dillinger grinned sardonically at the man who was going to prosecute him for murder.

It was the end of Estill's political ambitions—and the beginning of an even more audacious Dillinger legend.

The man who had started it all was still on the outside, however, looking in. Matt Leach had been effectively blocked from the main action by his political enemies. The best he could manage was the journey back to Indiana by train with the rest of the captured gangsters. There were fair to middling crowds along the route, and press conferences were held at each of the larger whistle stops. At one a U.S. Senator came aboard to meet the captives, and Harry Pierpont got off a widely quoted line. He said, "My conscience doesn't hurt me. I stole from the bankers. They stole from the people. All we did was help raise the insurance rates." But, all in all, it was small potatoes compared to what was going on at Crown Point.

Whole armies seemed to be deployed there.

Sheriff Holley had buttressed her defenses with armed members of the local Farmers' Protective Association. A squad of National Guardsmen had been called in. At night floodlights illuminated the area around the large, three-story brick jail. A patrol plane circled the Crown Point area by day, on the watch for motorcades of gangsters bent on releasing Dillinger.

"There will be no jail delivery," announced the *Lake County Star:* "there will be no repetition of the Lima, Ohio, jail delivery in which Dillinger was liberated . . ."

"A hundred men couldn't get him out of that jail," added Judge William Murray, who was scheduled to try his case.

Dillinger said nothing. He just sat whittling on a piece of wood in his cell in the jail's new second-floor "escape-proof" section.

Between him and the street were a half-dozen barred doors, more than fifty armed guards.

He was arraigned for trial on February 6, 1934. Prosecutor Estill said that five men had positively identified Dillinger as Officer O'Malley's killer. Dillinger's lawyer, Louis Piquett, announced that he had six Florida residents who would testify that his client had been living in Daytona Beach as late as January 14.

Dillinger told the press, "I'm innocent, but it looks like I'll get the works, though. They got me charged with everything from strangling gold fish to stealing the socks off a blind man."

A woman identified only as "Mrs. Dillinger" was allowed to visit him for a few minutes on February 26. The jailer who monitored their conversation could make little sense of it—it was mostly numbers. Later, the "mystery woman" was identified as Billie Frechette.

Around 9:15 A.M. on March 3 Dillinger suddenly jammed something that felt mighty like a gun into the back of cell-block turnkey Sam Cahoon. "Open up," he ordered. Cahoon opened. "Call Blunk," he said. Cahoon called. As Deputy Sheriff Ernest Blunk approached, Dillinger leaped out from behind Cahoon and leveled what looked like a real gun at him. "Call Baker," he ordered. Blunk called. As Warden Lou Baker entered, Dillinger braced him.

And so it went—with the outlaw methodically working his way through the half-dozen barred doors and fifty armed guards.

Only one other inmate chose to accompany him to freedom—Herbert Youngblood, a Negro from Gary awaiting trial for murder. Youngblood was armed with one of the submachine guns that they had taken from a couple of National Guardsmen. Dillinger had the other. Driving Ernest Blunk ahead of them, the two men strolled out of the jail and into the back door of the Main Street Garage.

"Which is the fastest car here?" Dillinger asked mechanic Ed Saager. The mechanic, thinking that they were members of a posse, pointed to Sheriff Holley's V-8. "Okay, get inside," Dillinger told him. Saager said he was busy.

"Better do as he asks," said Blunk. Saager climbed into the back seat resentfully, thinking that he had been deputized.

Dillinger told Blunk to drive. Youngblood got in the back seat with Saager. Gradually the truth of the situation began to dawn on the mechanic. "My God, you're John Dillinger!" he said.

"Right," snapped Dillinger. "So do as I tell you."

The car pulled out of the garage and headed north on Main Street. As they passed the First National and Commercial Banks,

Dillinger chuckled and said that he was tempted to stop and hold them up.

"Then he began asking about highways," Blunk recalled later. "He wanted to turn west on State Route 8, but I was past it, so we turned on the macadam road just north of the Pennsylvania Railroad tracks on the edge of town. Dillinger was as cool as could be. He hummed and whistled 'The Last Roundup.' As we were driving away from Crown Point he showed me a dummy gun and said, 'You wouldn't think a guy could make a break with a peashooter like this, would you?' Then he laughed. I looked at it, but I couldn't see much but the machine gun. Every time we hit a bump the barrel of the machine gun bumped me in the side."

Controversy still surrounds the "wooden gun escape"—as it does every other event in Dillinger's career.

A Lake County grand jury decided that the outlaw's only gun, at least when the break started, was a wooden one that he had fashioned from a washboard during his endless whittling sessions. Dillinger brought such a gun home to Mooresville in April, and was photographed holding it. It remained in his sister's possession until 1959, when a souvenir hunter walked off with it. "Johnnie wouldn't have been apt to go to all the trouble of making a wooden gun for our benefit," she told reporters later.

The Justice Department thought otherwise. After an independent investigation they announced that Dillinger's lawyer, Louis Piquett, paid $3,900 to "a small town Indiana police official and a Crown Point man" and that a real gun was sneaked to Dillinger by Evelyn Frechette, who also made the final arrangements for the delivery and a hideout.

A third investigation, made by the Hargrave Secret Service of Chicago, differed on the amount of money and to whom it was paid, but agreed that the gun was real.

Real or not, Dillinger was out and heading west in what must have been the most leisurely getaway of the whole Public Enemy Era. "Take your time," he kept telling Blunk. "Thirty miles an hour is enough. There's no hurry. What's time to me?"

"We went on the Peotone road about two miles," Ed Saager later remembered, "and Dillinger said, 'There ain't no telephone along here. It's a good place to let you guys out.' So we got out and he shook hands with us and he handed me four dollars for carfare. 'I'd give you more,' he said 'but I only got fifteen dollars. But I'll remember you at Christmas.' Then Dillinger slipped behind the wheel and told Youngblood to lie down in the back, and they took off south . . . I never saw him again. They got him before Christmas. I was hoping they wouldn't. I thought he'd come through. He seemed like an honest fellow."

The national reaction to the Crown Point escape was strangely divided. Politicians, law enforcement officials, church leaders, and prominent newspapers all thundered their outrage. "An object lesson of scandalous futility or corruption or the two in combination," *The Literary Digest* editorialized, and J. Edgar Hoover called it "a damnable outrage." The head of the Chicago Crime Commission said, "I'm speechless! The idea of a man with a record like his getting away! I can't understand it!"

But the voice of the people—or at least that portion of it that made itself known in the letters-to-the-editor columns—reacted differently:

"Why not give Dillinger a gold medal and a pardon?" a typical letter said. "He deserves both. Hurray for you, John. May you never be caught!"

"These politicians can sit in a nice little office every day," said another, "and make comments about a fellow who does get caught doing something in the open when they sit around plotting to keep the people from finding out what they really are."

Dillinger drove Sheriff Holley's car across the Indiana line into Illinois, abandoning it on the outskirts of Chicago. There he parted company with Youngblood. (Thirteen days later Youngblood would be slain in a gun duel in Port Huron, Michigan, taking a local sheriff along with him.)

Dillinger went straight to his lawyer's office, where he met Billie Frechette. "I told him it was my duty to advise him to surrender," Piquett said afterward, "and to let me take him to Town Hall station. He said he would do it later."

He and Bille left the same night for St. Paul, where John Hamilton and Homer Van Meter were waiting for him.

In crossing a state line in a stolen car, Dillinger had committed a Federal offense. The FBI now swung into action. Typewriters blazed, and the headlines were suddenly filled with the clamor of a "great all-out federal war" on the new national menace—Dillinger. "Act first, talk afterward," Hoover told his men, ordering them "to shoot straight and get the right man." Attorney General Cummings rubber-stamped the execution order: "Shoot to kill—then count ten," he advised.

A few thoughtful people objected to this kind of talk. Clarence Darrow, the famed defense attorney, was one. He said he didn't believe that Dillinger should even receive a life sentence if caught, and criticized the government's "shoot to kill" policy.

Hoover immediately spoke out against "sob sisters" and "sentimental yammerheads." Dillinger was a "craven beast," a "public rat," and those who aided him "vermin," "vultures," and "scum from the boiling pot of the underworld."

Although Hoover's bestiary didn't really fit Dillinger, it did the man with whom he was about to join forces.

Baby Face Nelson was something out of a bad dream. Compared to him, Clyde Barrow was a snowbank. Barrow killed to avoid capture, but Baby Face killed for the sheer hell of it.

He was the most blood-smeared figure of the Public Enemy Era, the only one about whom nothing decent can really be said. The underworld itself spoke of him in Hoover-like terms: he was a "bedbug," a "crazy cockroach," a "poisonous toad." The concensus was: "Don't prod that squirt—he's poison."

Nelson's real name was Lester Gillis, and Chicago made him. He was the only major Depression bandit who was city born and bred, and for that matter, the underworld never considered him a professional thief, anyway. He was a gangland torpedo who had fallen on hard times, a refugee from organized crime.

Gillis was a stocky five foot five, a strutting little tough with a face shadowed by a cap, a lit cigarette usually dangling from his lip. He had a squeaky voice and, beneath the cap, a peach-smooth angelic face—hence the famous nickname.

It was worth a man's life to call him it, though. Typically enough, Gillis wanted to be known as "Big George" Nelson. He would answer to plain George, though, and even to Jimmy.

He was born near the Chicago Stockyards in 1908, the son of a tanner. He didn't have to go to jail to learn the facts of life. They were right there, openly on display in the seamy South Side neighborhood where he was raised. He got his start heisting bookie joints and brothels, then selling protection to the places he had knocked off. Later he became a Capone gunman.

A spark of decency, of human emotion, entered his life with Helen Wawzynak. She worked in the neighborhood Woolworth's. He called her his "Million Dollar Beauty in the Five and Ten Cent Store." In 1928 he married her. She bore him a son. He didn't really deserve her, but in his own queer way he actually cared for his sickly, sad-faced child bride. There were other women, of course, but Helen always forgave him. She knew that sex, and plenty of it, was the only foolproof prescription for his vicious temper.

In 1931 the cops nabbed Nelson for a jewelry heist, and the mob, who had warned him about his extracurricular activities, refused to spring him. He did some time at Joilet, then escaped and went to California, where he became a hired gun for the Joe Parente mob.

It was there that he picked up his faithful sidekick, John Paul Chase—later described by J. Edgar Hoover as "a bit of human vermin with a poetically patriotic name." Chase, a former speakeasy operator, became Nelson's general handyman. He chauffeured him places, delivered messages, arranged hideouts, and even cleaned up after him.

When Repeal came along, Parente went out of business, and Nelson decided that if hicks like the Barrows and Pretty Boy Floyd could stick up banks, so could he.

He went back east and set up headquarters at Long Beach, Indiana, a haven for Chicago hoodlums along the shores of Lake Michigan. There he recruited a gang. Tommy Carroll, a happy-go-lucky ex-boxer, became the center fielder, and Eddie Green, a former Holden-Keating gangster, became the "jug-marker"—the man who fingered the banks that they were to rob.

The gang was fairly successful. They hit some good-sized banks in Wisconsin, Iowa, and Nebraska during the fall and winter of 1933. Nelson was beside himself, though—each job that he pulled was credited to the Dillinger gang.

He finally decided that if he couldn't beat them he would join them. He approached Homer Van Meter with the idea of a merger in December. He was turned down flat—the Dillinger boys didn't know him, didn't trust him.

But by February 1934 the picture had changed. Hamilton and Van Meter were the only Dillinger gangsters still at large. So this time it was Van Meter who approached Nelson with the idea of a merger. He told Baby Face that Dillinger would be busting out of jail any day and that he would "want action fast."

Nelson said that he had the action—a Sioux Falls job and a Mason City one, both fingered by Eddie Green. But, he added: "Can Dillinger take orders?"

The implication was clear. Van Meter was furious. So was Hamilton. But there wasn't much they could do about it. Nelson's was the only big-time game in town. "Johnnie will go along with it," Van Meter said quietly.

The five of them met at Eddie Green's apartment in St. Paul the morning after Dillinger's Crown Point escape. It was an edgy gathering. Nelson, obviously in awe of Dillinger but doing his best to hide it, blustered and ranted as he explained his theories of bank robbing. They were pretty simple: come in the door shooting, kill everybody in sight, and grab the dough. Van Meter laughed sarcastically, and Nelson leaped toward his submachine gun. Dillinger quickly stepped between the two men, and they simmered down.

The next day Dillinger got still another taste of what he was in for. Nelson was driving him over to Van Meter's place when he ploughed into another car. Eddie Green, who was with them, told what happened. The driver of the other car, Theodore Kidder, a young salesman, climbed out of his machine and came over. "Are you blind?" he said angrily. "You had a stop sign—"

Nelson whipped out his .45 and shot Kidder between the eyes. As they roared away, Dillinger said, "Did you have to do that?"

"Hell, yes!" squeaked Nelson. "He recognized you."

"Well, a citizen got your number back there," said Dillinger, looking out the rear window.

Nelson cursed wildly and almost lost control of the car a second time.

That night he sent John Paul Chase to clean out his old apartment, had the plates switched on the car and sent Helen to Bremerton, Washington, to stay with relatives. "I'm going to be busy as hell for the next few weeks," he told her.

The following day, March 6, the gang hit the Security National Bank and Trust Company in Sioux Falls, South Dakota. Jack Hamilton was the wheelman. Tommy Carroll held down the front of the bank. Dillinger led the other three inside. Nelson triggered the job by shouting shrilly, "This is a holdup. Lay on the floor."

A clerk pushed a button and the burglar alarm on the side of the building began clanging. Dillinger, Van Meter, and Eddie Green ignored it as they scooped up bills from the cages. They worked quietly, methodically, Dillinger pausing occasionally to ask a teller, "Is this all of it?"

Baby Face, meanwhile, was hopping around the lobby like Yosemite Sam. "I'm going to kill the man who hit the alarm!" he screamed over and over.

Dillinger and Van Meter finished off the cages and went to work on the vaults.

Suddenly Nelson spotted an off-duty policeman in the crowd outside. He hurdled a railing, jumped atop a desk, and began firing through the plate glass window. The policeman fell, four bullets in him. Nelson leaped up and down excitedly. "I got one of them!" he shouted gleefully. "I got one of them!"

Outside, even Tommy Carroll was surprised by that one. He had already captured two carloads of police, including the chief, without firing a shot.

Dillinger, Green, and Van Meter were ready now. They had collected $49,500. They rounded up ten employees as hostages and moved out.

A crowd of more than a thousand pressed around them as they emerged. "It's Dillinger!" they shouted excitedly. Baby Face Nelson swung around and fired over their heads angrily, starting a wild stampede that almost resulted in some serious injuries.

There was a wild auto chase after the gang dropped the hostages off, but they switched cars and made it back to the Twin Cities in one piece.

There, disaster almost struck again. They were in Green's apartment for the division of the loot. Baby Face saw Eddie dividing the money into six equal piles. He leaped toward his submachine gun. "Let Jimmy count it," Dillinger suggested diplomatically.

Dillinger's share came to $7,600 in currency and bonds. Faithful to his friends as always, he sent $2,000 of the cash to Mary Kinder. It was to help Pierpont and the others pay for an attorney. "Maybe later I can get them out," he wrote.

The same thought had occurred to the authorities in Lima, Ohio, where the three were being tried for Sheriff Sarber's killing. The jail was ringed by barbed wire. Machine guns had been placed at strategic intervals behind sandbag barricades. They were manned by grim-faced Guardsmen with steel helmets, gas masks, and drawn bayonets. At night searchlights restlessly probed the darkness, searching for what one newspaper called "the fearsome Dillinger and his underworld hordes."

Dillinger and his "hordes" were far away, though—in Iowa. On March 13 they hit the First National Bank in Mason City, Iowa.

The take ($52,000) was bigger than at Sioux Falls, but so was the trouble. A bank guard sitting in a bulletproof enclosure over the lobby dropped tear gas on them, and then snipers opened up at them from the roofs of nearby buildings as they emerged from the bank. Hamilton was hit in the shoulder; Dillinger in the left leg.

Baby Face, who had already shattered a retired school teacher's legs with a Tommygun burst, sprayed both sides of the street with fire. Windows tinkled, masonry flew. Bystanders scurried in panic.

Back in St. Paul Eddie Green took Dillinger and Hamilton to an underworld sawbones. He patched their wounds and prescribed rest.

The FBI had been on Dillinger's trail amost three weeks now, with nothing to show for it but bad press notices. As Will Rogers remarked acidly: "They had (Dillinger) surrounded in Chicago, but he robbed a bank in Sioux Falls that day. So they was right on his trail. Just three states behind."

By the end of March the Feds had the search area narrowed down to St. Paul. On March 30 the manager of the Lincoln Court Apartments phoned the U.S. Attorney's office. He had a suspicious tenant in Number 303—never went out, never let anyone in.

It was just one of many Dillinger reports. FBI agents R. L. Nalls and R. C. Coulter checked it out. They watched the building that night, then decided on a closer look the following morning. Together with city detective Henry Cummings they climbed the stairs to apartment 303 and knocked on the door.

Billie Frechette opened it a crack. "We're police," said Cummings.

"I'm not dressed," said Billie. She slammed the door and bolted it, and ran in to tell Dillinger.

"Keep your shirt on and get dressed," he said brusquely. Then, seeing that she was petrified, he added soothingly, "Never mind, never mind."

At that moment Homer Van Meter appeared at the head of the stairs. "Who are you?" demanded Coulter.

"A soap salesman," said Homer, smiling.

"Where are your samples?"

"In my car. Come down there and I'll prove my identity to you." Van Meter started down the stairs followed by the FBI agent. At a turn Homer suddenly bolted. When Coulter reached the ground floor, Van Meter's gun was out and blazing. He missed the FBI man but gained enough time to sprint out the rear door and leap onto a passing ash wagon. He pulled the surprised driver's cap off, put it on his own head, and went clip-clopping out of danger. When he left the wagon at Fourth and Pleasant, he was still wearing the cap.

Upstairs the gunfire flushed Dillinger. He came out with his submachine gun blazing, driving Nalls and Cummings around a corridor corner. Then, as Billie ran down the unguarded rear stairs and out the back way with a suitcase, Dillinger followed unhurriedly, covering their flight.

Cummings took careful aim and fired, winging Dillinger in the leg. It didn't seem to bother him. He waited calmly, facing the building, as Billie frantically backed a big Hudson out of the garage. Then he got in, and they roared off.

The press called it a '"Justice Department fiasco." It wasn't a total loss, though. Agents found Eddie Green's phone number among Dillinger's papers. They raided his apartment. Eddie and his wife, Bess, weren't home, but the place contained clothes and luggage. The Feds took up residence. Pretty soon two women appeared—Holden-Keating gang molls. They were all innocence. They had been told to take the clothes and luggage to their place. Somebody would pick them up that afternoon.

A small army of agents staked out the neighborhood around the molls' apartment. The G-men were still smarting from the criticism they had received for letting Dillinger get away. Eddie Green *wasn't* going to get away, no matter what happened.

He didn't. When he stepped out of his car late that afternoon, they drilled him.

They told a coroner's jury later that Green had been shot when he had ignored a shouted command to halt, and that he had reached for his hip as though to pull a gun. He had no gun, though. He was unarmed. Despite a lot of criticism, the coroner's jury decided that the G-men had been justified in their actions. (The case continued to attract controversy for some time afterward. In 1936 U.S. Secret Service agents began an investigation of Green's death, a move that was interpreted in the press as an effort to discredit the FBI men as trigger-happy amateurs. By 1936 the Bureau was sacrosanct, however, and nothing came of the investigation.)

Justified or not, Eddie Green's shooting turned out to be the luckiest break the FBI had ever had.

Eddie took eight days to die. He had been shot through the head, and the bullet had short-circuited some wires in his brain. He couldn't remember being shot. He thought he had been in an auto accident. He thought the nurse was his wife, and that the FBI men around his bed were fellow gangsters. He talked freely, babbling incoherently at times, lapsing into a coma at others, but giving the agents enough information to fill a book. Names, dates, places. The works.

It was the turning point in the Dillinger case.

John was already on the run. He had been recuperating from his leg wound in an underworld sanitarium in Minneapolis, but news of Green's capture had sent him fleeing first to Chicago, then on to Mooresville with Billie Frechette.

There was a family reunion at the Dillinger farm on Sunday, April 8. "I made him coconut cream pie," his sister remembered later, "fried chicken, everything that goes with it. All our family was there. There must have been a dozen of us. The FBI played all around the place, and a plane came down and nearly knocked a piece off the house while we were walking across the lawn. John was as relaxed as anyone could be. He never seemed concerned except when the airplane pulled over. When a car came into the driveway, he grabbed a gun off the bed and said, 'You get in back of the house. I'll take care of this.' But it backed out and went away."

Mary Hancock, his favorite niece, recalled walking through the woods with him that afternoon. "We walked hand in hand for a long time, a couple of miles along the lane, not a soul but he and I. He said, 'You believe what's in the papers if you want to, but take it from me, I haven't killed anyone and I never will.' He said, 'Take about half of it with a grain of salt, believe half of what's left, and you've got it made.'"

He and Billie returned to Chicago that night. The following day he had an appointment in a tavern at 416 North State Street. When he went to keep it, he found out how really extensive Eddie Green's ramblings had been. He sent Billie in ahead to look things over, and she never came back out. A squad of Feds led by Melvin Purvis had grabbed her.

Dillinger got out of town—fast. He went to Fort Wayne, where he hid out with Homer Van Meter. Both men were now low on money, but before they could hit a bank, they had to build up their arsenal once again.

Shortly after midnight on April 13 Dillinger and Van Meter invaded the Warsaw, Indiana, police station. They disarmed the lone duty officer and departed with three bulletproof vests and several submachine guns.

By dawn 5,000 lawmen were combing the northeast corner of the state. All highways had been sealed off. That day the Associated Press counted two hundred separate Dillinger "sightings" in half a dozen states.

Dillinger was on everybody's mind, everybody's lips. There was even a Dillinger fan club now, its members busy writing poems celebrating his deeds. And the hucksters were moving in on the legend, too. A Pennsylvania restaurant-owner had erected a billboard that read: HELLO, DILLINGER—YOU'LL LIKE LEE HOFFMAN'S FOOD! LEE HOFFMAN'S TAVERN, LORETTO, PA.

Dillinger was far away, though, in the north woods of Wisconsin.

The gang had assembled at the Little Bohemia Lodge, thirteen miles south of Mercer, to discuss upcoming jobs.

Baby Face Nelson had returned from the West Coast, bringing his wife with him. Homer Van Meter was there with Marie Conforti. Hamilton had come from Sault Ste. Marie with Makley's old flame, Pat Cherrington. Tommy Carroll had driven in from his tourist cabin hideout near Cedar Rapids, Iowa. He had Jean Delaney Crompton with him.

The lodge's owner, Emil Wanatka, was suspicious. Late April was too early in the season for tourists. Snow was still heaped in the timberlands; the roads were rivers of mud. But the men were friendly and easygoing, and the women pitched in and helped Mrs. Wanatka with the food, so he kept his suspicions to himself.

That night, as he was playing poker with the men, the one called "Johnnie" leaned forward, and his coat opened. Wanatka saw two guns in shoulder holsters. He excused himself, went to the kitchen, and checked the pictures on the front page of the Chicago *Tribune*. The next morning he took "Johnnie" aside. "You're John Dillinger," he said.

The man looked at him calmly and said, "You're not afraid, are you?"

"No. But everything I've got is tied up in this place. I don't want a shooting match."

"Emil," said Dillinger, "all we want is to eat and rest for a few days. We'll pay you well and get out. There won't be any trouble."

"From then on we got very friendly," Wanatka remembered later. "He even tried to satisfy me by playing pinochle with me, and I cheated him every hand. It was very friendly."

But Wanatka decided to turn him in anyway. He thought he would be in more trouble with the authorities if he didn't than with the gang if he did.

On Sunday, April 22, Melvin Purvis's phone rang in Chicago. A man who identified himself as Mrs. Wanatka's brother-in-law said, "The man you want most is up here."

"You mean Dillinger?" snapped Purvis.

The brother-in-law, Henry Voss of Rhinelander, Wisconsin, said that's who he meant and he added that the gang was planning to leave that night, so the G-men better hurry.

A phone call to Wisconsin authorities would have expedited matters at this point, but Purvis was under strict instructions to bring no one else in on the Dillinger case. The "Nation's Number One Menace" was to be the FBI's baby and theirs alone.

Purvis phoned the Bureau's St. Paul office and told Assistant Director H. Hugh Clegg to round up all available men and to meet him in Rhinelander. Then he and eleven other Chicago-based agents took off for the wilds of Wisconsin in two chartered planes.

At Rhinelander the two forces borrowed five automobiles and set out along the rutted, backcountry roads. They had no local lawmen with them and therefore had only the haziest notion of where they were going.

The FBI men reached the lodge around seven. The attack plan called for five agents to close in from the left, five from the right. This left only the rear of the lodge uncovered, but since the building was on a lake and there were no boats, the agents didn't worry about that.

Local lawmen could have told them that there was a steep bank along the lake shore that would effectively mask the gang's flight around the ends of the FBI pincers. They could also have warned them that there was a deep ditch along the left side of the lodge and a barbed wire fence along the right, and that the lodge was guarded by a couple of husky watchdogs.

As the FBI men approached, the dogs began to bark furiously. With all chance of surprise gone, the agents sprinted toward their assigned stations on the wings of the lodge. Those on the left plunged into the ditch. Those on the right became entangled in the barbed wire fence. As they were struggling to extricate themselves the front door of the lodge opened, and three men came out. They were the gas station operator and two CCC men on their way home. Two bartenders also stopped outside to see why the dogs were barking.

Seeing five men emerging from the lodge together, the FBI agents concluded that they were the Dillinger gang and called on them to halt.

Upstairs the gang heard shooting and left immediately by the rear windows.

Purvis's account of the raid would later tell of heavy fire from within the lodge, fire that continued for some time. According to Wanatka, that was unadulterated poppycock. He was in the bar when the shooting began and heard the gang's footsteps overhead. "They cleared out right away," he said. "They didn't waste any time shooting back."

Wanatka rushed to the cellar with his two bartenders to escape the murderous FBI fusillade that now came pouring into the lodge itself. He was joined there by Helen Gillis, Marie Conforti, and Jean Delaney Crompton.

The male members of the gang, meanwhile, went sliding down the steep bank to the lake's edge and slipped off into the night.

Tommy Carroll walked from Little Bohemia to Kuhnert's Northern Lights resort in Manitowish Waters. He stole a Packard from the front yard there and drove to St. Paul.

Dillinger, Hamilton, and Van Meter walked through the woods, circling the attacking forces, then crossed the road to a resort run by E. J. Mitchell. They knocked on the door, gained admittance and, after jerking the telephone connection loose, demanded a car. They got one, a Model A, plus the owner's services as a chauffeur. "For an outlaw," Mitchell later said, "that Dillinger was a gentleman. He made the others behave. No foul language, and cool as a cucumber."

The same couldn't be said for Baby Face Nelson, who at that moment was hopping up and down like an enraged bantam rooster at Alvin Koerner's store, a few miles down the road from Little Bohemia. "I want a car and I want it fast!" he squeaked.

One of the men he was covering, George LaPorte, said that his Ford was standing outside. "Let's go, then," snarled Nelson, herding LaPorte and a couple of hostages out the door.

At that moment, two FBI men, Agents J. C. Newman and W. Carter Baum, came driving toward Koerner's store. With them was Carl Christensen, a constable from Spider Lake who had been called in to aid them. The three had heard there was "trouble at Koerner's place" and were on their way to investigate.

As they approached the store they saw the men getting into LaPorte's car. They pulled up beside it and said, "Halt! We're Federal officers."

Nelson came running around the front of the car, pulled the door open, and snarled, "I know you bastards are wearing bullet-proof vests, so I'll give it to you high and low!" His gun, a .45

Colt converted into a machine gun with a long clip and a pistol grip, blazed away. Newman was hit over the eye by a bullet and rolled out. Baum and Christensen piled out the other side and started running. Baum was killed by a bullet through the throat. Christensen caught slugs in the lungs, liver, chest, hip, arm, and ankle but somehow survived. Baby Face looked around for new targets, saw none, jumped into the FBI Ford, and roared off.

Dillinger and his companions had dropped their chauffeur off near the Pixley power station, meanwhile, and were on their way to St. Paul.

Near Hastings, Minnesota, they ran into a roadblock. When they went roaring through it, the lawmen gave chase. During the gun battle that followed, a bullet fired by one of the deputies hit a fender brace and ricocheted into Jack Hamilton's back. It proved to be a mortal wound.

Back at Little Bohemia the FBI men now had the lodge surrounded. In Washington J. Edgar Hoover announced that Dillinger's end was imminent. When daylight came, the government agents moved cautiously toward the silent lodge. They tossed tear gas into the building. Out came the three women, coughing and crying, their hands in the air.

It was—in Attorney General Homer Cummings's words—"a rather depressing episode."

The FBI was attacked on all sides. Once again there were rumors that Hoover would be replaced. A petition circulated in Mercer County demanded Melvin Purvis's head and protested the "irresponsible conduct of federal operatives" for having raided the lodge "in such a stupid manner as to bring about the deaths of two men and injury to four others"—none of them criminals.

The only reply from the Justice Department was an "admission" on April 23 that Federal agents would probably kill Dillinger on sight rather than risk another gun battle by trying to take him alive.

Dillinger was hiding in Chicago with members of the Barker-Karpis gang when he heard the execution order passed. He had tried to get Doc Moran, the Barkers' sawbones, to help Hamilton but had been turned down flat. Gangrene set in, and on April 29 Hamilton died in Volney Davis's apartment in nearby Aurora. He was buried in a gravel pit outside town. As Dock Barker and the others watched, Dillinger poured lye on Hamilton's face and hands to prevent identification. "I hate to do this, Red," he said, "but I know you'd do the same to me."

The Justice Department now declared Dillinger "Public Enemy Number One."

Ironically, he had never been more popular with the public. In Mooresville a petition was gotten up urging Governor McNutt to issue Dillinger a pardon if he surrendered and pledged to remain within the law. The petition cited a precedent—the pardon of Frank James in Missouri—and declared that Dillinger "has never manifested a vicious, revengeful, or bloodthirsty disposition, there being considerable doubt as to whether he ever committed a murder." It added that "many of the financial institutions of the State have just as criminally robbed our citizens without any effort being made to punish the perpetrators."

There's evidence that Dillinger was so heartened by this petition that he tried to arrange a "truce" with Indiana authorities through his lawyer. There was talk of a "peaceful surrender" and of "amnesty." The lawyer said later that pressure from the Justice Department torpedoed the negotiations in their opening stages.

The Department was gravely concerned at the rising tide of Dillinger's popularity. They appealed to President Roosevelt, and he took to the air shortly after this to ask the public's cooperation in the war against crime. "Law enforcement and gangster extermination," said FDR, "cannot be made completely effective while a substantial part of the public looks with tolerance upon known criminals, or applauds efforts to romanticize crime."

On May 26 the governors of five midwestern states each posted a $1,000 reward "to provide additional incentive" for Dillinger's capture. Shortly after that the U.S. Attorney General announced that the Federal government was posting a reward of $10,000 for Dillinger's capture or $5,000 for information leading to it. That put a total of $20,000 on his head. It ended any lingering hopes that he may have had of an amnesty.

On May 27 Dillinger asked his lawyer to find a doctor who would be willing to alter his face and mutilate his fingerprints. Piquett did so, and Dillinger paid this underworld surgeon $5,000 to reshape his cheeks and eyebrows and carve up his fingertips.

Homer Van Meter underwent a similar operation.

Neither man was pleased with the results. Dillinger complained of "looking like he'd been in a dogfight." But Piquett put a reassuring arm around his shoulder and said, "John, you look wonderful. Nobody would recognize you." Dillinger was placated and paid the balance of what he owed.

The molls who had been captured at Little Bohemia were released, meanwhile. The Feds hoped that they would lead the law to their men. Marie Conforti went home to her parents, and Helen Gillis was smart enough to stay away from her husband. But Jean Delaney Crompton went rushing to Tommy Carroll's side at Waterloo, Iowa.

"Spotted for a bullet the day he was born," early acquaintances had said of Tommy. He absorbed six of them altogether and still lingered on long enough to whisper to lawmen, "Take care of the little girl. She doesn't know what it's all about. I've got seven hundred dollars on me. Be sure she gets it." She didn't. She got a year at the Federal Reformatory for Women in Alderson, West Virginia, instead.

Dillinger made plans to escape to Mexico. A Chicagoan was to drive him there for $3,500 in advance and $6,500 on crossing the border. He was to pose as a member of the man's family.

To raise the money Dillinger joined Van Meter, Baby Face Nelson, Pretty Boy Floyd and (some say) John Paul Chase in a raid on the Merchants National Bank in South Bend, Indiana.

It was Homer's baby. He had fingered it, cased it, and had worked out the details right down to the farmer's straw hats and overalls that the gang wore to distract attention from their faces. But Nelson made his presence felt, too. It was one of the wildest, bloodiest shoot-'em-ups of '34—a vintage year for violent bank robberies.

The take was disappointing. Homer had figured it for $20,000 a share. "This will be the last one, John," he'd told Dillinger as they had strapped on their bulletproof vests that morning. The take was nowhere near that. It worked out to a measly $4,800 each. But he was right. It was Dillinger's last job.

He returned to Chicago, hungry—as always—for a woman. A cabdriver steered him to the home of Mrs. Anna Sage. Mrs. Sage sent for Polly Hamilton Keele, a shapely twenty-six-year-old redhead. "I was crazy about him," Polly said later. "He had a marvelous personality. He really *couldn't* have been kind and good and do the things he did, but he was kind and good to me."

Polly eventually moved into the Sage apartment. So did Dillinger. They were with each other almost constantly during the last two weeks of his life. Dillinger called himself John Lawrence and posed as a clerical worker at the Chicago Board of Trade. Both women knew his real identity, though; they had guessed it almost immediately. "I don't think he was careless," Polly said later. "He just made one mistake. He trusted her" (meaning Anna Sage).

Anna had problems. Twice she had been arrested and convicted for running disorderly houses in Gary and East Chicago, Indiana. Twice she had been pardoned by the governor. Then had come a third arrest—and Anna, who was born in Rumania, now faced deportation by the Federal government. Anna didn't want to go back, but she had no bargaining power—none, that is, until the most wanted man in America dropped into her lap.

She went to see an old friend in East Chicago, Police Sergeant Martin Zarkovich, and presented her proposition: she would turn Dillinger over to the law in return for the $10,000 reward and a promise that she wouldn't be deported. Zarkovich took her proposition to his superior, Captain Timothy O'Neill, and O'Neill telephoned Melvin Purvis.

Hoover had sent Samuel N. Cowley from Washington to take supreme command of the FBI's special Dillinger squad, but Purvis still ran the Chicago office. Purvis conferred with Cowley and then, with Hoover's approval, met with Anna Sage. Deportations, he explained to her, were handled by the Labor Department, not the Justic Department, but if she helped, he would do all he could to help her.

Anna Sage agreed, and now events began to move swiftly. She told Purvis that she often accompanied Polly Hamilton and Dillinger to neighborhood movie houses. They were going, she thought, the next night. She would wear an orange skirt so that they could see her in the crowd.

Cowley summoned all the FBI agents in the Chicago area to a meeting and briefed them on the trap.

The night of July 22 was suffocatingly hot. The mercury had climbed to 108 degrees at the municipal airport that day and no relief was in sight. Crowds thronged the beaches along Lake Michigan. Taverns and air-cooled movie houses did a brisk business.

At 7 P.M. Anna Sage called the FBI office. "He's here," she whispered. "He's just come. We'll be leaving in a short while. I still don't know if we're going to the Biograph or Marbro." She hung up.

Purvis led a squad to the Biograph while Sergeant Zarkovich and four East Chicago officers accompanied other FBI agents to the Marbro. Cowley and the main squad waited at headquarters for the final word.

Dillinger selected the Biograph. *Manhattan Melodrama* was playing, and he was a Clark Gable fan. The FBI men and East Chicago police converged on the theater. Dillinger and the two women were already inside, watching the film. The G-men decided they would get him on the way out.

Purvis took up his station in a doorway just to the left of the entrance. In his hand he held a cigar. As soon as he spotted Dillinger coming out, he was to light the cigar as a signal to the agents to close in.

The crowd of strange men around the theater got the management nervous. They phoned Chicago police. Three plainclothesmen were sent to investigage. They were quietly but firmly informed that the strangers were there on "government business."

The movie ended, and Dillinger and his two companions strolled out. They turned to the left—as expected. As they walked past Purvis he raised a match and lighted his cigar. The ring of FBI agents started to close.

None of the government men spoke, but Dillinger suddenly sensed that something was wrong. Anna Sage had dropped behind the other two. Polly Hamilton, seeing men with guns, also broke away.

Purvis later claimed that he shouted something like "Stick 'em up, Johnnie," and that Dillinger pulled his gun and darted down an alleyway.

Eyewitnesses tell a different story. Mrs. Esther Gousinow's account is typical. She was sitting in the window of her second-story apartment at 2427 Lincoln Avenue. She had been watching the front of the Biograph for some time and had noticed a group of men waiting, as though for girl friends.

"Then I saw a young man walk out of the theater, accompanied by two girls," she told reporters later. "They were only about ten feet from the alley and I was looking right down at them when I saw three men walk up behind them. I heard two shots—there may have been more—and the man with the two girls fell to the sidewalk. I thought at first that it was a holdup and that the victim was killed. Then I thought of Dillinger, and because it appeared to me that the three men shot without giving a warning, I thought immediately that the victim was Dillinger."

Four bullets had struck Dillinger, one in the back of the neck, virtually at point-blank range. He had been driven forward and down, landing on his face in the alleyway, his own gun still uncleared. Purvis leaned over him and spoke. There was no answer.

Anna Sage and Polly Hamilton hurried away. Under the marquee lights the older woman's orange skirt looked red—blood red.

The next day an anonymous scribbler added the finishing touches to the legend—four lines scrawled in chalk on the brick wall of the alleyway where Dillinger had fallen:

Stranger, stop and wish me well,
Just say a prayer for my soul in Hell.
I was a good fellow, most people said,
Betrayed by a woman all dressed in red.

Dillinger was as big a hit in death as in life. A pushing, shoving mob dipped handkerchiefs in his blood, and later at the morgue thousands streamed by his body, continuing "on through the night," according to the Associated Press, "in a seemingly never-ending line."

The funeral, a few days later in Mooresville, was another madhouse scene with thousands trampling down flower beds in an effort to reach his coffin. "Instead of keeping the usual mourners' pace on the way to the hearse," *Newsweek* reported, "(the pallbearers) had to travel at a dogtrot, using one arm for carrying and one for fighting off spectators."

The Justice Department was pleased at the outcome of the "greatest manhunt since Pershing chased Pancho Villa." Said Attorney General Cummings: "Organized society has triumphed, as it must over one who would defy its laws."

The FBI didn't totally escape criticism for its method of dispatching Dillinger, however. One Virginia newspaper assailed the killing as the work of cowards. "Any brave man," the editorial said, "would have walked down the aisle and arrested Dillinger . . . why were there so many cowards afraid of this one man?"

Actually, when the Justice Department embarked on its "shoot to kill" campaign, Dillinger had commited no offense under Federal law except to drive a stolen car across a state line, for which, as Turner Catledge of *The New York Times* observed acidly, "the offender is seldom shot on the spot."

Even such mild criticism made J. Edgar Hoover bristle. "He was just a yellow rat that the country may consider itself fortunate to be rid of," he said of Dillinger.

And when an aide, in private, suggested that "rat" was perhaps an undignified word, Hoover demanded, "Well, wasn't he a rat? Wasn't he everything that was low and vile? Didn't he hide behind women? Didn't he shoot from ambush? Wasn't his whole career as filthy as that of any rat that ever lived?"

And then, almost as an afterthought, he added: "There are other rats still to be gotten, however."

CHAPTER SIX

Baby Face Nelson Heads the Rodent List

At the top of Hoover's rodent list was Baby Face Nelson.

Now that Dillinger was dead, Nelson became Public Enemy No. 1. It's said that he exulted in the title but was peeved that the Federal reward on his head was only half that offered for Dillinger.

Nelson went west after Dillinger was killed. He had important mob contacts along the Pacific Coast.

The cross-country trip was made by car. Nelson, John Paul Chase, and Helen traveled with "Fatso" Negri, a Joe Parente mobster who was now Nelson's chauffeur. "Fatso's" wife and three-year-old son went along, too, adding valuable camouflage to the group. To the casual eye, they appeared to be a carload of vacationing tourists.

On the Coast, where the fix was in, Nelson shuttled freely between his resort cottage home at El Verano and Sausalito, Oakland, and San Francisco.

G-men thought they had him on a couple of occasions, but Nelson knew exactly where they were at all times and followed their futile maneuverings gleefully.

He was safe. Organized crime took care of its own.

Back in the Midwest Homer Van Meter was in deep trouble. He had always been a free-lance bandit, and Dillinger's death had marked the beginning of the open season on freelancers. The mob had seen which way the wind was blowing outside the Biograph Theater. Now they were the Justice Department's staunchest allies in the war against unorganized crime.

One of the mob's "bankers" decided to do his part and co-operate with the law. The $10,000 he was holding for Van Meter helped him decide.

On August 23, 1934, the St. Paul Police Department and a couple of dozen spectators seemed to know that Van Meter would appear at Marion and University Avenues at precisely 6 P.M. When he did, they were ready for him. Homer was driven up a blind alley by the combined fire of four automatic rifles and machine guns. Fifty shots were fired in all, and the alley was so narrow that few of them missed their mark. The crowd surged forward, delighted at the free show.

In Fort Wayne, Indiana, Van Meter's brother, Harry, nodded grimly when reporters brought him news of Homer's death. "I knew he'd get the same thing that John Dillinger got," he said.

A month later Makley and Pierpont also went down before the law's guns. Sentenced to die for the Sarber killing, they managed to escape from death row at the Ohio State Prison in Columbus.

Using "pistols" they had carved out of soap, they overpowered one guard and were beating on the door leading out of the death house when a riot squad opened up on them through the bars. Makley died in the blaze of gunfire, but Pierpont survived. He was nursed back to full health, then was strapped into the electric chair on October 17, 1934. He was smiling when they pulled the switch.

Russell Clark wanted to die, too. He told officers taking him back to prison after the Tucson roundup, "Do me a favor—shoot me." He was sentenced to life imprisonment instead.

"The Woman in Red," Anna Sage, was taken to California for safekeeping after Dillinger was killed. She received half of the $10,000 reward she had originally been promised, then was deported to Rumania, where she died in 1947.

Melvin Purvis, the man who had promised to do all he could for her, resigned from the FBI in 1935. Mrs. Sage's lawyer claimed that it was because the government had refused to honor its promise to his client. J. Edgar Hoover said that no promise had been made. Purvis wrote a book about his experiences, worked briefly as a screen writer, then organized nearly a million youngsters in "Melvin Purvis' Junior G-Men" for Post Toasties. In 1938 he returned home to Florence, South Carolina, married his childhood sweetheart, and settled down to publishing the local paper. In 1960 he shot and killed himself in his home.

Matt Leach also had his later differences with the FBI. Bitter at having his prize creation stolen out from under his nose, he kept sniping at the Bureau for their handling of the Dillinger case. In 1937 he was fired as head of the Indiana State Police. The Police Board announced that the action had been taken at the request of J. Edgar Hoover. The official decapitation was described as "the first result of a drive" by Hoover to get the cooperation of local police forces. Leach was killed in an auto accident in 1955.

In September 1934 Baby Face Nelson was still feeling so secure in California that he drove down to San Francisco, walked in a

Van Ness Avenue auto agency, and bought a new car under his real name, Lester Gillis.

With John Paul Chase at the wheel, Nelson now headed east, nonchalantly puffing a cigar in the rear seat, his arm around his wife. Baby Face had run low on money. He intended to stick up some more banks.

The Feds, meanwhile, went to work with what he had given them. They traced "Lester Gillis" backward from the auto agency to his El Verano hideout. There they pounced on John Paul Chase's girl friend, Sally. "You know Nelson's crazy," they told her. "He'll get your man killed if we don't stop him soon. Why not help us?"

She decided they were right—and did. She retraced their trips, named contacts, harborers, and helpers.

In the Midwest Nelson began to feel the heat. He started running, moving from hideout to hideout. But the heat was everywhere. He was like a drop of water skittering atop a sizzling stove.

He headed back west to Reno, Nevada, where he had the fix on, but discovered that the Feds, in their eagerness to get him, had even roughed up the mob. "Do us a favor," the big shots told him. "Die."

The FBI sat back to wait. All the "ratholes" had been plugged. A detailed description of Nelson's car, right down to its current license number, had been relayed to every Bureau office in the U.S. On November 27, 1934, the report they had been waiting for came in. The car had been seen near Lake Geneva, Wisconsin.

Inspector Cowley, who had led the FBI's Dillinger Squad, pulled two special agents off the investigation of the Bremer kidnapping and sent them north. He and Special Agent Herman Hollis would follow shortly, he said.

The two agents, William Ryan and Thomas McDade, sped toward Wisconsin on the Northwest Highway. Nelson's license number, Illinois 639578, was pinned over the sun visor. Suddenly, just beyond Fox River Grove, a Ford sedan came speeding in the opposite direction. There were two men and a woman in it, and the license number was—"Five-seven-eight!" they both exclaimed simultaneously. McDade, who was driving, made a screeching U-turn.

Nelson saw the car turn and said, "Heat." John Paul Chase, who was sitting in the back seat, snatched up a Browning automatic rifle. Nelson made a U-turn, and the two cars passed each other once again, the occupants staring hard at each other. Then Nelson swung around a second time and came roaring after the FBI car.

The agents let it catch up with them. As it pulled abreast, Baby Face, sporting a mustache and wearing a cap and sunglasses, leaned across his wife and shouted, "Pull over!" Then, suddenly, with no warning, he yelled, "Let 'em have it!" and Chase opened up with the BAR.

The two cars roared along the highway side by side, guns blazing away. Nelson was firing with his left hand and his shots were going wild. The dumdum bullets from Chase's rifle were mushrooming as they went through the windshield of their own car. The G-men's shots were also off target.

After a few seconds of this, and everybody still intact, Nelson slowed and the FBI car pulled away. The two agents tried to swing off the highway to reach a phone, but they were going too fast and crashed. They hurriedly extricated themselves from the wreckage and drew their guns, but Nelson had vanished.

He was farther down the highway, speeding toward Chicago. Inspector Cowley and Special Agent Hollis passed him now. They made a quick U-turn and started after his car. One of Ryan's shots had already hit its water jacket. It was spouting steam, and the engine was beginning to overheat.

Nelson jammed on the brakes just outside Barrington, Illinois, swung right into a gravel road, and stopped. Helen jumped out and ran into a field. Baby Face came leaping out with a submachine gun. Chase had the BAR.

The FBI car screeched to a stop fifty yards past the turn-off. Bullets were already thudding into its frame as the two agents jumped clear. Hollis hunched down behind the car with a shotgun. Cowley leaped into a ditch, clutching his submachine gun.

A group of highway workers who had been planting trees several hundred feet down the road hit the dirt as bullets suddenly filled the air. Then, to their awed amazement, they saw Baby Face walk slowly toward the FBI car, his submachine gun blazing from his hip—"Just like Edward G. Robinson," one of them said later.

Cowley fired from the ditch, hitting Nelson a number of times, but he didn't fall. He kept on coming, sweeping the ditch with bullets until Cowley dropped, fatally wounded. Hollis blazed away with his shotgun. Half a dozen slugs tore into Baby Face—but he still plodded forward, submachine gun roaring. Hollis dropped his empty shotgun, pulled out a pistol, and ran toward a telephone pole for cover. Nelson's submachine gun cut him down, killing him instantly.

Nelson climbed into the FBI car and backed it up to where the Ford was parked. Chase transferred the weapons to it, and Helen climbed in. Baby Face, in what was perhaps the only understatement of his career, said, "You'll have to drive. I've been hit." He had, at that moment, seventeen slugs in him.

The next morning his body—stripped to prevent immediate

identification—was found in a ditch near St. Peter's Cemetery in Niles Center, Illinois.

Only his wife mourned his passing.

The Feds grabbed her in Chicago shortly after that, and she was sent to Madison, Wisconsin, where she served a year for her part in the Battle of Little Bohemia. Her whereabouts today is unknown.

John Paul Chase was arrested on December 27, 1934, when he visited a fish hatchery where he had once worked in Mount Shasta, California. He was tried and convicted for the murder of Inspector Cowley and was sentenced to life in Alcatraz. He is still in Federal custody today.

Chase's arrest closed the book on the Dillinger gang, but not on the Public Enemy Era. One more "rat pack" still had to be "exterminated" before the tumultuous epoch could be considered officially over.

CHAPTER SEVEN

The End of an Era

The Barker-Karpis outfit was scattered by December 1934, and on the run.

The Hamm kidnapping had marked the turning point. "Chicken before it, feathers afterwards," Ma was quoted as saying.

She had advised against a second snatch, but Fred, Alvin, and Dock had ignored her. She had refused to help them and had sat sulking in her Chicago apartment while the boys had gotten themselves into a king-size mess up in St. Paul.

Fred had started the ball rolling. On the very eve of the snatch he noticed a car containing three uniformed men on his tail. He hit the brakes and came out shooting. Two of the "pursuers" were wounded, one critically. They weren't cops, though, just employees of Northwest Airways.

Harry Sawyer, St. Paul's criminal boss, hit the panic button. The snatch was off, he declared. The public outcry following the shooting would force the police into action. His man at headquarters had told him that every known criminal was going to be rounded up for questioning; every known hideout combed.

Dock Barker managed to calm him down. They would delay the snatch, not scrub it completely. The public had a short span of attention. The whole thing would be quickly forgotten.

It was—and on January 17, 1934, the gang struck.

The victim, Edward G. Bremer, president of the Commercial State Bank of Minneapolis, was grabbed after he dropped his daughter off at a fashionable girls' school.

He resisted, and Fred Barker sapped him. Barker slid behind the wheel of his car while Harry Campbell and Alvin Karpis pulled the unconscious banker into the back seat and bracketed him between them. "Let's go," said Karpis.

The car pulled away. It was followed by a second car containing Dock Barker, Volney Davis, William Weaver, and Willie Harrison, all armed with submachine guns.

Bremer was transferred to the second car at the city limits and was driven to Bensenville, Illinois. For twenty-one days he sat blindfolded in a bedroom of Harold Alderton's House while the gang mismanaged the kidnap negotiations.

It was mostly Harry Sawyer's fault. His nervousness infected them all. Bremer's car had been found by the local police. The numerous bloodstains convinced lawmen that Bremer was already dead. The FBI was called in.

Sawyer was frantic. "The town's crawling with Feds," he told the gang. "Get the women out. Send them to Chicago. Hold up the negotiations until things cool off."

Dock Barker and Karpis tried to argue with him. He was beyond reason, though. They were forced to break off contact with the kidnapped man's family only hours after it had been established.

When contact was finally renewed, Sawyer's constant meddling in the mechanics of the operation almost brought the whole structure crashing down on them. Once again negotiations were broken off.

As the days passed, the victim's family became desperate. Bremer's father, Adolph, made a newspaper plea to the kidnappers to return his son alive. He had the $200,000 they were demanding, but he didn't know how to get it to them.

A ransom pickup was worked out. Everything went smoothly until the go-between reached the prearranged transfer point—the Jefferson Lines bus station in Des Moines, Iowa. Then another Sawyer-inspired epidemic of jitters swept the gang. The pickup wasn't made.

Alvin Karpis gave up in disgust. He traveled to Chicago with Fred Goetz and begged Ma Barker to reconsider. "Come in on it," he told her, "before Sawyer gets us all killed."

It was a triumphant moment for Ma. They should have listened to her in the first place, she nagged. She had never trusted Harry Sawyer. He was a weakling and his wife, like most women, was treacherous. She didn't like any of the new crowd, she went on. They weren't the solid, dependable heist men that she was used to working with.

Karpis sat patiently through her tirade, and when he returned to St. Paul the next morning, he had what he wanted—a shrewd pickup plan that bore Ma's unique stamp of genius.

Karpis announced that he was taking over. This was the plan they were going to follow, and his advice to Harry Sawyer was to stay scarce for the next few days.

On the night of February 6 a solid contact was established with Walter Magee, a wealthy contractor who was a friend of the Bremer family.

Magee was told to prepare a parcel of $200,000—$84,000 of it in 5s, the balance in 10s. The bills were to be unmarked, of course, but the gang realized that their serial numbers would be forwarded to the FBI. There was no way to get around that.

Magee's next set of instructions was to take the ransom money in his own car and drive down University Avenue in St. Paul until he came to a parked 1933 Chevrolet coupe with Shell Oil Company signs on each door. He was to park his own car, transfer the money to the coupe and then drive it south on State Highway No. 1 to Farmington.

Magee did all this. When he reached Farmington, he waited until the 9:15 bus to Rochester came through, then followed it out of town. He was to look for four red lights.

He spotted them five miles outside Zumbrota. They were on a hill to his left. He turned off onto a gravel road and drove slowly for about a half a mile. A car approached from the rear. Its headlights flashed five times. Magee stopped, placed the two cardboard boxes containing the ransom money on the right-hand side of the road, and drove off.

The following morning Edward Bremer was loaded into a car for the long trip home. He was still blindfolded. The car stopped to refuel several times, and Bremer heard the clank of gas cans, which the kidnappers had cached along the route.

Around eight o'clock that night, as they approached Rochester, Minnesota, Dock Barker told Bremer that they were going to set him free. He was to count to fifteen, then remove the blindfold. Dock gave him a few dollars and told him to take the 9:40 bus to St. Paul.

As soon as Bremer turned up, the FBI swung into action. They distributed a printed list of serial numbers to all banks in the U.S. and to those in several foreign countries. They retraced Magee's route and found four flashlights fitted with red lenses on the gravel road near Zumbrota. They also questioned Bremer carefully and learned about the gas cans.

On February 10 a farmer near Portage, Wisconsin, found four empty gasoline cans plus a funnel in a ditch on his property. FBI men sent the cans to their Technical Laboratory in Washington. The lab found a fingerprint. An exhaustive check of FBI files disclosed that it had been made by the right index finger of one Arthur (Dock) Barker.

The FBI had next to nothing on Barker. As far as they were concerned, he was just an Oklahoma parole violator. He had a brother, Fred, who was wanted for murder in Missouri, and Fred traveled with another ex-con named Alvin Karpis. There was also a mother on the scene somewhere, a woman named Kate Barker, who was thought to harbor criminals. But that was the extent of their information.

The Hamm kidnapping was still considered a Touhy job (even

though a St. Paul jury had acquitted him of it in November), and the gang's other capers—the bank raids, the payroll snatches, and the armored car holdups—were divided evenly among Frank Nash, Harvey Bailey, and John Dillinger.

That's how well the Barker-Karpis outfit had covered their tracks—until the Bremer kidnapping.

Word of Dock's fingerprint reached the gang. It was an alarming development. He was on the FBI's wanted list now, described as a "Dillinger gangster." (The Bremer snatch was thought to have been engineered by members of the Dillinger gang while their leader languished in jail.)

The Barker-Karpis outfit scattered. Fred and Paula Harmon went to Toledo. Volney Davis and Edna Murray rented a place in Aurora, Illinois. The rest of the mob spread out through the Chicago area. Some dyed their hair and took to wearing dark glasses: several grew mustaches.

Karpis and Fred Barker, whose faces decorated wanted posters for the murder of that Missouri sheriff, decided on more drastic measures. Through Russell Gibson, the drug addict, they contacted Dr. Joseph P. Moran, an underworld sawbones, who had offices on the ground floor of the Irving Park Hotel. Moran assured them that he could alter their fingerprints and change their faces.

Moran was a dipsomaniac. He had started out as a "pin artist" (abortionist), and had been sent to Joliet. There he had met Ollie Berg, a Louie Alterie-Bugs Moran mobster. Berg had put Doc Moran into contact with the "big boys" and, on his release, he had become an underworld surgeon. By 1934 Moran's clientele was almost exclusively bank bandits. Although he was only thirty-nine years old, he was already a physical wreck. Whiskey failed to steady his nerves; his befuddled brain seemed unconnected to the rest of his body. He did little more than butcher Karpis and Fred Barker, then inject them with morphine.

Ma Barker and Doris Delaney nursed them. Their fingers had been whittled almost to the bone. The agonizing pain caused Fred to scream by the hour. He had to be restrained, then injected with more morphine. Karpis was stoical but could touch nothing for weeks. His girl, Doris, had to become an extension of his hands. As for their faces—they were mutilated with scars but otherwise unchanged. "I'm going to kill that guy," Fred panted, "soon as I can hold a gun."

Ma told him to hold off, at least for the time being. Doc Moran was going to help fence the ransom money.

The bulk of the $200,000 had been hidden by Fred Goetz in the garage of his wife's uncle. It was to stay there until things got cooler.

Something funny had happened to the college-boy pilot, though. He was drinking heavily and talking wildly. Other gang members had warned him about it a couple of times, but he couldn't seem to stop. Gradually it dawned on them—the strain of the Hamm and Bremer jobs had gotten to Goetz. He was slowly losing his marbles.

They listened in horror one night as Goetz reminisced in public about the St. Valentine's Day Massacre, the Hamm kidnapping, even the Bremer job.

The following night, March 20, Goetz received a phone call. The caller asked him to come out to a restaurant owned by an old friend on Cermak Road in Chicago. The owner wanted to buy him a couple of drinks, talk about the good old days. Goetz kept the appointment, surprising his old friend, who knew nothing about the visit. They talked for a while, then Goetz left. As he stepped out the restaurant door a half dozen sawed-off shotguns roared. Goetz was literally blown apart. It took two days to put enough pieces together to identify him.

Goetz was as big a threat dead as he had been alive, however. The former engineering student had been a neat, methodical man. He had kept written records of his part in the Hamm and Bremer kidnappings. FBI agents read them with interest.

The ransom money—recovered from the garage where Goetz had hidden it, quite possibly with the notion of keeping it all for himself—was now in the process of being converted to clean currency. Ollie Berg was working on it, and so was John J. "Boss" McLaughlin, the Chicago ward heeler. Nearly $100,000 of the tainted loot was exchanged for Cuban gold, which a well-known bank then converted into $1,000 in American bills at a discount of one quarter of one percent.

Some of the money got loose locally, though, and McLaughlin panicked. He sent a suitcase full of the hot loot back to the gang, saying that he didn't want to handle any more of it.

Doc Moran's office now became the clearing house for the huge, complicated money-passing operation. Russell Gibson had talked Moran into doling out the hot stuff on a percentage basis to the various underworld figures who streamed through his office. The operation had hardly gotten under way, though, when bad news arrived.

The Feds had Boss McLaughlin. They had traced a hundred-dollar bill from the City National Bank and Trust Company to the bookie who had tried to pass it, then on back to Ollie Berg and the Chicago politician.

"This is the blow-off," said Doc Moran as he stuffed the hot loot into a suitcase and fled.

The whole mob was on the run now. The boat was springing

leaks right and left. Up in St. Paul, Eddie Green lay dying with a bullet in his brain. Eddie was a Dillinger gangster now, but he had been on the fringes of the Barker-Karpis outfit and he had been a Frank Nash, Holden-Keating associate before that. Eddie was a walking encyclopedia of underworld information. The bullet had short-circuited some wires in Eddie's head, and he was talking around the clock. A battery of FBI stenographers struggled to keep up with the endless flow of information.

On the day that he finally died, the Associated Press reported from St. Paul that "authorities seeking Dillinger have uncovered operations of a criminal gang which has taken five lives and $500,000 loot. Ten persons have been connected with the gang. The information was given by persons caught since Dillinger's escape" (meaning Eddie).

It was the first public disclosure of the Barker-Karpis gang.

Its members were widely separated at the moment, some as far afield as Glasgow, Montana; Las Vegas; and Allandale, Florida.

In August they converged on Toledo, Ohio, where remnants of the Licavoli mob had arranged a temporary sanctuary in exchange for some $50,000 of the tainted loot.

This was the end of the line for Doc Moran. The strain of being a fugitive had begun to affect his brain, too. One night, as he sat with some members of the gang in the Casino Club, he began to boast drunkenly about his ability to alter fingerprints.

"We'll forget that finger-fixing stuff," warned Russell Gibson. "It's lousy."

"Who are you crowding?" demanded Moran. "Think I'm afraid of you? You can't hurt me! I've got this gang in the hollow of my hand—right there!" He regarded his cupped palms. "In the hollow of my hand!"

"There, there, Doc. Take it easy," said Fred Barker. "Listen, you're a swell guy, but you're a little tight, that's all. How about a nice motorboat ride on the lake to clear your head?"

When Russell Gibson and Fred Barker returned from the motorboat excursion, Doc Moran wasn't with them. One of the molls later testified that Fred told an associate, "Doc will do no more operating. The fishes probably have eat him up by now."

The gang refused to let Moran's death spoil an otherwise delightful vacation. Everybody, even Ma, went swimming and boating on Lake Erie. Karpis went fishing and also took some golf lessons from gang member Willie Harrison, who had once been a pro. Dock Barker also took lessons from a pro—a red-headed *poule de luxe* he had met at his lakefront hotel.

On September 8 the vacation came to an abrupt end. Paula Harmon and Harry Campbell's girl got drunk in a hotel suite with Gladys Sawyer. There was a disturbance. Police were called. They tipped off local FBI agents, who raided the hotel. They nailed the three molls but missed Harry Sawyer, Alvin Karpis, Fred Barker, and Harry Campbell by seconds.

It was too close for comfort. The gang started traveling. They went west, then deployed towards the East again. Their nerves began to wear thin. Volney Davis had a falling out with them and went his own way. Back in Bensenville, Illinois, Harold Alderton and Elmer Farmer were arrested for their part in the Bremer kidnapping.

The temperature continued to climb. Since Dillinger's death the FBI had been striding across the nation's headlines in what one critic has called "a blaze of gunfire, heroics, and publicity." No sooner had one "national menace" been eliminated than another sprang up to take his place. On October 21 Pretty Boy Floyd went down before the G-men's guns. A month later, on November 27, Baby Face Nelson bit the dust. Now it was the Barker-Karpis gang's turn.

They got the full FBI buildup. The press began to blossom with stories about "Ma Barker and her Viper Brood." Some of the wilder accounts of their doings had Ma herself leading them on raids, submachine gun in hand.

The gang read the handwriting on the wall and scattered. Ma and Fred went to Florida. Dock returned to Chicago with Russell Gibson and Byron Bolton. Alvin Karpis decided to get out of the country altogether. His eighteen-year-old girl friend, Dolores, was five months' pregnant, and he wanted her to give birth in peaceful surroundings.

He took her to Havana, where he was able to sell his share of the hot money to the Cuban underworld. He rented a villa at Varadero Beach for $300 a month and let his fishing mania take full possession of him.

Alvin spent every day out in the Gulf Stream, wrestling the big ones in. He was so thrilled when he landed a 400-pound swordfish on an 80-pound test line that he wrote Ma and Fred about it.

They came to visit him at Christmastime, bringing a layette with them. The other molls had chipped in and bought it for Dolores's baby. Ma and Fred stayed with them awhile, then returned to Florida on New Year's Eve.

Alvin went into town a couple of days later—and got a shock. Havana was crawling with Feds. The kidnap money had been traced there. He put Dolores on a plane for Miami, then slipped across to Key West on the ferry. He rented a house in Coral Gables, installed Dolores in it, and got back to his fishing.

In Chicago, meanwhile, the FBI had hit pay dirt. They had learned from underworld sources that Bolton, Gibson, and Dock Barker were living somewhere on the North Side. One of the gang's molls was pointed out to them, and the Feds trailed her to an apartment building on Pine Grove Avenue.

On the night of January 8, 1935, Melvin Purvis led a squad of heavily armed agents in a raid on the building. The Feds quickly surrounded it, covering every exit and alley. Purvis went to the speaking tube in the hallway, buzzed the apartment and ordered the occupants to come out with their hands up.

Byron Bolton and two women appeared a few minutes later and were taken into custody without gunfire. Russell Gibson decided to run for it. He put on a bulletproof vest, snatched up a BAR, and went down the rear fire escape. The vest was no match for bullets from .351 rifles, though. It looked like a cheese grater when the G-men had finished. The effects of the bullets' expansion had left the top half of Gibson unrecognizable, but Byron Bolton identified him for the Feds.

They asked Bolton where Dock Barker was. Byron said he lived in an apartment house on Surf Street, fourteen blocks south of Pine Grove. The G-men poured into that neighborhood. Dock was taken completely by surprise. He was out for his evening constitutional when they surrounded him. He was searched, but no weapons were found. "Where's your gun?" Melvin Purvis asked him.

"Home," chuckled Dock, "and ain't that a hell of a place for it?"

The Feds took Dock down to their headquarters in the Bankers' Building and tried to grill him. He was no help at all. As Melvin Purvis remembered it later, "He sat in a chair, his jaw clenched, and looked straight ahead. He was not impressive-looking; only his eyes told the story of an innate savagery." Dock later claimed that the Feds kept him handcuffed to a chair for eight days and nights.

Byron Bolton was much more helpful. Byron's job had been to take care of the women in the gang, to transport them from city to city, arrange reservations, make sure they didn't go out on the town while their men were busy. He told the Feds everything he knew and later, in court, turned state's evidence.

In Dock's apartment G-men found a map of Florida on which the Ocala area, including Lake Weir, was circled in pencil. Dock would say nothing about it, but Byron Bolton told them that Ma and Fred Barker were holed up somewhere in that area. Dock and Russell Gibson had gone down to visit them, he went on, and had come back talking about an alligator nicknamed "Old Joe." They had tried to catch him by placing a pig in a barrel with hooks on it, but "Old Joe" had grabbed the pig and had gotten clean away. They had laughed about it.

Special agents poured into the Ocala area. Their questions

finally led them to a man in Oklawaha who had heard of "Old Joe" the alligator. "He's dead now," he said. "He used to hang out in a bayou just down the road." The agents went down the sand road he had pointed out. They came to a two-story white cottage. They watched it through binoculars for a couple of days and one morning they finally saw what they were looking for—Ma Barker standing beside a rowboat, framed against a background of Spanish moss and still, sluggish water.

Planeloads of extra agents were flown in from Chicago and Jacksonville. All roads in the vicinity of the house were blocked. By seven o'clock the following morning, January 16, 1935, they had the place surrounded.

Special Agent in Charge E. J. Connelley stepped out into an open area in front of the white house. "Fred!" he shouted through cupped hands. "Kate Barker! We are officers of the U.S. Department of Justice. The house is surrounded. Come out one at a time with your hands raised and you won't be hurt."

There was a half-minute of silence, then the agents heard Ma Barker shout hoarsely, "All right! Go ahead!"

They thought she was telling Fred to go ahead and surrender. But suddenly bullets chopped into the earth at Connelley's feet. He dived for cover, and the G-men opened up with rifles and machine guns. The fire was returned from the house. The agents calculated its source inside the rooms, then saturated those sections with bullets. They also fired tear gas bombs through the windows.

After some forty-five minutes of silence from inside the house, Connelley cautiously approached it. A Negro handyman who had worked for Ma was sent inside to find out if the Barkers were injured or dead. The handyman, whose name was Willie, stuck his head out of a second-story window a few seconds later and yelled (according to Melvin Purvis): "Dey's heah, boss. Dey's dead."

The FBI men entered. They found Fred and Ma Barker on the floor of an upstairs room. Empty submachine gun drums lay scattered about. Fred's gun, a Thompson carrying a 50-round drum of overloaded .45 caliber pistol ammunition, was still in his hands. He had been hit eleven times.

Ma Barker's weapon, a Lewis .300 gas-operated automatic rifle, lay across her body. It was still hot. Forty of its ninety-four rounds were gone. Ma had been hit by three bullets. One of them had drilled her squarely through the heart. (There was talk later, at the inquest, of this shot having been self-inflicted.) In Ma's pocketbook G-men found $10,200 in bills of large denomination. It was clean currency, not Bremer ransom loot.

Alvin Karpis got the news in Miami that evening. He'd been out fishing with Harry Campbell. A car came weaving crazily toward the dock. Dolores Delaney was at the wheel, her face gray with fright. "There was a gunfight up at Oklawaha," she said. "Ma's dead. So is Fred Barker."

Karpis knew what that meant. He rushed Dolores to the station and put her aboard a train to Atlantic City. Wynona Burdette, Harry's girl, would meet her there and arrange a hideout. The two men would follow later.

Karpis was now Public Enemy No. 1. His picture was in every paper. He was called "Old Creepy" and "Killer Karpis." Reporters visited Topeka, Kansas, where he had grown up, and managed to find the usual unidentified neighbor who could remember his torturing cats as a boy.

In Karpis's case the heat was unusually intense. He was the last major figure of the Public Enemy Era—and that Era was already over. It had ended at Oklawaha. Big-time bandits were suddenly as scarce as passenger pigeons. Tremendous prestige would accompany Karpis's capture; ten thousand sheriffs and police chiefs, as well as squads of G-men, were aching to see him.

Officer Elias Saab of the Atlantic City force figured he was going to be the lucky man. He spotted a car with Florida plates on a street near the boardwalk on January 20 and checked the plates against his list. It was the car the FBI had reported stolen; the one that Karpis was believed to have driven north.

Saab did a little high-grade sleuthing and located the apartment where Campbell and Karpis were staying. He and three other officers marched up to it with drawn guns. Karpis came to the door in his underwear. "You're under arrest," said Saab.

Karpis nodded. "I suppose you want the man with me also," he said. "He's just inside. I'll get him."

Saab made the mistake of letting him go back into the room. When Alvin came out, he had Harry Campbell with him—and two machine guns.

The press later reported a battle equal to Oklawaha. Karpis was more casual about it. "Oh, I guess we shot a couple of times in the air," he reminisced later. "The cops fired a few times, but the bullets didn't come anywhere near us. One hit my girl in the leg."

The two men raced through the icy streets in their underwear, leaped into their car, and roared off. In Allentown, Pennsylvania they kidnapped Dr. Horace Hunsicker and forced him to drive them to Wadsworth, Ohio. There they removed his suit, divided it between them, and left the doctor tied up in an abandoned schoolhouse. His car was found the next day in Monroe, Michigan.

No further sightings came in. Karpis and Campbell had gone to ground—presumably in the Toledo area, where they still had the fix on.

Dolores Delaney had her baby a few weeks later. It was a seven-pound boy. She named him Raymond Alvin Karpavicz. She was allowed to hold him for a few hours; then the baby was sent to Karpis's parents for safekeeping, and Dolores was wheeled back into the prison ward at Milan, Michigan, to serve five years for harboring the last of the Public Enemies.

On April 15, 1935 the Bremer kidnapping trial opened in St. Paul. On hand for the occasion were two star witnesses, Byron Bolton and Wynona Burdette. Wynona had wanted to be a radio singer but had never made the grade. G-men convinced her that she had a fine voice anyway, and she used it freely at the trial.

John J. "Boss" McLaughlin was found guilty and sentenced to five years. He died in prison. Ollie Berg was sent back to Leavenworth for parole violations. Harold Alderton, in whose house Bremner had been held, got twenty years. So did Elmer Farmer. Jess Doyle and Edna Murray were freed for lack of evidence; but Edna, "The Kissing Bandit," had twenty-five years left of a sentence she was serving when she escaped from the Missouri Penitentiary, and Jess Doyle was wanted for bank robbery. Dock Barker and "Lapland Willie" Weaver each got life. (Dock was later killed while trying to escape from Alcatraz in 1939.) After turning state's evidence, Byron Bolton received four three-year sentences to run concurrently, and Wynona got a three-to-five set at Alderson.

While the trial was in progress Harry Sawyer was nabbed in New Orleans and Volney Davis in Chicago. Their trials were held over for the next term of court, when it was expected that the rest of the gang would be cleaned up.

The rest of the gang—Alvin Karpis and Harry Campbell—were doing some cleaning up of their own, meanwhile. Together with Fred Hunter, a 32-year-old Oklahoma bandit, and another man, they held up a mail truck in Warren, Ohio, on April 24, 1935, and escaped with $70,000.

Hoover was enraged. He put every available G-man on Karpis' trail and heaped torrents of verbal abuse on him. Karpis, he told reporters, headed the "shrewdest, most cold-blooded gang in America"; he was "Former Enemy Number One" who had become "Public Rat Number One."

In November the gang struck again, raiding Erie Train No. 622, bound from Detroit to Pittsburgh, at Garrettsville, Ohio. They held up postal employees, seized some $36,000, and escaped in a waiting airplane.

The FBI traced the plane to Hot Springs, Arkansas. Agents flooded the area in the guise of sportsmen, hunters, and fishermen. But Karpis hadn't contributed $6,500 to the local Mayoralty campaign for nothing. He was warned in plenty of time and pulled out.

He wandered through Texas, Mississippi, and Florida, moving back and forth along the Gulf Coast, dodging the law.

Hoover said later that the persistent pursuit made Karpis edgy. In a fit of rage the outlaw decided to liquidate the entire FBI. His battle plan (still according to Hoover) called for the use of fast cars and airplanes to speed him from one slaying to the next. First he would knock off the top agent in Los Angeles, next the agent in charge in Chicago, then New York. Then, Hoover said, Karpis decided that the Special Agents were just employees, after all. Their boss was the one he wanted to kill—"that fellow Hoover."

The FBI said it received a letter from Karpis, postmarked Dayton, Ohio, in which he threatened Hoover's life. When this information reached the Director, he demanded that every tid-bit of information about Karpis' whereabouts and activities be expedited directly to his personal desk.

Karpis' mail robberies, meanwhile, had brought a second powerful Federal force, the postal inspectors, into the nationwide hunt. According to the subsequent report of the Postmaster General, they made the next big score. In March 1936 they joined forces with the Kansas State Police and tracked down the fourth member of the gang. He told them that Karpis, Campbell, and Hunter were back in Hot Springs, Arkansas.

The postal inspectors told the FBI, and Hot Springs was raided for the second time. In the early dawn of March 30 heavily armed agents stalked through the brush to surround a small cabin. A barrage of tear gas bombs was released—but the cabin was empty. The men had been warned, as usual, and had already fled.

Evidence found in the cabin implicated two local women. According to *Uncle Sam's Gang Smashers*, a popular FBI book of the period, "three weeks after the Hot Springs bushwhacking the special agents had one woman on the grill. She sang, and the Gang Smashers wrote the lyrics. It was the swan song of Alvin Karpis."

Miffed postal inspectors told a different story. They accused the G-men of acting on leads that they had developed. Hoover denied it but never offered a satisfactory counter-explanation of how the FBI learned that Karpis was in New Orleans.

At any rate, Karpis was located there. He was posing as a "Mr. O'Hara" and living with Fred Hunter and his girl in an apartment on Canal Street.

Every agent in the Justice Department wanted to be in on the historic pinch but Hoover decided to make it himself—personally.

He was still smarting from a head-butting contest that he had had with Senator Kenneth D. McKellar, Democrat, of Tennessee, in April. Hoover had appeared before McKellar's Senate Appropriations Committee and had received a severe grilling. McKellar's purpose was to show that Hoover had never personally made an arrest, that he had little personal experience in crime detection, and was virtually an amateur. McKellar, *Time* Magazine said, "wanted to know why G-man Hoover wasn't out risking his own neck." Hoover was livid at this slur on his personal courage and decided to show McKellar up.

He gathered together a raiding party and took off by airplane from Washington on the night of April 30, 1936. The group arrived in New Orleans the following morning and plans were drafted for the raid on the Canal Street apartment. Hoover himself and four agents were to crash the front door while his men ringed the apartment house.

The G-men had hardly taken up their posts when Karpis altered their plans. The front door of the apartment house opened, and there was Alvin, accompanied by Fred Hunter, striding down the front steps.

Just as the Feds were about to attack, an old man on a white horse came ambling through the boulevard traffic. He passed between them and their quarry. The G-men had to wait. By that time Karpis and Hunter were seating themselves in their car. The Feds sprinted forward. Hoover ran to the left side of the car and grabbed the surprised "Public Rat Number One" before he could reach for a rifle lying on the back seat.

"Put the cuffs on him, boys," said Hoover.

But nobody had remembered to bring any. So two of the agents bound Alvis's hands with their neckties.

"To the Post Office Building," said Hoover.

But it turned out that none of the agents knew where it was. "Mr. Hoover," said Karpis, speaking for the first time, "if you mean the new Post Office, I know where that is, because I was just going to rob it."

"Fortunately for the dignity of the Federal Bureau of Investigation," Hoover wrote later, "it was the old Post Office where the prisoners were to be taken, and we didn't have to accept the proffered guidance. We did, however, have to ask the way from a passing pedestrian."

Six days later, in Toledo, Ohio, G-men captured Harry Campbell. He received a life sentence for his part in the Bremer kidnapping. So did Volney Davis and Harry Sawyer.

Charles J. Fitzgerald and Jack Peifer had been nabbed, meanwhile, and were sent to St. Paul to stand trial for the Hamm kidnapping. Both received life sentences. Peifer escaped serving his by chewing poisoned gum in his cell.

Karpis' involvement in the Hamm job was easier to establish than his part in the Bremer snatch, so he too was flown to St. Paul to stand trial.

He was found guilty and was sentenced to life imprisonment.

He served most of it at Alcatraz and the McNeil Island Federal Penitentiary at Tacoma, Washington. He was finally paroled in August 1967 and now lives in Montreal, Canada, the city where he was born.

Hoover's personal arrest of "Public Rat Number One" resulted in his riding higher than ever. He and the FBI were eulogized in eight-column headlines. The G-men could do no wrong; to criticize them was to fling mud at the flag.

When Senator McKellar's recommended cut of Hoover's budget was brought up on the floor, Senator Arthur H. Vandenberg arose and denounced him as a miser "who would cause the threat of kidnapping to hang once more over every cradle in America." When Vandenberg was finished, one Democrat after another got up and lavishly eulogized the G-men for their work. The proposed cut was defeated by a throaty roar of noes. "McKellar sat apart in Catilinian silence," reported *The New Yorker*, "shunned by friend and foe alike."

It would be a long time before anyone else dared criticize the FBI.

J. Edgar Hoover accompanied Karpis on the flight to St. Paul. At one point in the journey, the Director referred to his prize catch as a "hoodlum."

"I'm no hood!" snapped Karpis. "And I don't like to be called a hood. I'm a thief."

"As far as I'm concerned, you're a hoodlum," replied Hoover.

Karpis shrugged. "You don't understand," he said, "I was offered a job as a hoodlum and I turned it down cold."

Hoover said nothing, so Karpis tried to explain the difference. "A thief is anybody who gets out and works for his living," he said, "like robbing a bank, or breaking into a place and stealing stuff, or kidnapping somebody. He really gives some effort to it. A hoodlum is a pretty lousy sort of scum. He works for gangsters and bumps guys off after they have been put on the spot. Why, after I'd made my rep, some of the Chicago Syndicate wanted me to go to work for them, as a hood—you know, handling a machine gun. They offered me two hundred and fifty dollars a week and all the protection I needed. I was on the lam at the time and not able to work at my regular line. But I wouldn't consider it. 'I'm a thief,' I said, 'I'm no lousy hoodlum'."

It was a significant little story, for it illustrated perfectly the difference between the Public Enemies of the early '30s and the gray, anonymous functionaries of big-time crime who came before and after them.

But Hoover, who had built the FBI's reputation on the roundup of colorful figures like Karpis and Dillinger, not on the Lucianos and Frank Costellos who really ran things, preferred not to understand. 'From my standpoint," he said coldly, "you're still a hoodlum."

It was a rather shabby way to treat the man who had just contributed the final touches to the FBI's most glorious legend.